Mastering TypeScript
From Basics to Expert Proficiency

Contents

Introduction

TypeScript has rapidly emerged as a powerful tool in the modern software development landscape. Developed and maintained by Microsoft, TypeScript was designed to address some of the fundamental shortcomings of JavaScript by introducing a statically typed superset of the language. With its robust type system, TypeScript enables developers to catch errors early in the development process, improve code maintainability, and enhance overall productivity.

TypeScript extends JavaScript by adding static types, which can be used to define variables, function parameters, and return types, among other elements. The typing system helps in identifying type mismatches, thereby reducing runtime errors. This feature is particularly beneficial in large-scale applications where the complexity of code can make manual error detection challenging.

Another significant advantage of TypeScript is its toolset. The TypeScript compiler (tsc) offers seamless integration with popular code editors and IDEs, including Visual Studio Code, JetBrains WebStorm, and Microsoft Visual Studio. These tools provide intelligent code completion, real-time type checking, and advanced refactoring capabilities that streamline the development process.

TypeScript also introduces modern JavaScript features and syntactic sugar that may not yet be available in all browsers. This includes features from ECMAScript 6 (ES6) and later versions, such as classes, modules, arrow functions, and template literals. TypeScript's transpilation process ensures that code written in TypeScript is converted to plain JavaScript that can run in any environment, providing backward compatibility and performance optimization.

Moreover, TypeScript supports a range of programming paradigms, including object-oriented, functional, and reactive programming. Its flexibility allows developers to choose the best approach for their specific use case, making it suitable for a variety of applications, from small scripts to large-scale enterprise applications.

TypeScript has also gained substantial traction in the open-source community. Projects like Angular, Vue.js, and React offer first-class TypeScript support, which has contributed to its widespread adoption. The active development community continually contributes to improving type definitions for popular JavaScript libraries, enhancing TypeScript's utility.

With TypeScript, teams can enforce coding standards and consistency across their codebase through configurable compiler options. This enforces a level of discipline in code writing, leading to clean, understandable, and maintainable code. Additionally, TypeScript's ecosystem includes tools for testing, linting, and formatting, which further enhance code quality.

In this book, we will explore TypeScript from the ground up, beginning with setting up the development environment, understanding basic types and variables, and progressing towards advanced topics such as generics, asynchronous programming, and error handling. Each chapter is designed to provide a comprehensive understanding of the topic, complete with practical examples and real-world use cases.

We aim to equip you with the knowledge and skills necessary to harness the full potential of TypeScript in your projects. By the end of this book, you should be proficient in writing type-safe, scalable, and efficient TypeScript code that adheres to industry standards.

Chapter 1

Introduction to TypeScript

TypeScript is a statically typed superset of JavaScript that introduces strong typing and modern JavaScript features to improve code quality and developer productivity. Originating from Microsoft, it offers advantages such as early error detection, enhanced code maintainability, and seamless integration with popular development tools. Throughout this chapter, we will explore the history, key differences from JavaScript, component types of the TypeScript ecosystem, and practical use cases, culminating in writing your first TypeScript program and understanding the resources and communities available for continued learning.

1.1 What is TypeScript?

TypeScript is defined as a statically typed superset of JavaScript, developed and maintained by Microsoft. It introduces static typings, classes, and interfaces to JavaScript, thus bringing the power of modern programming languages such as Java and C# to the web development arena.

The primary distinction between JavaScript and TypeScript is its type system. While JavaScript is a dynamically typed language, TypeScript is statically typed. This means that type-checking is performed at compile-time instead of run-time, allowing developers to catch potential errors earlier in the development cycle.

TypeScript code is transpiled into standard JavaScript code via the TypeScript compiler, enabling it to run anywhere JavaScript runs. The file extension for TypeScript files is .ts, whereas JavaScript files have the extension .js. The transpilation process can be handled using the TypeScript compiler, which is typically installed via Node Package Manager (npm).

The TypeScript type system supports various types, both primitive and user-defined. Primitive types include number, string, and boolean. Additionally, TypeScript introduces type annotations, which provide a way to declare variable types explicitly. This is especially useful for maintaining large codebases by improving readability and reducing the potential for bugs.

```
let isDone: boolean = false;
let decimal: number = 6;
let color: string = "blue";
```

In the example above, isDone is declared as a boolean, decimal as a number, and color as a string. These type annotations are useful documentation within the code and provide a mechanism for the TypeScript compiler to ensure variables are used consistently.

Beyond primitive types, TypeScript allows the definition of complex types through interfaces and classes. Interfaces in TypeScript enforce contracts on classes or objects, ensuring that they adhere to a particular structure. Below is an example of defining and using an interface in TypeScript:

```
interface Person {
    firstName: string;
    lastName: string;
}

function greet(person: Person) {
    return `Hello, ${person.firstName} ${person.lastName}`;
}

let user = { firstName: "John", lastName: "Doe" };

console.log(greet(user));
```

In this example, the interface Person defines the structure of a person object, ensuring that any object of type Person must have firstName and lastName properties of type string. The greet function enforces the use of this structure, providing certainty about the shape of person parameter it receives.

TypeScript also supports object-oriented programming paradigms with features such as classes, inheritance, and access modifiers. Classes in TypeScript can have properties and methods, and they can extend other classes to inherit their behaviors. Below is an example demonstrating the use of a simple class:

```
class Student {
    fullName: string;

    constructor(public firstName: string, public middleInitial: string, public lastName:
          string) {
        this.fullName = `${firstName} ${middleInitial} ${lastName}`;
    }
}

let student = new Student("Jane", "M.", "Doe");
console.log(greet(student));
```

In the example above, a Student class is defined with a constructor that initializes the object's firstName, middleInitial, and lastName properties. The Student class can be instantiated, and its fullName property is initialized upon creation.

TypeScript's powerful tooling integration allows for superior development experiences. Enhanced code navigation, refactoring, and autocompletion are realized through editors such as Visual Studio Code, which natively supports TypeScript. Furthermore, TypeScript's rich type inference mechanism reduces the amount of required type annotations, thus simplifying code while maintaining its robustness.

Overall, TypeScript aims to provide a more robust development experience by overlaying a strong type system onto JavaScript, resulting in improved early error detection, code maintainability, and seamless tool integration.

1.2 History and Evolution of TypeScript

Microsoft released TypeScript publicly on October 1, 2012, introducing it as a free and open-source programming language developed to address shortcomings in JavaScript, particularly for large-scale application development. Developed under the leadership of Anders Hejlsberg, a prominent software engineer known for his work on Turbo Pascal, Delphi, and C#. TypeScript was designed to enhance the tooling and development experience with JavaScript, effectively by bringing static typing capabilities, advanced IDE features, and early error detection.

The need for TypeScript stemmed from the growing complexity of web applications. While JavaScript is a powerful and flexible language, it lacked the robust type system found in traditional programming languages such as Java or C#. The absence of static type checking in JavaScript meant that developers often had to deal with runtime errors that could be detected and corrected at compile time in statically typed languages. TypeScript emerged to provide a statically-typed layer atop JavaScript, enabling the development of more robust, maintainable, and scalable applications.

Initial Release and Features

Upon its initial release, TypeScript encompassed basic, yet significant, extensions to JavaScript, including:

- Static Typing: Allowing developers to specify types for variables, function parameters, and return values.
- Classes and Interfaces: Bringing object-oriented programming constructs that align with ES6 standards.
- Type Inference: Automatically deducing types to lessen the verbosity for the developer while still benefiting from type safety.
- ES6 Support: Compatibility with ECMAScript standards, enabling forward compatibility and the use of modern JavaScript features.

These features aligned with the vision of improving developer productivity by providing better tooling support, such as enhanced code navigation, refactoring, and auto-completion features in Integrated Development Environments (IDEs).

Evolution and Milestones

TypeScript's progression has been marked by a series of major releases, each incorporating advancements driven by both user feedback and ECMAScript standard evolution. Here are key milestones in its development:

- *TypeScript 1.0* (April 2014): The first stable version, TypeScript 1.0 solidified its initial features and garnered a growing developer community.
- *TypeScript 1.5* (July 2015): Introduced support for ES6 modules, decorators, and better tooling integration.

- *TypeScript 2.0* (September 2016): Marked a leap forward with the introduction of non-nullable types, control flow analysis, and improved module resolution. Key additions included:
  - null and undefined types: Types that provide additional compile-time safety checks.
  - Read-only property support: Enabling better immutability patterns.
  - Declaration file acquisition: Simplifying the use of JavaScript libraries without TypeScript typings.
- *TypeScript 2.1* (December 2016): Implemented async functions and object spread/rest syntax, mirroring JavaScript advancements.
- *TypeScript 2.4* (June 2017): Introduced dynamic import expressions for lazy module loading, an essential factor in optimizing large applications.
- *TypeScript 3.0* (July 2018): This milestone included:
  - Project references: Allowing large codebases to scale more efficiently.
  - Unknown and never types: Enhancing type safety and control flows.
  - Richer tuple types: Providing variadic tuple elements and improved destructuring.
- *TypeScript 3.7* (November 2019): Highlighted by features such as optional chaining and nullish coalescing, borrowing from the latest ECMAScript proposals.
- *TypeScript 4.0* (August 2020): Continued to refine the language with variadic tuple types, labeled tuple elements, and new tooling support.
- *TypeScript 4.5* (November 2021): Added support for ECMAScript module support in Node.js, template literal types, and improved performance.

Community and Ecosystem

Beyond the language itself, TypeScript has fostered a vibrant community and ecosystem. The DefinitelyTyped repository, a crowdsourced collection of type definitions for JavaScript libraries, vastly improves TypeScript's utility by providing typings for thousands of JavaScript packages.

Integration with popular frameworks and libraries has also been a crucial aspect of TypeScript's rise. Angular adopted TypeScript as its primary language, which significantly boosted TypeScript's visibility and credibility. In addition, frameworks like React and Vue provide extensive support for TypeScript, further solidifying its importance in modern web development.

TypeScript's evolution continues to be aligned with the advancements in the JavaScript ecosystem. The open-source model and the collaboration with the developer community ensure that it remains poised to address current and future challenges in software development. Through each iteration, TypeScript refines its capabilities, maintaining a balance between rigorous type systems and JavaScript's dynamic nature, making it an indispensable tool for developers across the globe.

1.3 Benefits of Using TypeScript

TypeScript offers multiple advantages that contribute to improved code quality, developer productivity, and efficient project management. As a statically typed superset of JavaScript, it incorporates strong typing, robust tooling support, and modern JavaScript features. These attributes enable developers to detect errors early, maintain large codebases more effectively, and integrate seamlessly with existing JavaScript projects.

1. Early Error Detection

One significant benefit of TypeScript is its ability to identify errors during development rather than at runtime. By introducing static typing, TypeScript helps catch type-related errors early in the development process. Developers can define explicit types for variables, function parameters, and return types, which dramatically reduces the probability of encountering type-related bugs.

```
// TypeScript Code Example
function addNumbers(a: number, b: number): number {
    return a + b;
}
addNumbers(5, '10'); // Error: Argument of type 'string' is not assignable to parameter
    of type 'number'.
```

In the above example, TypeScript immediately flags the incorrect argument type (a string instead of a number), preventing the execution of potentially erroneous code. This timely feedback minimizes debugging efforts and enhances code reliability.

2. Improved Code Maintainability

TypeScript's strong typing system aids in long-term code maintainability, especially in large codebases with extensive developer collaboration. By defining and enforcing data types, function signatures, and class structures, TypeScript makes it easier to understand the code's intent and structure. This self-documenting nature simplifies code reviews, refactoring, and onboarding new developers.

- Interfaces - Enforce consistent API structures across modules and components.
- Type Aliases - Define complex types in a readable manner.
- Enums - Cater to clearly defined sets of named constants.

```
// TypeScript Code Example
interface User {
    name: string;
    age: number;
    role: UserRole;
}

enum UserRole {
    Admin,
    Editor,
    Viewer
}

const newUser: User = {
    name: "Alice",
    age: 30,
    role: UserRole.Admin
};
```

The clear definition of user properties and roles in the above example ensures consistent data handling and reduces ambiguity.

3. Enhanced Tooling and IDE Support

The rich tooling ecosystem of TypeScript significantly enhances the developer experience. With features such as IntelliSense, code navigation, and automated refactoring, TypeScript-aware Integrated Development Environments (IDEs) increase productivity and minimize the chance of introducing errors.

- IntelliSense - Offers smart code completion, parameter info, quick info, and member lists.
- Code Navigation - Facilitate quick jumps to definitions, references, and implementations.
- Refactorings - Enable safe and automated code modifications.

Most popular IDEs, such as Visual Studio Code, WebStorm, and Sublime Text, provide first-class TypeScript support, making it easier for developers to manage complex projects effectively.

4. Modern JavaScript Features

TypeScript incorporates features from the latest ECMAScript standards, ensuring that developers can utilize modern JavaScript capabilities regardless of the runtime environment's support. TypeScript transpiles these features to compatible JavaScript versions, enhancing backward compatibility and future-proofing development efforts.

```
// TypeScript Code Example
class Employee {
    private name: string;
    constructor(name: string) {
        this.name = name;
    }

    getName(): string {
        return this.name;
    }
}

const emp = new Employee("John Doe");
console.log(emp.getName()); // Output: John Doe
```

In the above example, TypeScript seamlessly integrates modern JavaScript features such as classes, access modifiers, and template literals.

5. Seamless Integration with JavaScript

TypeScript's design aims to be highly compatible with existing JavaScript codebases. Developers can gradually adopt TypeScript and incrementally apply typing to their projects. TypeScript files can coexist with JavaScript files, facilitating a smooth transition without necessitating complete rewrites.

```
// JavaScript Code
function multiply(a, b) {
    return a * b;
}
```

```
// TypeScript Code
import { multiply } from './multiply';

const result: number = multiply(5, 10);
console.log(result); // Output: 50
```

This interoperability ensures that existing JavaScript libraries and frameworks can continue to be used alongside TypeScript code, optimizing development workflows and leveraging past investments.

6. Robust Community and Ecosystem

TypeScript's growing popularity has cultivated a robust ecosystem, with extensive libraries, frameworks, and tooling support. The proactive community and comprehensive documentation provide valuable resources for learning, troubleshooting, and staying updated with best practices.

- DefinitelyTyped - Offers type definitions for popular JavaScript libraries.
- TsLint/ESLint - Facilitate code linting and style consistency.
- Testing Frameworks - Supported by Jest, Mocha, and other testing tools.

This thriving ecosystem elevates the overall developer experience, enriching the toolkit available for building scalable and maintainable applications.

By leveraging these benefits, developers can achieve higher code quality, better maintainability, and enhanced productivity. TypeScript's compatibility with modern JavaScript features, extensive tooling support, and strong community presence make it a valuable asset for contemporary software development.

1.4 Key Differences Between TypeScript and JavaScript

TypeScript (TS) is a statically typed superset of JavaScript (JS) that compiles to plain JavaScript. Understanding the key differences between TypeScript and JavaScript is crucial for leveraging the advantages TypeScript offers. This section delineates the primary distinctions in type system, compilation, tool support, and language features.

1. Type Annotations

TypeScript introduces type annotations to enable static type checking. In JavaScript, types are determined at runtime, making it difficult to catch type-related errors during development. TypeScript's type annotations allow developers to specify types explicitly.

```
let message: string = "Hello, TypeScript";
let count: number = 42;
let isValid: boolean = true;
```

In JavaScript, the same variables would be declared without any type information:

```
let message = "Hello, JavaScript";
let count = 42;
let isValid = true;
```

2. Compilation

TypeScript code is compiled, or transpiled, to JavaScript. This step identifies type errors before the code is run, improving reliability and reducing debugging time. The TypeScript compiler (tsc) performs this transpilation.

```
tsc app.ts
```

The above command compiles the app.ts file into a JavaScript file, app.js. JavaScript does not have a build step like this unless specifically set up with tools like Babel.

3. Interfaces and Type Aliases

TypeScript introduces interfaces and type aliases that allow more advanced type definitions. Interfaces define the structure of an object, ensuring it adheres to a particular format.

```
interface Person {
    name: string;
    age: number;
}

function greet(person: Person) {
    return `Hello, ${person.name}`;
}
```

JavaScript does not support interfaces directly. Instead, developers validate object structures manually or use libraries for this purpose.

4. Enums

TypeScript supports enumerated types (enum), which are not natively available in JavaScript. Enums allow a variable to be one of a set of predefined constants.

```
enum Direction {
    Up,
    Down,
    Left,
    Right
}

let move: Direction = Direction.Up;
```

In JavaScript, enums must be simulated using objects.

```
const Direction = {
    Up: 0,
    Down: 1,
    Left: 2,
    Right: 3
};

let move = Direction.Up;
```

5. Generics

TypeScript supports generics, which provide a way to create reusable components. Generics allow functions, classes, and interfaces to operate with specific types without losing type information.

```
function identity<T>(arg: T): T {
    return arg;
}

let output = identity<string>("Generic String");
```

JavaScript does not natively support generics, so developers often rely on untyped workarounds.

```
function identity(arg) {
    return arg;
}

let output = identity("Generic String");
```

6. Advanced Type Features

TypeScript includes features like union and intersection types, allowing for more precise type definitions.

```
type ID = number | string;

function display(id: ID) {
    console.log(`ID: ${id}`);
}
```

JavaScript does not have built-in support for such advanced types.

7. Null and Undefined Handling

TypeScript enforces stricter null and undefined handling compared to JavaScript. By enabling the –strictNullChecks compiler option, TypeScript ensures null or undefined values are not assignable to other types.

```
let name: string = null; // Error with --strictNullChecks
```

JavaScript allows null and undefined values implicitly unless explicitly checked.

```
let name = null; // No error
```

8. Modules

Both TypeScript and JavaScript support modules, but TypeScript builds on top of JavaScript's module system by allowing type-safe imports and exports.

```
// file: module.ts
export const pi = 3.14;

// file: app.ts
import { pi } from "./module";
console.log(pi);
```

JavaScript uses similar syntax for modules, but lacks type safety.

```
// file: module.js
export const pi = 3.14;

// file: app.js
import { pi } from "./module.js";
console.log(pi);
```

9. Tooling and Editor Support

TypeScript's integration with modern editors like Visual Studio Code provides enhanced features such as autocompletion, refactoring tools, and in-line type-checking. While JavaScript has some of these capabilities through additional extensions and tools, the advancements in TypeScript stem from its richer type information enabling more intelligent tooling.

These distinctions underline the enhancements TypeScript brings to JavaScript, particularly in terms of type safety and developer tooling. Understanding these differences aids developers in choosing the right language for their projects and fully leveraging the benefits TypeScript offers.

1.5 TypeScript's Type System

TypeScript's type system is one of the fundamental aspects that distinguish it from JavaScript. The type system introduces static typing to the otherwise dynamically typed JavaScript language, allowing for early detection of errors, improved code navigation, and better IDE support. In TypeScript, you can define types for variables, function parameters, return values, and object properties, leading to more robust and maintainable code.

Basic Types

TypeScript provides several basic types which include boolean, number, string, array, tuple, enum, any, void, null, undefined, and never. These types serve as the building blocks for more complex type definitions.

```
// Boolean
let isDone: boolean = false;

// Number
let decimal: number = 6;
let hex: number = 0xf00d;
let binary: number = 0b1010;
let octal: number = 0o744;

// String
let color: string = "blue";
color = 'red';

// Array
let list: number[] = [1, 2, 3];
let anotherList: Array<number> = [1, 2, 3];

// Tuple
let x: [string, number];
x = ["hello", 10]; // OK
x = [10, "hello"]; // Error

// Enum
enum Color {Red, Green, Blue}
let c: Color = Color.Green;

// Any
let notSure: any = 4;
notSure = "maybe a string instead";
notSure = false; // OK, definitely a boolean

// Void
function warnUser(): void {
    console.log("This is my warning message");
}
```

```
// Null and Undefined
let u: undefined = undefined;
let n: null = null;

// Never
function error(message: string): never {
    throw new Error(message);
}

// Object
declare function create(o: object | null): void;
create({ prop: 0 }); // OK
create(null); // OK
```

Type Inference and Type Annotations

TypeScript's type inference capability allows the compiler to infer types when they are not explicitly defined. This feature can make code shorter and more readable while still maintaining type safety.

```
let count = 10; // inferred type is number

// Function with inferred return type
function add(a: number, b: number) {
    return a + b;
}
```

However, TypeScript also allows for explicit type annotations to ensure that variables and function signatures adhere to specified types.

```
let message: string = "Hello, TypeScript!";
function greet(name: string): string {
    return "Hello, " + name;
}
```

Type Aliases and Interfaces

Type aliases and interfaces in TypeScript are powerful ways to define custom types that can be reused throughout an application. Type aliases allow developers to create new names for existing types, while interfaces define the structure of an object.

```
type StringOrNumber = string | number;
let sample: StringOrNumber = "hello";
sample = 42; // OK
```

```
interface Person {
    firstName: string;
    lastName: string;
    age?: number; // optional property
}

function welcome(person: Person) {
    console.log("Hello, " + person.firstName);
}
```

```
let user = { firstName: "John", lastName: "Doe" };
welcome(user); // OK
```

Generics

Generics enable the creation of reusable components that can work with a variety of types. Generics provide a way to define functions, classes, and interfaces that operate with type variables, allowing for greater flexibility and type safety.

```
// Generic function
function identity<T>(arg: T): T {
    return arg;
}

let output = identity<string>("myString"); // type of output is 'string'
let anotherOutput = identity<number>(100); // type of anotherOutput is 'number'
```

Generics can also be used in class and interface definitions to create flexible and type-safe data structures.

```
class GenericNumber<T> {
    zeroValue: T;
    add: (x: T, y: T) => T;
}

let myGenericNumber = new GenericNumber<number>();
myGenericNumber.zeroValue = 0;
myGenericNumber.add = function(x, y) { return x + y; };
```

Union and Intersection Types

Union types allow a value to be one of several types, providing flexibility in type definitions without sacrificing type safety.

```
function getLength(input: string | number): number {
    if (typeof input === "string") {
        return input.length;
    } else {
        return input;
    }
}
```

Intersection types combine multiple types into one, allowing an object to satisfy multiple type requirements.

```
interface A {
    a: string;
}

interface B {
    b: string;
}

type C = A & B;
```

```
let example: C = { a: "hello", b: "world" };
```

Type Guards and Type Assertions

Type guards are used to narrow down the type within a conditional block, improving code reliability and reducing runtime errors.

```
function isString(x: any): x is string {
    return typeof x === "string";
}

function example(x: string | number) {
    if (isString(x)) {
        console.log(x.length); // x is string
    } else {
        console.log(x.toFixed(2)); // x is number
    }
}
```

Type assertions allow developers to inform the compiler about the specific type of an expression, thus bypassing type checks.

```
let someValue: any = "this is a string";
let strLength: number = (someValue as string).length;
```

TypeScript's type system significantly enhances code quality by leveraging static typing. Through basic types, type annotations, type inference, type aliases, interfaces, generics, union and intersection types, type guards, and type assertions, developers can write clear, concise, and reliable code that is easier to maintain and debug.

1.6 Use Cases and Real-World Examples

TypeScript's rigorous type system and support for modern JavaScript features make it suitable for a variety of real-world applications. Its robust nature ensures applications are maintainable, scalable, and less prone to runtime errors. This section explores prominent use cases and real-world examples demonstrating the advantages of adopting TypeScript.

Web Applications:

TypeScript is extensively used in web development, particularly with frameworks such as Angular, React, and Vue.js. Angular, an open-source framework created by Google, was one of the first major libraries to integrate TypeScript comprehensively. The following example demonstrates a simple component in Angular using TypeScript:

```
import { Component } from '@angular/core';

@Component({
  selector: 'app-hello-world',
  template: '<h1>Hello, {{name}}!</h1>'
})
export class HelloWorldComponent {
  name: string;

  constructor() {
    this.name = 'TypeScript';
  }
}
```

In this example, the HelloWorldComponent defines a template binding to the name property. The type system ensures name is always a string, preventing runtime errors.

Server-Side Development:

With the advent of Node.js, JavaScript has expanded beyond the realm of client-side scripting, allowing developers to build server-side applications. TypeScript enhances Node.js applications by enforcing types and modern JavaScript syntax.

```
import * as express from 'express';

const app: express.Application = express();
const port: number = 3000;

app.get('/', (req: express.Request, res: express.Response) => {
  res.send('Hello TypeScript');
});

app.listen(port, () => {
  console.log(`Server running on port ${port}`);
});
```

The use of type annotations (express.Application, express.Request, express.Response) and ES6 features (e.g., modules, arrow functions) help in building a safe and clean server setup.

Large-Scale Applications:

One of TypeScript's strengths is in managing large codebases, where the static type checking can catch potential issues early in the development cycle. Companies like Microsoft, Asana, and Slack use TypeScript in their applications for improved code maintainability and minimized bug tracking.

Consider a scenario involving complex business logic and multiple interconnected components:

```
interface IUser {
  id: number;
  name: string;
  email: string;
}

class UserService {
  private users: IUser[] = [];

  addUser(user: IUser): void {
    this.users.push(user);
  }

  getUserById(id: number): IUser | undefined {
    return this.users.find(user => user.id === id);
  }
}

const userService = new UserService();
userService.addUser({ id: 1, name: 'Alice', email: 'alice@example.com' });

const user = userService.getUserById(1);
console.log(user);
```

TypeScript's interface (IUser) and class (UserService) structures ensure that the users array strictly adheres to the user data contract and the logic for adding and retrieving users is robust.

Library and Framework Development:

TypeScript is also ideal for developing libraries and frameworks due to its strong typing and code clarity benefits. Creating a library ensures that developers integrating it will benefit from IntelliSense and early error detection.

```
export function sum(a: number, b: number): number {
  return a + b;
}

export function multiply(a: number, b: number): number {
  return a * b;
}
```

When incorporated into a project, TypeScript consumers will experience increased confidence in using these functions due to the inherent type safety.

Tooling and Developer Experience:

Besides applications, TypeScript significantly enhances the developer experience through better tooling. Editors such as Visual Studio Code offer rich IntelliSense, autocompletion, and refactoring support when TypeScript is in use.

Consider automatic type inference and type suggestions:

```
let numbers = [1, 2, 3, 4];
let doubled = numbers.map(n => n * 2);

console.log(doubled);
```

Even without explicit type annotations, TypeScript infers that numbers is an array of numbers, and doubled is correspondingly inferred as number[].

TypeScript's diverse applicability—from frontend to backend, utility libraries to large-scale applications, and improved developer tools—demonstrates its flexibility and efficacy in modern software development.

1.7 Installing and Running TypeScript

To begin developing in TypeScript, it is essential to first install the necessary tools and configure the development environment. TypeScript can be installed and run on various platforms and accommodates different project structures and workflows. This section will guide you through the installation process, configuring a TypeScript project, and compiling and executing TypeScript code.

1. Installing TypeScript

TypeScript installation typically leverages npm (Node Package Manager), part of Node.js environment. Ensure Node.js and npm are installed. You can verify this by running:

```
node -v
npm -v
```

To install TypeScript globally, use the following npm command:

```
npm install -g typescript
```

Verify the installation by checking the TypeScript compiler version:

```
tsc -v
```

2. Setting Up a TypeScript Project

A TypeScript project can be initiated by creating a configuration file named tsconfig.json. This file specifies compiler options and includes/excludes files from the compilation process. Let's start by creating a basic tsconfig.json file:

```
{
  "compilerOptions": {
    "target": "es6",
    "module": "commonjs",
    "strict": true,
    "outDir": "./dist"
  },
  "include": ["src/**/*"]
}
```

Details of the compilerOptions used:

- target: Specifies the ECMAScript target version. In this case, es6.
- module: Determines module system. Common options are commonjs and esnext.
- strict: Enables all strict type-checking options.
- outDir: Specifies the output directory for compiled JavaScript files.
- include: Array of glob patterns to specify files that should be compiled.

3. Writing TypeScript Code

Create a source directory structure, typically src/. Within this directory, create a file named index.ts:

```
function greet(name: string) {
  return `Hello, ${name}!`;
}

console.log(greet('World'));
```

This code snippet defines a simple function greet that takes a string argument name and returns a greeting message. The console.log statement invokes this function with World as the argument.

4. Compiling TypeScript Code

Compile TypeScript code using the TypeScript compiler tsc. Run the following command from the project's root directory (where tsconfig.json is located):

```
tsc
```

This command reads tsconfig.json and compiles the .ts files specified in the include section. The compiled JavaScript files are output to the directory specified in outDir (in this case, dist/).

5. Running Compiled JavaScript

Execute the compiled JavaScript file using node:

```
node dist/index.js
```

Expected output:

Hello, World!

6. Automating Build Process

To streamline the development process, consider using tools like tsc –watch or integrating with task runners/build automation tools like Gulp, Webpack, or npm scripts.

Using tsc –watch, the TypeScript compiler monitors files for changes and recompiles automatically:

```
tsc --watch
```

For automation with npm scripts, add the following in package.json:

```
"scripts": {
  "build": "tsc",
  "start": "node dist/index.js"
}
```

Use these npm commands for building and running the application:

```
npm run build
npm run start
```

The npm run build command triggers the TypeScript compiler as defined, while the npm run start command executes the compiled JavaScript file.

This methodical approach to installing and running TypeScript ensures that you are well-equipped to manage TypeScript projects efficiently and effectively. It forms a strong foundation for delving deeper into TypeScript's advanced features and capabilities in subsequent chapters and sections.

1.8 Your First TypeScript Program

To get started with TypeScript, we need to go through a few basic steps: setting up the environment, writing our first TypeScript code, compiling it to JavaScript, and running it. This process will help solidify the concepts introduced in previous sections and provide a practical foundation for further development.

Before we dive into writing our first TypeScript program, ensure that you have Node.js and npm installed, as they are prerequisites for installing TypeScript. You can verify their installation by running the following commands in your terminal:

```
node -v
npm -v
```

If you do not have Node.js installed, download and install it from the official website (https://nodejs.org/).

Next, install TypeScript globally on your machine using npm:

```
npm install -g typescript
```

Verify the installation by checking the TypeScript version:

```
tsc -v
```

Once TypeScript is installed, you can proceed to write and run your first program.

Create a new directory for your TypeScript project and navigate to it:

```
mkdir my-first-typescript-project
cd my-first-typescript-project
```

Inside this directory, create a new file named hello.ts. The .ts extension indicates that this is a TypeScript file.

Open hello.ts in your preferred text editor and add the following code:

```
function greeter(person: string) {
    return "Hello, " + person;
}

let user = "World";

console.log(greeter(user));
```

This is a basic TypeScript function that greets a user. Let's break down the code:

- The greeter function accepts a single argument, person, which is explicitly typed as a string.
- The function returns a greeting message concatenated with the person argument.
- We declare a variable user and assign it the value "World".

- Finally, we call the greeter function with user as the argument and print the result to the console using console.log.

The next step is to compile the TypeScript code to JavaScript. TypeScript provides a compiler, tsc, which converts TypeScript code to JavaScript. Run the following command in your terminal to compile the hello.ts file:

```
tsc hello.ts
```

This command generates a file named hello.js in the same directory. You can open hello.js to inspect the JavaScript code generated by the TypeScript compiler. You will notice that the TypeScript-specific syntax (such as type annotations) has been removed.

To execute the compiled JavaScript code, use Node.js:

```
node hello.js
```

The output of the program will be:

```
Hello, World
```

This simple example demonstrates the basic flow of writing, compiling, and running a TypeScript program. TypeScript's type annotations (e.g., person: string) help catch errors early and provide better tooling support.

Consider another example to dive deeper into TypeScript's capabilities. Create a new file named person.ts and add the following code:

```
class Person {
    fullName: string;

    constructor(public firstName: string, public middleInitial: string, public lastName:
        string) {
        this.fullName = firstName + " " + middleInitial + " " + lastName;
    }
}

function greeter(person: Person) {
    return "Hello, " + person.fullName;
}

let user = new Person("John", "D.", "Doe");

console.log(greeter(user));
```

Explanation of the code:

- This example defines a Person class with a constructor that initializes three public fields: firstName, middleInitial, and lastName.

The fullName field is created by concatenating these attributes.

- The greeter function now expects a Person object instead of a string.
- We create a new instance of Person and pass it to the greeter function.

Compile and run this TypeScript code following the same steps as before:

```
tsc person.ts
node person.js
```

You will see the output:

```
Hello, John D. Doe
```

This section showcases the power of TypeScript's static types and class-based object-oriented features, which are particularly useful for building large-scale applications. The improved code clarity and error detection capabilities offer significant advantages over vanilla JavaScript.

1.9 Helpful Resources and Communities

TypeScript's rapidly growing adoption by developers worldwide has fostered a wealth of resources and vibrant communities. Various online platforms offer extensive materials ranging from official documentation to community-driven tutorials, forums, and code repositories. For developers seeking to deepen their understanding of TypeScript or find specific solutions, these resources and communities provide invaluable support and knowledge.

Official TypeScript Documentation

The most authoritative source for understanding TypeScript is the TypeScript Official Documentation, maintained by Microsoft at https://www.typescriptlang.org/docs/. This comprehensive resource offers detailed explanations on every aspect of TypeScript, including:

- **Basic Concepts**: Introduces fundamental concepts, helping beginners get started with TypeScript.

- **Advanced Topics**: Delve into more complex topics such as type guards, decorators, and generics.
- **Handbook**: A guided tour through both basic and advanced features of TypeScript.
- **Project Configuration**: Instructions on TypeScript project configuration using tsconfig.json.
- **Compiler Options**: Detailed descriptions of compiler flags and their effects.

TypeScript GitHub Repository

The TypeScript GitHub Repository is located at https://github.com/microsoft/TypeScript. It serves as the central hub for the TypeScript source code, issue tracking, and contributions. Key resources available here include:

- README.md: Provides an overview of the repository and basic setup instructions.
- Issues: A platform for reporting bugs, requesting features, and discussing problems.
- Pull Requests: For contributing code or documentation improvements.
- Wiki: Additional technical resources and community guidelines.

Online Tutorials and Guides

Numerous online resources provide tutorials and in-depth guides to help developers at various levels:

- **TypeScript Deep Dive** (https://basarat.gitbook.io/typescript/): A comprehensive e-book written by Basarat Ali Syed, covering both foundational and advanced topics.
- **Microsoft Learn** (https://docs.microsoft.com/en-us/learn/): Interactive courses and modules from Microsoft, including TypeScript.

- **TypeScript Course on Codecademy** (https://www.codecademy.com/learn/learn-typescript): An interactive course designed for learners to practice TypeScript through hands-on exercises.
- **TypeScript Programming with Visual Studio Code** (https://code.visualstudio.com/Docs/languages/typescript): Specific guides on using TypeScript in Visual Studio Code, with tips and best practices.

Community Forums and Discussion Platforms

Engaging with the TypeScript community through discussion platforms provides developers with a venue to ask questions, share knowledge, and network:

- **Stack Overflow** (https://stackoverflow.com/questions/tagged/typescript): A popular Q&A site where developers can ask and answer TypeScript-related questions.
- **Reddit** (https://www.reddit.com/r/typescript/): A community-driven forum where users discuss TypeScript news, tips, and projects.
- **TypeScript Gitter Chat** (https://gitter.im/Microsoft/TypeScript): A chatroom where developers can interact in real-time and discuss various aspects of TypeScript.
- **Discord Communities**: Several Discord servers such as #typescript on the dev.to Discord provide community support and discussion.

Open Source Projects

Participating in open source projects that use TypeScript can be an excellent way to learn from real-world codebases:

- **DefinitelyTyped** (https://github.com/DefinitelyTyped/DefinitelyTyped): A repository containing TypeScript type definitions for popular JavaScript libraries.

- **Angular** (https://github.com/angular/angular): The Angular framework, written in TypeScript, offering insights into building large-scale applications.
- **React with TypeScript** (https://github.com/typescript-cheatsheets/react): Community-driven cheatsheets and best practices for using React with TypeScript.
- **NestJS** (https://github.com/nestjs/nest): A progressive Node.js framework built with TypeScript, showcasing advanced Type-Script patterns.

Conferences and Meetups

Attending TypeScript conferences and meetups provides an opportunity to learn from experts and network with other TypeScript enthusiasts:

- **TSConf** (https://tsconf.io/): An annual conference dedicated to TypeScript, featuring talks by TypeScript team members and prominent community contributors.
- **Meetup Groups**: Look for local meetup groups focused on Type-Script or JavaScript to join discussions and collaborative coding sessions.
- **Microsoft's Virtual Events** (https://techcommunity.microsoft.com/): Online events and webinars hosted by Microsoft, often covering TypeScript-related topics.

Exploring these resources and engaging with the TypeScript community can greatly enhance one's understanding and proficiency with TypeScript. As the TypeScript ecosystem continues to evolve, staying connected with these resources will ensure access to the latest developments and best practices.

Chapter 2

Setting Up the TypeScript Environment

This chapter guides you through the process of setting up an efficient TypeScript development environment, including installing necessary tools such as Node.js, npm, and the TypeScript compiler. Key configurations such as setting up a TypeScript project, understanding the tsconfig.json file, and integrating build tools will be covered. Additionally, it will detail how to configure and use popular integrated development environments (IDEs) like Visual Studio Code to compile and manage TypeScript code effectively, ensuring both flexibility and productivity.

2.1 System Requirements

Before delving into the intricacies of setting up a TypeScript development environment, it is imperative to ensure that your system meets certain fundamental requirements. This section details these prerequisites, focusing on operating system compatibility, hardware specifications, and essential software installations. Adhering to these recommendations will facilitate a smooth and efficient setup of TypeScript and the associated development tools.

Operating System Compatibility

TypeScript, along with necessary tools such as Node.js and npm, is compatible with major operating systems including Windows, macOS, and various distributions of Linux. Ensure that you are running one of the following:

- **Windows:** Windows 10 or later.
- **macOS:** macOS 10.12 (Sierra) or later.
- **Linux:** Any modern distribution such as Ubuntu 18.04 LTS or later, Fedora 29 or later, or CentOS 7 or later.

Hardware Specifications

While TypeScript compilation is not heavily demanding on hardware, certain minimum specifications are recommended for optimal performance:

- **Processor:** Dual-core CPU (Intel/AMD) with a clock speed of at least 2.0 GHz.
- **Memory:** A minimum of 4 GB of RAM is recommended, though 8 GB or more is preferable for handling larger projects and multitasking efficiently.
- **Storage:** At least 10 GB of free disk space to accommodate the installation of Node.js, npm, TypeScript, and related dependencies.
- **Network:** An internet connection for downloading the required software packages and dependencies.

Essential Software

Several software installations are requisites for setting up a TypeScript development environment. Detailed steps for installation will be covered in subsequent sections; however, the following list provides an overview:

- **Node.js and npm:** Node.js is a JavaScript runtime environment that allows you to run JavaScript on the server-side, while npm (Node Package Manager) is used to manage libraries and dependencies. Both are integral for running and managing TypeScript projects.

- **TypeScript Compiler:** The TypeScript compiler (tsc) converts TypeScript code into JavaScript. It is crucial for project development and is installed via npm.
- **Integrated Development Environment (IDE):** An IDE such as Visual Studio Code, IntelliJ IDEA, or WebStorm is recommended for writing, compiling, and debugging TypeScript code. These IDEs offer rich support for TypeScript and other web technologies.

Node.js and npm Versions

Ensuring you have the correct versions of Node.js and npm is essential as certain features and performance improvements are tied to specific versions. The recommended versions are:

- **Node.js:** Version 14.x or later. Long Term Support (LTS) versions are preferred for their stability and ongoing support.
- **npm:** Version 6.x or later, typically bundled with the recommended Node.js versions.

To verify the versions installed on your system, you can use the following commands in your command line interface (CLI):

```
node -v
npm -v
```

Correct output confirming appropriate installations might look like:

```
v14.17.0
6.14.13
```

Permissions and Administrative Rights

During the installation and configuration process, administrative rights may be required, especially on Windows and certain Linux distributions. Ensure you have the necessary permissions to install software and modify system settings to avoid interruptions during the setup process.

Environment Variable Configuration

On some systems, especially Windows, it may be necessary to configure environment variables to add the paths to Node.js and npm. This ensures that the CLI can access these tools from any directory. Typical steps include:

- **Windows:** Open Environment Variables in System Properties and add C:\Program Files\nodejs\ to the PATH variable.
- **macOS/Linux:** Modify the PATH variable in your shell configuration file (.bashrc, .zshrc, or .bash_profile) to include the directory where Node.js and npm are installed:

```
export PATH=/usr/local/bin:$PATH
```

Ensuring that these system requirements are met lays a stable foundation for the subsequent steps involved in setting up an efficient TypeScript development environment.

2.2 Installing Node.js and npm

To establish a robust TypeScript development environment, the installation of Node.js and npm (Node Package Manager) is imperative. Node.js is a JavaScript runtime that enables server-side execution of JavaScript, while npm is the default package manager for Node.js, facilitating the management of libraries and dependencies. The following instructions delineate the process for installing Node.js and npm on various operating systems.

For Windows:

- Navigate to the official Node.js website at https://nodejs.org.
- Download the Windows Installer corresponding to the latest Long Term Support (LTS) version.
- Execute the downloaded MSI installer file.
- Follow the installation prompts and ensure that the Add to PATH option is checked during the setup process. This ensures accessible command-line execution of Node.js and npm.
- Verify the installation by opening a Command Prompt and running the following commands:

```
node -v
npm -v
```

```
$ node -v
v16.13.0

$ npm -v
8.1.0
```

The version numbers may vary with the latest releases. Successful execution of these commands with version outputs confirms the correct installation.

For macOS:

- Visit the Node.js website and download the macOS Installer.
- Open the downloaded .pkg file and run through the installer steps.
- To verify the installation, open the Terminal and input:

```
node -v
npm -v
```

```
$ node -v
v16.13.0

$ npm -v
8.1.0
```

The above outputs indicate a successful installation.

Alternatively, macOS users can employ Homebrew for a streamlined installation process. Ensure Homebrew is installed, then execute the following commands in Terminal:

```
brew install node
```

Reconfirm the installation with the same version check commands mentioned above.

For Linux:

Different Linux distributions have various package managers and steps to install Node.js and npm. Below are guidelines for popular distributions:

- **Ubuntu/Debian-based:**

  ```
  sudo apt update
  sudo apt install nodejs npm
  ```

  Conduct the version verification process using:

  ```
  node -v
  npm -v
  ```

- **Fedora:**

  ```
  sudo dnf install nodejs npm
  ```

  Verify with:

  ```
  node -v
  npm -v
  ```

- **Arch Linux:**

  ```
  sudo pacman -S nodejs npm
  ```

  Again, verify installation:

  ```
  node -v
  npm -v
  ```

Using Node Version Manager (nvm):

For users who require multiple versions of Node.js, nvm provides an efficient solution. Begin with the installation of nvm:

```
curl -o- https://raw.githubusercontent.com/nvm-sh/nvm/v0.39.0/install.sh | bash
```

Reload the shell configuration to make nvm available in the terminal:

```
source ~/.nvm/nvm.sh
```

Install Node.js using nvm:

```
nvm install node
```

Verify the installation:

```
node -v
npm -v
```

Managing multiple versions becomes seamless with nvm:

```
nvm install [version]
nvm use [version]
nvm ls
```

For instance, to switch to Node.js version 14.x:

```
nvm install 14
nvm use 14
```

Ensuring Node.js and npm are installed correctly serves as the foundation for developing and managing TypeScript applications. Multiple methods and tools facilitate the process, allowing flexibility for different operating systems and user preferences.

2.3 Installing TypeScript Compiler

To develop applications using TypeScript, the first essential step is to install the TypeScript compiler. The TypeScript compiler, also referred to as tsc, translates TypeScript code into JavaScript, which can then be executed in any JavaScript runtime environment such as a web browser or Node.js. The following instructions outline the installation process of TypeScript using Node Package Manager (npm).

- **Prerequisites**

Before installing the TypeScript compiler, ensure that Node.js and npm are installed on your system. To verify the installation, open your command-line interface (CLI) and execute the following commands:

```
node -v
npm -v
```

These commands should return the installed versions of Node.js and npm, respectively. If Node.js and npm are not installed, refer to the previous section on *Installing Node.js and npm*.

- **Global Installation**

One common approach is to install TypeScript globally. This setup allows you to utilize the tsc command from any directory on your system. To install TypeScript globally, execute the following command in your CLI:

```
npm install -g typescript
```

The -g flag specifies a global installation. After the installation completes, verify the installation by checking the TypeScript compiler version:

```
tsc -v
```

A successful installation will return the Version number of the TypeScript compiler.

- **Local Installation**

In some projects, it might be preferable to install TypeScript locally, especially when different projects require incompatible TypeScript versions. To install TypeScript as a local dependency, navigate to your project directory and run:

```
npm install typescript --save-dev
```

The -save-dev option ensures that TypeScript is added as a development dependency in your package.json file. You can then access the TypeScript compiler via npx, a tool that npm provides to run binaries from the local node_modules directory.

To verify the local installation, execute the following command:

```
npx tsc -v
```

This will display the installed version of TypeScript if the installation was successful.

- **Compiler Configuration**

Once the TypeScript compiler is installed, you can configure your project to specify compiler options by creating a tsconfig.json file. This file houses configuration options that control the TypeScript compiler behavior. To generate a basic tsconfig.json file, run:

```
tsc --init
```

This command generates a tsconfig.json file with default values. Modifying this file to suit your project's requirements is essential, and its structure will be further discussed in the *Understanding tsconfig.json* section.

- **Upgrade TypeScript Compiler**

To upgrade the TypeScript compiler to the latest version, use npm update commands. For a global installation, use:

```
npm update -g typescript
```

For a local project installation, navigate to the project directory and run:

```
npm update typescript
```

- **Uninstalling TypeScript Compiler**

If you need to uninstall the global TypeScript compiler, you can do so by executing:

```
npm uninstall -g typescript
```

Likewise, to uninstall TypeScript from a specific project, navigate to the project directory and run:

```
npm uninstall typescript
```

Following this, it is advisable to remove TypeScript references from the package.json file to maintain clean project dependencies.

Installing the TypeScript compiler is an essential step in setting up your TypeScript development environment. With the compiler appropriately installed and configured, you can effectively translate TypeScript code into JavaScript, ensuring compatibility across various execution contexts.

2.4 Setting Up a TypeScript Project

Setting up a TypeScript project involves a series of steps that ensure your development environment is conducive to efficient coding, testing, and debugging. We will walk through initializing a new project, creating essential configuration files, and organizing your project's structure.

1. Initializing a New Project

The first step in setting up a TypeScript project is to create a new project directory and initialize it with npm. This can be achieved through the following commands:

```
mkdir my-typescript-project
cd my-typescript-project
npm init -y
```

The npm init -y command generates a package.json file with default settings, which is essential for managing project dependencies.

2. Installing TypeScript

With your project initialized, the next step is to install TypeScript as a development dependency. This ensures that TypeScript is available for compiling your code but isn't bundled into your final project:

```
npm install typescript --save-dev
```

3. Creating the tsconfig.json File

The tsconfig.json file is crucial for defining TypeScript compiler options and specifying the files to be included in the project. You can create this file manually, or by running:

```
npx tsc --init
```

Executing npx tsc –init generates a tsconfig.json file with default configurations. Here is an example of a basic tsconfig.json file:

```
{
    "compilerOptions": {
        "target": "ES6",
        "module": "commonjs",
        "strict": true,
        "esModuleInterop": true,
        "skipLibCheck": true,
        "forceConsistentCasingInFileNames": true
    },
    "include": ["src"]
}
```

This setup specifies that the target JavaScript version is ES6 and the module system is CommonJS. The inclusion of src ensures that all TypeScript files within the src directory are included.

4. Creating Project Structure

A well-organized project structure enhances maintainability and clarity. A typical TypeScript project structure might look like this:

```
my-typescript-project/

  src/
     index.ts
     components/
        exampleComponent.ts

  .gitignore
  tsconfig.json
```

Here's a brief explanation of the different components:

- src/: Contains all TypeScript source files.
- index.ts: Typically the entry point of the application.
- components/: A directory for organizing different components if the project has a modular structure.

- .gitignore: A file that specifies which files and directories should be ignored by Git.

5. Writing Your First TypeScript File

With the project structure in place, you can now create your first TypeScript file. Open src/index.ts and add the following code:

```
function greet(name: string): string {
    return `Hello, ${name}!`;
}

console.log(greet('World'));
```

This simple function demonstrates TypeScript's type annotations and template literals. The greet function takes a name parameter of type string and returns a greeting message.

6. Compiling the TypeScript Code

To compile your TypeScript code into JavaScript, run the TypeScript compiler using the following command:

```
npx tsc
```

If everything is correctly set up, this will create a dist directory (or another directory specified in outDir option in tsconfig.json), containing the compiled JavaScript files that mirror your src structure.

7. Running the Compiled Code

To execute the compiled JavaScript, you can use Node.js as follows:

```
node dist/index.js
```

```
Hello, World!
```

This confirms that your TypeScript code was successfully compiled and executed, thus completing the basic setup of a TypeScript project.

Ensuring a methodical setup for your TypeScript project facilitates a robust development workflow and paves the way for easy scaling and maintenance.

2.5 Understanding tsconfig.json

The tsconfig.json file is a crucial configuration file in TypeScript projects. It serves as the foundation for configuring the TypeScript compiler (tsc) with various options that dictate how your TypeScript code gets compiled. Within this section, we will meticulously explore the structure and options available in a tsconfig.json file, aimed at refining your understanding and mastery over this integral component.

At the most basic level, a tsconfig.json file in the root directory of your project might look like this:

```
{
    "compilerOptions": {
        "target": "es6",
        "module": "commonjs"
    },
    "include": [
        "src/**/*"
    ],
    "exclude": [
        "node_modules",
        "**/*.spec.ts"
    ]
}
```

Compiler Options

The compilerOptions object allows you to specify multiple settings that direct the TypeScript compilation process. Understanding and appropriately setting these options is critical for achieving desired build outputs.

- target: Specifies the JavaScript language version for the emitted JavaScript. Common targets include ES5, ES6/ES2015, ESNext.
- module: Defines the module code generation method. Options include commonjs, amd, es6, es2020, system, umd, among others.
- outDir: Specifies the directory where the compiler outputs the compiled files.
- rootDir: Identifies the root directory of input files, which is used for the compilation context.
- strict: Enables all strict type-checking options. This flag is a shorthand for various other flags such as strictNullChecks, strictFunctionTypes, and more.

Example:

```
{
    "compilerOptions": {
        "target": "es6",
        "module": "commonjs",
        "outDir": "./dist",
```

```
        "rootDir": "./src",
        "strict": true
    }
}
```

Files, Include, and Exclude

Files: Specifies an array of relative or absolute file paths to include in the project.

Include: Specifies an array of file patterns to include. Useful for ensuring only certain files or directories are part of the compilation context.

Exclude: Specifies files or directories to exclude from the compilation. Typical defaults include node_modules.

Example:

```
{
    "files": [
        "src/main.ts"
    ],
    "include": [
        "src/**/*.ts"
    ],
    "exclude": [
        "node_modules",
        "dist"
    ]
}
```

Further Useful Compiler Options

- allowJs: Allows JavaScript files to be compiled alongside TypeScript files.
- sourceMap: Indicates if .map files should be generated, aiding in debugging by mapping the emitted code back to the source TypeScript.
- declaration: Generates corresponding .d.ts files alongside JavaScript output, aiding in TypeScript type-checking when these compiled types are used in other projects.
- noImplicitAny: Issues errors when variables have an any type. Enhances type safety by discouraging the easy escape of any conversion.

Example:

```
{
```

```
    "compilerOptions": {
        "allowJs": true,
        "sourceMap": true,
        "declaration": true,
        "noImplicitAny": true
    }
}
```

Advanced Compilation Options

- paths: Provides a way to specify module aliases, which can simplify module import paths.
- baseUrl: Configures the base directory to resolve non-relative module names.
- typeRoots: Specifies directories in which the TypeScript compiler should look for type definitions.

Example:

```
{
    "compilerOptions": {
        "baseUrl": ".",
        "paths": {
            "@models/*": ["src/models/*"],
            "@utils/*": ["src/utils/*"]
        },
        "typeRoots": [
            "./node_modules/@types",
            "./typings"
        ]
    }
}
```

tsconfig.json **Inheritance**

Inheritance is supported through extends, allowing for the creation of a base tsconfig.json that other configuration files can extend. The extends property is a relative or absolute path to another tsconfig.json file.

Example:

```
{
    "extends": "./base-tsconfig.json",
    "compilerOptions": {
        "outDir": "./build"
    },
    "include": [
        "src/**/*"
    ]
}
```

Execution and Validation

To use the tsconfig.json file, ensure it is placed in the project's root directory. Upon executing the tsc command in the terminal, the TypeScript compiler automatically locates and reads the tsconfig.json file to apply the specified configurations.

```
$ tsc
```

2.6 Integrating TypeScript with Build Tools

The incorporation of TypeScript into existing or new projects often necessitates the integration of build tools to automate tasks such as compilation, linting, and bundling. Efficient build tools streamline the development process, ensuring that your TypeScript code is consistently compiled and deployable. This section delves into integrating TypeScript with popular build tools, including gulp, webpack, and Grunt, illustrating how to configure each tool to work seamlessly with TypeScript.

Integrating TypeScript with gulp

gulp is a toolkit for automating painful or time-consuming tasks in your development workflow. It uses Node.js streams to facilitate fast builds. To set up a TypeScript project using gulp, follow these steps:

- Install gulp and necessary plugins:

```
$ npm install --save-dev gulp gulp-typescript typescript
```

- Create a gulpfile.js and configure the tasks:

```
const gulp = require('gulp');
const ts = require('gulp-typescript');
const tsProject = ts.createProject('tsconfig.json');

gulp.task('scripts', function() {
    return tsProject.src()
        .pipe(tsProject())
        .js.pipe(gulp.dest('dist'));
});

gulp.task('watch', function() {
    gulp.watch('src/**/*.ts', gulp.series('scripts'));
});

gulp.task('default', gulp.series('scripts', 'watch'));
```

In the above configuration, the scripts task compiles TypeScript files based on the settings in tsconfig.json and places the resulting JavaScript files in the dist directory. The watch task monitors changes in TypeScript files in the src directory and re-runs the scripts task when changes are detected. The default task is configured to run both the scripts and watch tasks.

Integrating TypeScript with webpack

webpack is a powerful module bundler. It takes modules with dependencies and generates static assets representing those modules. To integrate TypeScript with webpack:

- Install necessary dependencies:

```
$ npm install --save-dev webpack webpack-cli ts-loader typescript
```

- Create a webpack.config.js configuration file:

```
const path = require('path');

module.exports = {
    entry: './src/index.ts',
    module: {
        rules: [
            {
                test: /\.ts$/,
                use: 'ts-loader',
                exclude: /node_modules/,
            },
        ],
    },
    resolve: {
        extensions: ['.ts', '.js'],
    },
    output: {
        filename: 'bundle.js',
        path: path.resolve(__dirname, 'dist'),
    },
};
```

- Update package.json to include a build script:

```
"scripts": {
    "build": "webpack"
}
```

The configuration tells webpack to use ts-loader for files ending in .ts, ensuring they are processed by the TypeScript compiler. The entry point for the application is src/index.ts, and the bundled output will be dist/bundle.js. Running the build script compiles the TypeScript code and creates a single bundled file using webpack.

Integrating TypeScript with Grunt

Grunt is a JavaScript task runner, designed to automate repetitive tasks. To set up TypeScript with Grunt:

- Install Grunt and necessary plugins:

```
$ npm install --save-dev grunt grunt-ts typescript
```

- Create a Gruntfile.js configuration file:

```
module.exports = function(grunt) {

    grunt.initConfig({
        ts: {
            default : {
                tsconfig: './tsconfig.json'
            }
        },
        watch: {
            scripts: {
                files: ['./src/**/*.ts'],
                tasks: ['ts'],
            },
        },
    });

    grunt.loadNpmTasks('grunt-ts');
    grunt.loadNpmTasks('grunt-contrib-watch');

    grunt.registerTask('default', ['ts', 'watch']);
};
```

In the Grunt configuration above, the ts task loads the TypeScript configuration from tsconfig.json and compiles the TypeScript files. The watch task tracks changes to the TypeScript files in the src directory and reruns the ts task upon detecting modifications.

Each build tool offers specific advantages depending on the complexity and requirements of the project, and selecting the appropriate one can significantly enhance productivity. Proper integration of TypeScript into these tools ensures smooth and efficient project workflows, automating repetitive tasks and maintaining consistency in code management.

2.7 Setting Up an Integrated Development Environment (IDE)

A well-configured Integrated Development Environment (IDE) is crucial for enhancing productivity when working with TypeScript. This section details how to set up and configure an IDE, with a focus on Visual Studio Code (VS Code), one of the most popular choices for TypeScript development due to its rich feature set and extensibility.

Visual Studio Code can be downloaded from the official website. Installation is straightforward, with executables available for Windows, macOS, and Linux systems. Follow the platform-specific instructions:

- For **Windows**, run the installer and follow the setup wizard.
- For **macOS**, download the .dmg file, open it, and drag Visual Studio Code to the Applications folder.
- For **Linux**, you can use the package manager to install it:

```
sudo apt update
sudo apt install code
```

Once installed, launch Visual Studio Code. The initial screen prompts you to start a new file, open an existing directory, or clone a repository. For TypeScript development, open a directory where your TypeScript project resides or create a new one.

```
mkdir my-typescript-project
cd my-typescript-project
code .
```

This command opens the current directory in Visual Studio Code.

Extensions for TypeScript Development

To maximize the efficiency of working with TypeScript, the following extensions should be installed:

- TypeScript and JavaScript Language Features: Provides the necessary support for TypeScript syntax highlighting, IntelliSense, and other TypeScript-related features.
- ESLint: Integrates ESLint into VS Code to analyze TypeScript code for adherence to a defined style guide and catch syntax and formatting issues.

- Prettier - Code formatter: Automatically formats your TypeScript code based on predefined rules, ensuring consistency across your codebase.

Install these extensions via the Extensions view by clicking the Extensions icon in the Activity Bar on the side of the window. Use the search bar to find and install the extensions.

Configuring VS Code for TypeScript Development

Open the command palette via Ctrl+Shift+P (Windows/Linux) or Cmd+Shift+P (macOS). Execute the command TypeScript: Select TypeScript Version and select Use Workspace Version:

```
> TypeScript: Select TypeScript Version > Use Workspace Version
```

This ensures that VS Code uses the TypeScript compiler version specified in your project's node_modules directory, providing consistency with your development environment.

Configuration File: settings.json

The settings.json file in VS Code allows you to customize various settings, such as editor behavior and linter rules. Open the settings JSON file through the command palette:

```
> Preferences: Open Settings (JSON)
```

Include TypeScript-specific configurations in settings.json:

```
{
    "typescript.tsdk": "./node_modules/typescript/lib",
    "eslint.validate": [
        "javascript",
        "javascriptreact",
        "typescript",
        "typescriptreact"
    ],
    "editor.formatOnSave": true,
    "editor.tabSize": 2,
    "editor.insertSpaces": true
}
```

Debugging TypeScript in VS Code

VS Code offers powerful debugging capabilities. To debug your TypeScript code, create a launch.json file in the .vscode directory of your project:

```
> Debug: Open launch.json
```

Select Node.js as the environment. This auto-generates a basic configuration. Customize launch.json to align with your project's structure:

```
{
    "version": "0.2.0",
    "configurations": [
        {
            "type": "node",
            "request": "launch",
            "name": "Launch Program",
            "skipFiles": ["<node_internals>/**"],
            "program": "${workspaceFolder}/src/index.ts",
            "preLaunchTask": "tsc: build - tsconfig.json",
            "outFiles": ["${workspaceFolder}/dist/**/*.js"]
        }
    ]
}
```

This configuration specifies the entry file for debugging (src/index.ts) and ensures the code is compiled before launching the debug session.

Tasks Configuration: tasks.json

Defining tasks in VS Code streamlines your workflow by automating common operations like compiling TypeScript code. Create a tasks.json file in the .vscode directory:

```
> Tasks: Configure Task
```

Configure a task for TypeScript compilation:

```
{
    "version": "2.0.0",
    "tasks": [
        {
            "label": "tsc: build - tsconfig.json",
            "type": "shell",
            "command": "tsc",
            "args": [
                "-p",
                "tsconfig.json"
            ],
            "group": "build",
            "problemMatcher": ["$tsc"],
            "detail": "Compiles the entire project based on tsconfig.json"
        }
    ]
}
```

This task enables you to build your TypeScript project by running Ctrl+Shift+B, which invokes the TypeScript compiler with the specified tsconfig.json.

By following these steps to set up and configure Visual Studio Code, you will be prepared to manage TypeScript projects efficiently, taking full advantage of features like IntelliSense, debugging, and task automation.

2.8 Using TypeScript with Visual Studio Code

Visual Studio Code (VS Code) is a highly favored integrated development environment (IDE) for TypeScript development due to its robust features, including intellisense, debugging, and built-in version control. This section explores the configuration and utilization of VS Code to optimize your TypeScript development workflow.

To commence, ensure you have installed VS Code. The installation packages are available at the official https://code.visualstudio.com/ website. VS Code supports extensions, crucial for enhancing TypeScript development.

First and foremost, install the TypeScript and JavaScript language features. Open VS Code and navigate to the Extensions view by clicking on the Extensions icon in the Activity Bar on the side of the window or using the shortcut Ctrl+Shift+X. Search for Typescript in the search bar and select the installation option for "TypeScript and JavaScript Language Features". This extension provides rich support for interacting with TypeScript files.

An effective TypeScript project often requires specific configurations within VS Code. Create a tsconfig.json file in the root of your project if it does not already exist. This file informs the TypeScript compiler of your desired project settings.

```
{
  "compilerOptions": {
    "target": "es6",
    "module": "commonjs",
    "strict": true,
    "esModuleInterop": true,
    "skipLibCheck": true,
    "forceConsistentCasingInFileNames": true,
    "outDir": "./dist"
  },
  "include": ["src/**/*"],
  "exclude": ["node_modules", "**/*.spec.ts"]
}
```

The configuration above sets the compilation target to ECMAScript 6 and specifies the use of CommonJS modules. It enforces strict type-checking options and includes all TypeScript files in the src directory, excluding the node_modules directory and any test files ending in .spec.ts.

Visual Studio Code's task system allows defining tasks for development goals such as compiling TypeScript files. Create a tasks.json file within the .vscode directory. A sample tasks.json configuration for compiling TypeScript can be depicted as follows:

```
{
  "version": "2.0.0",
  "tasks": [
    {
      "label": "tsc: build",
      "type": "shell",
      "command": "tsc",
      "args": ["-p", "."],
      "group": {
        "kind": "build",
        "isDefault": true
      },
      "problemMatcher": ["$tsc"]
    }
  ]
}
```

In this configuration, a task labeled tsc: build invokes the TypeScript compiler from the shell with the project (-p) flag referencing the current directory. It defines this task as the default for the build group, automating the TypeScript compilation process. The problemMatcher links the task output to VS Code's problem reporting mechanism, facilitating debugging by highlighting errors directly in the editor.

Debugging TypeScript in VS Code is straightforward. Ensure a comprehensive launch.json configuration in the .vscode directory:

```
{
  "version": "0.2.0",
  "configurations": [
    {
      "type": "node",
      "request": "launch",
      "name": "Launch Program",
      "skipFiles": ["<node_internals>/**"],
      "program": "${workspaceFolder}/src/index.ts",
      "preLaunchTask": "tsc: build",
      "outFiles": ["${workspaceFolder}/dist/**/*.js"]
    }
  ]
}
```

This configuration specifies launching a Node.js program, setting the entry point to src/index.ts. The preLaunchTask key ensures TypeScript compilation occurs before debugging sessions. The outFiles key maps the source files to their compiled JavaScript equivalents in the dist directory.

To enhance productivity, consider additional VS Code extensions like TSLint for linting support and Prettier for code formatting. These can be installed similarly through the Extensions view. Place a settings.json file in your .vscode directory to configure the workspace settings:

```
{
  "editor.formatOnSave": true,
  "eslint.alwaysShowStatus": true,
  "files.autoSave": "afterDelay",
  "typescript.tsdk": "node_modules/typescript/lib",
  "javascript.validate.enable": false,
  "tslint.autoFixOnSave": true,
  "editor.codeActionsOnSave": {
    "source.fixAll.tslint": true
  }
}
```

This configuration file enables automatic file saving, TypeScript formatting on save, and disables JavaScript validation to prevent conflicts with TypeScript linting.

Implementing these configurations will enhance your development experience, ensuring a streamlined, efficient workflow within Visual Studio Code when working with TypeScript. The features and settings discussed provide an extensible, customizable environment, empowering developers to leverage TypeScript's advanced capabilities effectively.

2.9 Compiling TypeScript Code

The process of compiling TypeScript code is fundamental to transitioning from TypeScript to JavaScript. This section will provide an exhaustive description of the steps necessary to compile TypeScript code into JavaScript using the TypeScript Compiler (tsc). Adhering to these guidelines will ensure a robust and efficient compilation process.

To begin, the TypeScript compiler (tsc) is an integral tool, translating TypeScript files(.ts) into JavaScript files(.js). This translation ensures compatibility across different environments that execute JavaScript. The tsc command is used in the terminal (or command prompt) for compiling TypeScript files.

Firstly, we will illustrate compiling a single TypeScript file. Consider a basic TypeScript file named example.ts with the following content:

```
let message: string = 'Hello, TypeScript!';
console.log(message);
```

To compile this TypeScript file, navigate to the directory containing example.ts and execute the following command in the terminal:

```
tsc example.ts
```

Upon successful compilation, a JavaScript file named example.js will be generated in the same directory. The content of example.js will be as follows:

```
var message = 'Hello, TypeScript!';
console.log(message);
```

The command tsc example.ts invokes the compiler, translating .ts to .js. The output can be executed using Node.js or in any JavaScript runtime environment.

For scenarios involving multiple TypeScript files, compilation can be managed more efficiently using a tsconfig.json file. This configuration file specifies the root files and compiler options required to compile the project.

Consider the following project structure:

```
project-root

  src
     file1.ts
     file2.ts

  tsconfig.json
```

An example tsconfig.json is provided below:

```
{
    "compilerOptions": {
        "target": "es6",
        "module": "commonjs",
        "outDir": "./dist",
        "rootDir": "./src",
        "strict": true
    },
    "include": [
        "src/**/*"
    ]
}
```

This configuration specifies the src directory as the root directory, and the compiled JavaScript files will be output to the dist directory. The compilerOptions dictate the compilation behavior, such as targeting ECMAScript 6 (es6), using CommonJS module system, and enforcing strict type-checking.

To compile the entire project, run the following command in the terminal, from the project root directory:

```
tsc
```

This will reference the tsconfig.json file to compile all included TypeScript files, producing the corresponding JavaScript files in the specified output directory.

For watch mode, which recompiles TypeScript files upon changes, use the –watch option:

```
tsc --watch
```

This command observes changes to TypeScript files and automatically recompiles them, enhancing development efficiency.

Additionally, errors and warnings during compilation are part of TypeScript's static type-checking process. For instance, consider modifying example.ts to introduce a type error:

```
let message: string = 42; // Incorrect type assignment
console.log(message);
```

Running tsc example.ts will output an error message indicating the type mismatch:

```
error TS2322: Type 'number' is not assignable to type 'string'.

  let message: string = 42;
                        ~~
```

Address these type errors to ensure the TypeScript code adheres to the specified type constraints, fortifying code reliability and maintainability.

Lastly, generating source maps is beneficial for debugging compiled JavaScript code, allowing one to map errors back to the original TypeScript source. Enable source map generation by adding the "sourceMap": true option in tsconfig.json:

```
{
    "compilerOptions": {
        "sourceMap": true,
        "target": "es6",
        "module": "commonjs",
        "outDir": "./dist",
        "rootDir": "./src",
        "strict": true
    },
    "include": [
        "src/**/*"
    ]
}
```

This produces .map files alongside the compiled JavaScript files, facilitating effective debugging.

The discrete steps outlined here solidify a comprehensive understanding of compiling TypeScript code, ensuring that any project can benefit from a streamlined, error-free compilation process.

2.10 Configuring TypeScript for Different Environments

Configuring TypeScript appropriately across different environments ensures the reliability and adaptability of your TypeScript project. Each environment, whether it be development, testing, or production, requires different settings to optimize performance and usability. This section elaborates on how to tailor your TypeScript configuration for various environments using the tsconfig.json file.

The tsconfig.json file is pivotal in controlling the compiler options, file paths, and other configuration details. To facilitate configurations for multiple environments, you can use different tsconfig files or dynamically extend a base configuration file.

Base Configuration

Creating a base tsconfig.json file that contains the common settings across all environments simplifies the process. The base file focuses on shared settings, avoiding redundancy.

```
{
    "compilerOptions": {
        "target": "es5",
        "module": "commonjs",
        "outDir": "./dist",
        "rootDir": "./src",
        "strict": true,
        "esModuleInterop": true,
        "skipLibCheck": true,
        "forceConsistentCasingInFileNames": true
    },
    "include": ["src/**/*"],
    "exclude": ["node_modules"]
}
```

Extending the Base Configuration

To extend the base configuration for specific environments, leverage the extends property. Create separate configuration files for different environments that extend the base tsconfig.json.

```
{
    "extends": "./tsconfig.json",
    "compilerOptions": {
        "sourceMap": true,
        "outDir": "./dist/dev"
    }
}
```

In the development environment configuration (tsconfig.dev.json), sourceMap is enabled to aid in debugging by mapping the compiled JavaScript code back to the original TypeScript code. The outDir is set to ./dist/dev to separate it from other environments.

```
{
    "extends": "./tsconfig.json",
    "compilerOptions": {
        "removeComments": true,
        "outDir": "./dist/prod",
        "sourceMap": false,
        "declaration": false
    }
}
```

For production (tsconfig.prod.json), unnecessary debugging information is removed by disabling sourceMap and setting removeComments to true. Additionally, declaration generation is turned off to expedite the build process.

Environment-specific Build Scripts

To streamline switching between different configurations, employ npm scripts:

```
{
  "scripts": {
    "build:dev": "tsc -p tsconfig.dev.json",
    "build:prod": "tsc -p tsconfig.prod.json"
  }
}
```

Here, build:dev and build:prod scripts automate the compilation process using the respective tsconfig files for development and production environments.

Continuous Integration and Deployment (CI/CD)

In a CI/CD pipeline, managing environment-specific TypeScript configurations becomes crucial. Configure environment variables within your CI/CD tool of choice to dynamically select the appropriate tsconfig file. For example, in a Jenkins pipeline script:

```
pipeline {
    environment {
        ENVIRONMENT = 'development'
    }
    stages {
        stage('Build') {
            steps {
                script {
                    def tsconfig = "tsconfig.${ENVIRONMENT}.json"
                    sh "npm run build -- -p ${tsconfig}"
                }
            }
        }
    }
}
```

By setting the ENVIRONMENT variable, the CI/CD pipeline dynamically picks up the correct tsconfig file based on the deployment environment. Such configurations ensure that builds are consistent and environment-specific out of the box.

Testing Environment

For testing environments, additional compiler options tailored for testing frameworks like Jest or Mocha can be specified:

```
{
    "extends": "./tsconfig.json",
    "compilerOptions": {
        "outDir": "./dist/test",
        "sourceMap": true,
        "isolatedModules": true,
        "types": ["jest"]
    }
}
```

Configuring isolatedModules helps with single-file transpilation scenarios, and the types option includes type definitions for the Jest testing framework. A dedicated outDir ensures that the compiled code used for testing is kept isolated.

By adhering to these configuration nuances and practice, TypeScript can be optimally tailored to meet the demands of various projects and deployment scenarios.

Chapter 3

Basic Types and Variables

This chapter delves into the foundational concepts of TypeScript's type system, covering type annotations, type inference, and the various primitive types such as number, string, and boolean. It explains the use of special types like null, undefined, and void, along with arrays, tuples, and enums. Additionally, it addresses the any type, union and intersection types, literal types, and type assertions, providing a comprehensive understanding of variable declarations with let and const, and how TypeScript handles type compatibility and coercion.

3.1 Overview of TypeScript Types

TypeScript introduces a sophisticated, static type system to JavaScript, enabling developers to specify types for their variables, functions, and other structures. This ensures that the code adheres to the desired behaviors, leading to early detection of errors during development. Type annotations and type inference are key mechanisms in TypeScript, used for declaring and deducing the types of variables, respectively.

At a high level, TypeScript's type system can be divided into basic types, such as number, string, and boolean, along with more complex structures like arrays, tuples, enums, and special types. This type system plays a crucial role in ensuring code reliability and maintainability by catching type-related errors before the code is executed.

Here is an example to demonstrate type annotations:

```
let userName: string = 'Alice';
let userAge: number = 30;
let isPremiumUser: boolean = true;
```

In the above code, we explicitly declare the types for userName, userAge, and isPremiumUser as string, number, and boolean, respectively.

Type inference, on the other hand, allows TypeScript to deduce types based on the assigned value, without explicit annotations. For instance:

```
let city = 'New York'; // TypeScript infers the type as string
let population = 8419000; // TypeScript infers the type as number
```

When defining function parameters and return types, TypeScript encourages specifying types to ensure the function is used correctly:

```
function greet(name: string): string {
    return `Hello, ${name}`;
}
```

Here, the function greet takes a string parameter and returns a string value, ensuring correct usage.

Arrays in TypeScript can be typed to ensure that they hold consistent types of elements:

```
let scores: number[] = [85, 95, 76];
```

This defines an array named scores that should only contain numbers. Similarly, tuples enable arrays with fixed types and lengths:

```
let person: [string, number] = ['John', 26];
```

Enums provide a way to define a set of named constants, improving code readability and reducing errors:

```
enum Color {
    Red,
    Green,
    Blue
}

let favoriteColor: Color = Color.Green;
```

Special types include null, undefined, and void, which handle scenarios where a variable may lack a value or a function may not return a value:

```
let unknownValue: null = null;
let uninitializedValue: undefined = undefined;
```

```
function logMessage(message: string): void {
    console.log(message);
}
```

The any type offers flexibility by allowing variables to hold any type of value, but it should be used cautiously since it reduces type-checking benefits:

```
let dynamicValue: any = "hello";
dynamicValue = 42; // TypeScript accepts this due to 'any' type
```

Union and intersection types enable more sophisticated type operations by combining multiple types, either allowing a value to match one of several types or requiring it to meet all type criteria:

```
let mixedType: number | string;
mixedType = 10;
mixedType = 'Ten';

type Draggable = { drag: () => void };
type Resizable = { resize: () => void };

type UIElement = Draggable & Resizable;

let box: UIElement = {
    drag: () => {},
    resize: () => {}
};
```

Literal types allow exact value constraints, providing additional compile-time validation:

```
type CardinalDirection = 'North' | 'East' | 'South' | 'West';
let direction: CardinalDirection = 'North';
```

Type assertions enable developers to override inferred types when they have more specific knowledge about a value's type, sometimes referred to as type casting:

```
let value: any = 'TypeScript';
let stringLength: number = (value as string).length;
```

Variable declarations using let and const ensure proper scoping and immutability where applicable, aiding in robust code practices:

```
let variableName = 'mutable';
const constantName = 'immutable';
```

Type compatibility and type coercion rules, such as structural typing and type widening, manage how disparate types interact:

```
interface Employee {
    name: string;
    age: number;
    department?: string;
}

let employee: Employee = { name: 'Alice', age: 28 };

interface Developer extends Employee {
    programmingLanguage: string;
}

let developer: Developer = { name: 'Bob', age: 32, programmingLanguage: 'TypeScript'
      };
```

Understanding these foundational concepts enables effective use of TypeScript's type system, fostering development of reliable and maintainable software.

3.2 Type Annotations and Type Inference

TypeScript extends JavaScript by adding optional static types which can be specified using type annotations. This addition helps in catching errors early during development and provides a more robust and maintainable codebase. Type annotations explicitly define the expected type of variables, function parameters, and return values. By doing so, developers can leverage the editor's or integrated development environment's (IDE) type-checking capabilities for enhanced code clarity and debugging.

The general syntax for type annotations involves a colon followed by the type after the variable name. For example, to declare a variable, message, as a string, the following code can be used:

```
let message: string;
message = "Hello, TypeScript";
```

Here, message is annotated as a string type, ensuring that any non-string assignment to message will trigger a type error.

Function parameters and return types can also be annotated. The following example demonstrates how to specify that a function, greet, accepts a string argument and returns a string.

```
function greet(name: string): string {
    return `Hello, ${name}`;
}
```

When annotations are not provided, TypeScript uses type inference to infer types based on the values assigned. For example:

```
let inferredMessage = "Hello, TypeScript";
// inferredMessage is inferred to be of type string
```

Here, TypeScript infers that inferredMessage is of type string based on the initial assignment.

Type inference also works with function return types. In the absence of explicit return type annotations, TypeScript infers the return type from the return statements within the function:

```
function add(a: number, b: number) {
    return a + b; // TypeScript infers the return type as number
}
```

Although type inference can significantly reduce the need for explicit type annotations, there are cases where annotations are necessary to avoid ambiguity and to provide explicit documentation. For example, when declaring variables without immediate initialization:

```
let numberOrString: number | string;
numberOrString = 10; // valid
numberOrString = "ten"; // also valid
```

Variable numberOrString is annotated as either type number or type string, leveraging TypeScript's union types. This annotation helps in enforcing type safety when numberOrString is used later in the code.

Another scenario is generic functions where the type parameters can vary based on usage. Explicit type annotations provide the flexibility to define generic types:

```
function identity<T>(arg: T): T {
    return arg;
}
let result1 = identity<number>(42); // T is number
let result2 = identity<string>("Hello"); // T is string
```

Here, the identity function uses a type parameter T which can represent any type. The explicit type annotations while calling identity ensure that T is accurately inferred to be number and string respectively.

Using the const keyword can also help TypeScript infer more specific types. For instance:

```
const specificMessage = "Hello, TypeScript";
// specificMessage is inferred to be of type "Hello, TypeScript"
```

In this example, specificMessage is inferred to be of type "Hello, TypeScript" rather than a general string type due to the use of const, which indicates immutability.

While type inference simplifies the code, judicious use of type annotations can provide clarity and reduce the potential for errors, particularly in large-scale applications where the explicit documentation of types is beneficial for code maintenance and collaboration.

3.3 Primitive Types: Number, String, Boolean

In TypeScript, as in many other programming languages, primitive types represent the most basic forms of data. Unlike more complex types such as objects or arrays, primitives are immutable and are directly operated upon by the language's basic operators. TypeScript refines these constructs, enabling robust type-checking at compile-time to ensure a higher degree of code correctness and readability.

Numbers in TypeScript are represented using the number type. TypeScript follows the IEEE 754 standard for representing both integer and floating-point values. Consequently, the same number type is used for integers, decimals, and even hexadecimal values. Here is an example of declaring and using numerical variables:

```
// Declaration of numerical variables
let integerNumber: number = 42;
let floatingPointNumber: number = 3.14;
let hexadecimalNumber: number = 0x2A; // Hexadecimal for 42

// Arithmetic operations on number
let sum: number = integerNumber + floatingPointNumber;
let product: number = integerNumber * 10;
```

The values stored in the variables integerNumber, floatingPointNumber, and hexadecimalNumber are all of type number, regardless of their specific numerical form.

For scientific and financial calculations, it is essential to handle numbers accurately. TypeScript inherently manages various numerical bases and forms, and implicitly guarantees safe arithmetic operations within the IEEE 754 specifications. However, developers must remain aware of the limitations and potential rounding issues inherent in floating-point arithmetic.

Strings are sequences of characters and are represented using the string type. TypeScript allows the use of single quotes, double quotes, and template literals for string declarations:

```
// Declaration of string variables
let singleQuoteString: string = 'Hello, TypeScript!';
let doubleQuoteString: string = "Hello, TypeScript!";
let templateLiteralString: string = `Hello, ${singleQuoteString}`;
```

Template literals, enclosed by backticks (`), provide an advanced way to embed expressions within strings using the ${} syntax. This feature is particularly useful for constructing strings dynamically:

```
// Using template literals
let name: string = 'Alice';
let greeting: string = `Hello, ${name}!`;
console.log(greeting); // Output: Hello, Alice!
```

String operations such as concatenation, slicing, and length determination are consistent with JavaScript's string functions, owing to TypeScript's adherence to ECMAScript standards. For example:

```
// String operations
let concatenatedString: string = singleQuoteString + " Welcome!";
let stringLength: number = concatenatedString.length;
let substring: string = concatenatedString.slice(7, 17);
```

Booleans represent logical values and are expressed using the boolean type, which can take only one of two values: true or false. The use of booleans is crucial for control flow and conditional logic.

```
// Declaration of boolean variables
let isTypeScriptGreat: boolean = true;
let isJavaScriptSuperior: boolean = false;

// Using booleans in control structures
if (isTypeScriptGreat) {
    console.log("TypeScript enhances JavaScript.");
} else {
    console.log("TypeScript is not useful.");
}
```

Boolean operations, such as logical conjunction (&&), disjunction (||), and negation (!), are essential in conditionally evaluating multiple expressions:

```
// Boolean operations
let a: boolean = true;
let b: boolean = false;

let andOperation: boolean = a && b; // false
let orOperation: boolean = a || b; // true
let notOperation: boolean = !a; // false
```

Understanding these primitive types — number, string, and boolean — provides the foundation for working effectively with TypeScript. These types facilitate performing arithmetic operations, manipulating textual data, and controlling program flow, supporting a range of practical applications within the language's type system.

3.4 Special Types: null, undefined, and void

In TypeScript, the special types null, undefined, and void play critical roles in representing the absence of a value or the intentional omission of any type. Understanding how these special types work and when to use them is essential for writing robust and type-safe TypeScript code. This section explores these special types in detail, including their definitions, usage examples, and the differences between them.

null

The null type represents an intentional absence of any object value. It is one of JavaScript's primitive values and is used to indicate that a variable points to no object. In TypeScript, null has its corresponding type null, which can be assigned to variables explicitly declared to accept it.

```
let value: null = null;
```

By default, TypeScript treats null as a subtype of all other types. This means you can assign null to any variable that has another type unless you configure the strictNullChecks compiler option to be true. When strictNullChecks is enabled, null is only assignable to variables of type any, unknown, or explicitly null.

```
let value: string = null; // Allowed without strictNullChecks
```

When strictNullChecks is enabled, it ensures stricter null safety:

```
let value: string = null; // Error with strictNullChecks
```

undefined

The undefined type indicates that an uninitialized variable exists but has not been assigned a value. This is another primitive value in JavaScript and has its corresponding type undefined in TypeScript.

```
let value: undefined = undefined;
```

Similar to null, undefined is also a subtype of all other types by default but follows the same rules as null when strictNullChecks is enabled. If strictNullChecks is true, undefined can only be assigned to variables of type any, unknown, or explicitly undefined.

```
let value: number = undefined; // Allowed without strictNullChecks
```

With strictNullChecks enabled, this assignment is not allowed:

```
let value: number = undefined; // Error with strictNullChecks
```

void

The void type is used to represent the absence of any type, often used in the context of functions that do not return a value. In other words, a function declared with a void return type explicitly states that it returns nothing.

```
function logMessage(message: string): void {
  console.log(message);
}
```

Unlike null and undefined, void is not a subtype of any other type except any and can only be used in specific contexts:

- Functions that do not return a value
- Contexts where the omission of any return value is intentional

```
let unusable: void = undefined;
```

This assignment is always allowed because undefined is technically the only value you can assign to a void type:

```
let unusable: void = null; // Allowed in non-strictNullChecks mode
```

Interrelation between null, undefined, and void

When working with these special types, it is crucial to understand the following distinctions and similarities:

- Both null and undefined can be used to denote the absence of a value, but null typically signifies an intentional non-value, whereas undefined indicates an uninitialized state.
- When strictNullChecks is true, assigning null or undefined to variables of other types is not allowed, thereby catching potential runtime errors at compile-time.

- The void type is specifically used to indicate the lack of any return value from a function and is not meant for use as a general-purpose data type.

Understanding null, undefined, and void ensures greater type safety and avoids null reference errors, a common source of bugs in many programming languages. Using these types appropriately allows developers to write clearer, more predictable code.

3.5 Arrays and Tuples

Arrays and tuples in TypeScript are sophisticated structures that enhance the flexibility and robustness of data handling. An array is an ordered collection of items, where each item is identified by an index or key. Tuples, on the other hand, are a finite ordered list of elements. Both data structures allow for sophisticated type-checking and manipulation.

Arrays in TypeScript are declared using square brackets '[]' or using the generic Array<elementType> syntax. The array elements are typically of a single type, although it is possible to create arrays of complex types by defining an array with a union type.

```
let primeNumbers: number[] = [2, 3, 5, 7, 11];
let mixedArray: (number | string)[] = [1, 'two', 3, 'four'];
let genericArray: Array<number> = [10, 20, 30, 40];
```

TypeScript arrays can function both as stacks and queues. These array operations are evidenced by several built-in methods: 'push()', 'pop()', 'shift()', and 'unshift()'. Additionally, methods such as 'map()', 'filter()', and 'reduce()' enable functional programming paradigms.

```
let numArray: number[] = [1, 2, 3, 4, 5];

// Stack functionalities
numArray.push(6); // [1, 2, 3, 4, 5, 6]
numArray.pop(); // [1, 2, 3, 4, 5]

// Queue functionalities
numArray.shift(); // [2, 3, 4, 5]
numArray.unshift(1); // [1, 2, 3, 4, 5]
```

The enhanced safety and functionality come from TypeScript's ability to exhaustively type-check the operations performed on typed arrays, thus reducing runtime errors and boosting code reliability.

Tuples in TypeScript extend the capabilities of arrays by allowing fixed-size collections of elements where each element can be of a different type. This property is particularly useful when dealing with static collections, such as coordinates, which have a predictable and stable structure.

A tuple can be declared using square brackets enclosing the types of its elements.

```
let point: [number, number] = [10, 20];
let person: [string, number] = ['John Doe', 25];
let mixedTuple: [number, string, boolean] = [1, 'hello', true];
```

Tuples support destructuring, a convenient way to extract values from them.

```
let rgb: [number, number, number] = [255, 0, 0];
let [red, green, blue] = rgb;

console.log(red); // 255
console.log(green); // 0
console.log(blue); // 0
```

Adding elements to a tuple is restricted to ensure type safety and predictability. TypeScript provides tuple-specific methods to facilitate this.

```
let tuple: [number, string] = [10, 'TypeScript'];
tuple.push(20); // [10, 'TypeScript', 20]
// tuple.push(true); // Error: Argument of type 'true' is not assignable to parameter of
    type 'string | number'.
```

The distinction between arrays and tuples lies in the predictability and immutability of tuples. Where an array might fluctuate in length and types based on runtime operations, a tuple maintains a fixed type and length, presenting robust guarantees at compile time.

Combining arrays and tuples effectively addresses different scenarios encountered in software development. Using arrays for dynamic lists and tuples for structured data leads to a balanced and efficient approach to type-safe programming in TypeScript.

3.6 Enums: Numeric and String Enums

Enums, short for enumerations, are a feature in TypeScript that facilitates the definition of a set of named constants. This feature is highly advantageous for cases where a variable should have one out of a fixed set of possible values. TypeScript provides two main types of enums:

Numeric Enums and String Enums.

Numeric Enums are the most common form of enums in TypeScript. They allow associating an identifier with a numeric value. By default, enums begin numbering their members starting from 0. The syntax for defining a numeric enum is straightforward:

```
enum Direction {
    Up,
    Down,
    Left,
    Right
}
```

In this example, the Direction enum automatically assigns the values 0, 1, 2, and 3 to the Up, Down, Left, and Right members, respectively. Enum members can also be explicitly assigned numeric values.

```
enum Direction {
    Up = 1,
    Down,
    Left,
    Right
}
```

Here, Up is explicitly set to 1, and the subsequent members increment from that value. Therefore, Down, Left, and Right will have values of 2, 3, and 4, respectively. Enums can further contain a mix of explicitly and implicitly assigned values.

```
enum CustomDirection {
    Up = 3,
    Down = 7,
    Left,
    Right
}
```

In the CustomDirection example, Up is set to 3, Down is set to 7, while Left automatically takes the value 8, and Right takes 9 due to the incremental nature of enums when values are not explicitly specified.

Enums in TypeScript are reverse mapped, i.e., both the name and the value can be used to access members of the enum.

```
console.log(Direction.Up); // Outputs 1
console.log(Direction[1]); // Outputs "Up"
```

Moving on to String Enums, these are enums where each member is initialized with a string literal. Unlike numeric enums, these do not auto-increment. Each member must be explicitly set to a string value.

```
enum Response {
```

```
    Yes = "YES",
    No = "NO"
}
```

String Enums improve readability and are particularly useful when the textual naming of elements is essential for comprehensibility and maintenance. Note that string enums differ from numeric enums as they do not support reverse mapping.

To define a mixture of numeric and string values in an enum, one must ensure that an enum either consists of numeric members or string members. Enums cannot combine both types in TypeScript:

```
enum MixedEnum {
    No = 0,
    Yes = "YES" // Error: Enum member must have initializer.
}
```

Enums also provide a way to define constant members and computed members. The constant members use a constant enum expression:

```
enum FileAccess {
    None,
    Read = 1 << 1,
    Write = 1 << 2,
    ReadWrite = Read | Write
}
```

In the example above, Read is defined using bit-shifting, Write follows similarly, and ReadWrite combines both through a bitwise OR operation. None is implicitly set to 0.

Enums bring structure and clarity when choosing from a predefined set of values. Understanding how to utilize numeric and string enums effectively can better align your TypeScript code with these principles, ensuring consistency and reducing errors related to invalid values.

3.7 The Any Type

The advent of any type in TypeScript offers the flexibility to work with variables that may hold values of arbitrary types. Unlike the strict nature of other TypeScript types, any allows you to opt out of type checking for specific portions of your code. This can be particularly useful in scenarios where you are working with codebases that are either loosely typed, such as when interacting with third-party libraries, or during the process of migrating JavaScript codebases to TypeScript. It is important, however, to employ any judiciously as it may undermine the type safety that TypeScript aims to provide.

In TypeScript, declaring a variable with any is straightforward:

```
let looselyTyped: any = 4;
looselyTyped = "I can be any type now";
looselyTyped = false; // no error
```

Here, looselyTyped is first assigned a number, then a string, and finally a boolean, each reassignment occurring without generating any type errors. This clearly exemplifies how the any type effectively turns off type checking.

When dealing with APIs whose response types are not well-defined, any proves efficient. For instance:

```
function getAPIResponseData(url: string): any {
    // Assume fetch() to get data from an API
    // Parsed response structure is unknown
    return fetch(url)
        .then(response => response.json())
        .then(data => data);
}
```

Here, getAPIResponseData ensures that we can handle the data without enforcing any specific type constraints. It is vital to note that excessive use of any can ease initial development but might lead to potential runtime errors. Therefore, leveraging any should be carefully planned and restricted to scenarios where type safety cannot be reasonably ensured.

TypeScript also provides mechanisms for migrating JavaScript codebases where types are unknown initially. Utilizing any allows for a smoother transition phase:

```
function addNumbers(a: any, b: any): any {
    return a + b;
}
```

The any type here permits addNumbers to accept and return parameters of any type, similar to JavaScript's dynamic typing nature. Once a stable understanding of the incoming data structure is established, you can replace any with more specific types, enhancing type safety incrementally.

Another critical aspect to consider is how any propagates through your code. Any variable derived from a value declared as any will itself be typed as any:

```
let looselyTyped: any = { x: 0 };
let d: number = looselyTyped.a.b.c.d; // no error due to any propagating
```

This code does not trigger any compile-time errors, although it is prone to runtime exceptions due to accessing properties that may not exist. Therefore, it becomes imperative to audit the usage of any especially when it propagates in larger codebases, potentially leading to bugs that are harder to diagnose.

Type assertions can be utilized to inform the compiler about the expected type of a any variable, providing a blend of flexibility and type safety:

```
let looselyTyped: any = "this is a string";
let strLength: number = (looselyTyped as string).length;
```

Here, the as keyword asserts that looselyTyped should be treated as a string, enabling type-safe operations like accessing string properties.

Using any as a function parameter type also means that TypeScript will not enforce any constraints on the arguments passed to that function, maintaining consistency with the dynamic nature of JavaScript:

```
function logValue(value: any) {
    console.log(value);
}
logValue(5); // logs: 5
logValue("hello!"); // logs: hello!
```

While function logValue can accept and log any input due to the any type, this practice can potentially obscure programming logic where type constraints could provide more meaningful development errors and auto-completion suggestions from tools.

The any type plays a crucial role in easing the integration and transitioning processes within TypeScript projects. While it facilitates flexibility and aids initial migration from a loosely typed or dynamically typed approach, it should be applied with cautious deliberation to avoid negating the benefits of static typing that TypeScript offers. Leveraging any mindfully ensures that it serves as a transitory tool rather than becoming a crutch that compromises type safety.

3.8 Union and Intersection Types

TypeScript introduces two advanced types: *union types* and *intersection types*, which provide powerful ways to handle complex type definitions.

Union types enable a variable to hold more than one type. This is particularly useful when a value could be one of several types. It is declared using the vertical bar (|) between the desired types. A union type indicates that a value can be any one of these types. Consider the following example:

```
// Example of a Union Type
let value: number | string;
value = 42; // valid
value = "hello"; // valid
```

In this example, value can be either a number or a string. This allows for flexibility in variable assignment.

TypeScript's type system is sufficiently advanced to infer the types when processing unions. When working with union types, type guards and type assertions are typical strategies to deal with multiple type scenarios.

Type guards are expressions that perform a runtime check to verify a type. Common type guards include checking with typeof, instanceof, or custom type predicates. The following example demonstrates a typeof guard:

```
// Using typeof for type guard
function formatValue(value: number | string): string {
  if (typeof value === "number") {
    return value.toFixed(2); // Format number with two decimal places
  } else {
    return value.toUpperCase(); // Convert string to uppercase
  }
}

console.log(formatValue(123.456)); // Output: 123.46
console.log(formatValue("hello")); // Output: HELLO
```

In this function, typeof is used to check whether value is a number or a string before performing the respective operation.

TypeScript also supports *intersection types* using the ampersand (&) operator. An intersection type combines multiple types into one. A variable of an intersection type must satisfy all constituent types. This feature is beneficial for creating composite types. Consider the following example:

```
// Example of an Intersection Type
interface Person {
    name: string;
}

interface Employee {
    employeeId: number;
}

type EmployedPerson = Person & Employee;

const manager: EmployedPerson = {
    name: "Alice",
    employeeId: 1234
};
```

In this example, EmployedPerson is an intersection of Person and Employee. The object manager must have both name and employeeId properties to be valid.

Intersection types are particularly effective in scenarios requiring multiple interfaces or classes to cooperate, ensuring that an object adheres to several contracts at once.

Practically, one might also encounter complex scenarios involving both unions and intersections within type definitions. Here's a more involved example to illustrate this concept:

```
// Complex Example involving Union and Intersection Types
interface Drivable {
    drive(): void;
}

interface Runnable {
    run(): void;
}

type Vehicle = Car | Motorcycle;
type Car = { wheels: 4 } & Drivable;
type Motorcycle = { wheels: 2 } & Runnable;

function operateVehicle(vehicle: Vehicle) {
    console.log("Wheels: " + vehicle.wheels);
    if ("drive" in vehicle) {
        vehicle.drive();
    } else {
        vehicle.run();
    }
}

const sedan: Car = {
    wheels: 4,
    drive: () => console.log("Driving the car")
};

const bike: Motorcycle = {
```

```
    wheels: 2,
    run: () => console.log("Riding the motorcycle")
};

operateVehicle(sedan); // Output: Wheels: 4 / Driving the car
operateVehicle(bike); // Output: Wheels: 2 / Riding the motorcycle
```

Here, Vehicle is a union type comprising Car and Motorcycle. Car is an intersection type of having 4 wheels and being Drivable, while Motorcycle is an intersection type of having 2 wheels and being Runnable. The operateVehicle function then determines the type of vehicle through property presence checks.

Combining union and intersection types harmoniously integrates advanced and nuanced type manipulations, making TypeScript a robust tool for type-safe development.

3.9 Literal Types

Literal types in TypeScript are types that have a specific, fixed value. Rather than defining a type for a wide range of possible values, literal types refine the type system by allowing you to specify exact values the variable can hold. This brings an additional level of type safety and predictability to your code.

Literal types commonly fall into three categories: string literal types, number literal types, and boolean literal types.

String Literal Types are straightforward; they define specific possible values for strings.

```
let direction: "north" | "south" | "east" | "west";
direction = "north"; // Valid
direction = "up"; // Error: Type '"up"' is not assignable to type '"north" | "south" | "
    east" | "west"'.
```

In this example, the variable direction can only hold one of the four specified string values: "north", "south", "east", or "west". Attempting to assign a value outside of this set results in a type error, enhancing code safety and clarity.

Number Literal Types work similarly. They allow you to specify exact numeric values a variable can take.

```
let diceRoll: 1 | 2 | 3 | 4 | 5 | 6;
diceRoll = 3; // Valid
diceRoll = 7; // Error: Type '7' is not assignable to type '1 | 2 | 3 | 4 | 5 | 6'.
```

The diceRoll variable in this code can only hold numbers 1 through 6, which correspond to the faces of a standard die. Assigning a value such as 7 would trigger a type error.

Boolean Literal Types are even more specific, as they encompass only two values: true and false.

```
let isRaining: true | false;
isRaining = true; // Valid
isRaining = false; // Valid
isRaining = "yes"; // Error: Type '"yes"' is not assignable to type 'true | false'.
```

In this code snippet, the isRaining variable can only be assigned the boolean literals true or false. Any assignment that deviates from these two values will result in a type error.

TypeScript also allows composite literals using union and intersection types. Union types consolidate multiple literal types into a single type, facilitating more complex and expressive type declarations.

```
type CardinalDirection = "north" | "south" | "east" | "west";
type AllowedValues = 1 | "one" | true | "none";
let someValue: AllowedValues;
someValue = 1; // Valid
someValue = "one"; // Valid
someValue = true; // Valid
someValue = "none";// Valid
someValue = "other"; // Error: Type '"other"' is not assignable to type '1 | "one" |
    true | "none"'.
```

Here, someValue can take on any of the defined literals: 1, "one", true, or "none". Assigning a value outside of these specified literals will cause a type error, as shown with the value "other".

Intersection types, while less commonly used, allow the combination of multiple types, requiring that a variable satisfies all specified type constraints simultaneously.

```
type HasName = { name: string };
type HasAge = { age: number };
type Person = HasName & HasAge;
let person: Person = { name: "John", age: 30 };
```

In this example, the person variable must satisfy both the HasName and HasAge type constraints, ensuring that it contains both a name property with a string value and an age property with a number value.

Literal types integrate well with other TypeScript features, enhancing the type system's expressiveness and precision. Type assertions can be used to manually specify that a value matches a particular literal type:

```
let mixedValue: 5 | "five";
mixedValue = 5 as 5; // Valid
mixedValue = "five" as "five"; // Valid
```

By employing literal types in TypeScript, developers can gain finer control over variable values, leading to more robust and error-resistant code. Literal types contribute significantly to the type system's flexibility, enabling a more declarative and secure approach to handling variable assignment and type checking within TypeScript applications.

3.10 Type Assertions

Type assertions in TypeScript provide a mechanism to override the compiler's inferred and analyzed type, offering more control over the types of certain variables or expressions. This ability is crucial when dealing with type constraints and ensures that developers can indicate to the compiler the intended type of a value when the compiler is unable to correctly infer it.

When working with TypeScript, there can be scenarios where the developer knows more about the type of a variable than TypeScript's inferred type system does. Type assertions come into play precisely in such scenarios. It does not perform any runtime checks or conversions but it allows us to override TypeScript's inferred type.

Two syntaxes are available for type assertions: the *as* syntax and the angle-bracket <> syntax.

```
// Example using the "as" syntax
let someValue: unknown = "This is a string";
let strLength: number = (someValue as string).length;
console.log(strLength); // Outputs: 16
```

```
let someValue: unknown = "This is a string";
let strLength: number = (<string>someValue).length;
console.log(strLength); // Outputs: 16
```

In both examples above, someValue is initially of type unknown. By asserting its type to string, we gain access to string-specific properties and methods, such as length.

It is important to note that type assertions are purely a compile-time construct and, as such, do not alter the actual runtime type of variables. They merely inform the TypeScript compiler of a different type assumption about a given element.

Type assertions can be particularly useful in scenarios involving DOM manipulation in a browser environment:

```
let inputElement = document.querySelector('input[type="text"]') as
    HTMLInputElement;
inputElement.value = "Hello TypeScript!";
```

In this snippet, the querySelector method returns an element of type Element or null. By asserting its type to HTMLInputElement, we can access the value property specific to input elements.

Assertions provide benefits when interfacing with third-party libraries that may not have comprehensive TypeScript definitions. They offer developers flexibility, though with an implicit caveat: incorrect type assertions can lead to errors that TypeScript cannot catch.

Consider the following example:

```
let someValue: unknown = "This is a string";
let numberValue: number = someValue as number;
console.log(numberValue); // Compilation passes, but runtime error may occur
```

In this scenario, the code erroneously asserts someValue to a number, which bypasses type checking but could lead to runtime errors, given that the actual value is a string. Developers must ensure that the type assertions they make are logically sound and accurate.

It is often possible to avoid the need for type assertions by designing code with robust type information. However, when type assertions are indispensable, developers should utilize them judiciously, verifying correctness through comprehensive unit tests and ensuring clarity in code readability.

TypeScript also supports assertion signatures in function parameters. For instance:

```
function getSomeValue(value: unknown): asserts value is string {
  if (typeof value !== "string") {
    throw new Error("Not a string!");
  }
}
let value: unknown = "string";
getSomeValue(value);
console.log(value.length); // TypeScript now knows value is a string
```

In this example, the function getSomeValue uses the asserts keyword to narrow down the type of value. Upon returning from a successful call to getSomeValue, TypeScript understands that value must be a string.

By understanding and applying type assertions appropriately, developers can ensure a more predictable and interpretable type system, facilitating smoother integrations and optimized code bases.

3.11 Variable Declarations with let and const

In TypeScript, as in JavaScript, variables can be declared using three keywords: var, let, and const. Understanding the usage and behavior of let and const is crucial for writing reliable and maintainable code. Unlike var, let and const are block-scoped and bring additional advantages such as the mitigation of issues related to variable hoisting. This section covers the detailed workings of let and const, illustrating their benefits with examples.

The use of let enables block scoping, ensuring that a variable is only accessible within the block it is defined in. This can prevent unintended behaviors caused by variable hoisting.

```
function exampleWithLet() {
    let x = 10;
    if (true) {
        let x = 20;
        console.log(x); // Outputs 20
    }
    console.log(x); // Outputs 10
}
exampleWithLet();
```

In the snippet above, the let keyword ensures that the variable x inside the if block is different from the x declared in the function's outer scope, demonstrating block scoping.

The const keyword is used to declare variables that are to remain constant. Once a variable is assigned a value using const, it cannot be reassigned. However, if the variable holds an object, the properties of the object can still be modified.

```
const constantValue = 42;
// constantValue = 50; // Error: Assignment to constant variable

const constantObject = { key: "value" };
constantObject.key = "newValue"; // Allowed
```

While constantValue cannot be reassigned, constantObject can have its properties mutated, highlighting the difference between immutability of primitive values and objects.

The concepts of hoisting and temporal dead zone are important when understanding let and const. Unlike var, let and const are not hoisted to the top of their enclosing block. They exist in a "temporal dead zone" from the start of the block until the declaration is encountered, during which they cannot be accessed.

```
console.log(a); // ReferenceError: Cannot access 'a' before initialization
let a = 10;

console.log(b); // ReferenceError: Cannot access 'b' before initialization
const b = 20;
```

In the code above, accessing a or b before their declarations results in a reference error, demonstrating the temporal dead zone which helps in avoiding common bugs during variable initialization.

An important aspect of using const and let over var is enhancing code maintainability and readability. The deterministic behavior of let and const reduces side effects and makes the code more predictable. By default, it is advisable to use const for variables that should not be reassigned and let for variables with a changeable value.

let and const also improve performance by reducing scope pollution. Excessively using var leads to global scope pollution or function-level scoping, making it harder to track variable states and often resulting in unintended side effects. Adopting block scoping through let and const helps confine variables to their relevant contexts.

```
function calculateArea(radius: number) {
    const pi = 3.14159;
    let area = pi * radius * radius;
    return area;
}
console.log(calculateArea(5)); // Outputs 78.53975
```

In this example, pi is a constant value used for calculating the area of a circle and hence declared with const. The variable area, whose value is computed based on the function's input, is declared using let.

The choice between let and const is dictated by the necessity of reassignment. Using let should be reserved for variables that are expected to adopt new values during their lifecycle, while const should be employed to flag variables that once assigned, should remain unchanged. This differentiation helps communicate the intent of variables more clearly to other developers, fostering better collaboration and understanding.

The adoption of let and const leads to safer, more maintanable, and bug-free code, in alignment with the principles of modern JavaScript and TypeScript development practices.

3.12 Type Compatibility and Type Coercion

In TypeScript, understanding type compatibility and type coercion is crucial for ensuring that the code adheres to the expected type contracts and behaviors. Type compatibility focuses on whether a value of one type can be assigned to a variable of another type without type errors. Type coercion, on the other hand, involves implicit and explicit conversions between types. This section provides an in-depth examination of these concepts, which are essential for mastering TypeScript's type system.

TypeScript employs structural typing, where types are considered compatible if their shapes match. This concept, also known as "duck typing," simplifies type compatibility checks by focusing on the properties that a type possesses rather than the explicit type itself.

interface declarations and literal types often play a central role in type compatibility, as demonstrated in the examples below:

```
interface Person {
    name: string;
    age: number;
}

let student: Person = { name: "Alice", age: 21 };

// A compatible type with extra properties
let teacher = { name: "Bob", age: 35, subject: "Math" };

// Valid assignment due to structural compatibility
student = teacher;

// Error: Missing 'age' property in object literal
// student = { name: "Charlie" };
```

Note that teacher has an additional property subject, yet it is still assignable to student because student only requires name and age. However, assigning a value without the required properties would result in a compile-time error.

Type compatibility also extends to function types. The parameters and return types determine compatibility. Consider the following example:

```
let add = (a: number, b: number): number => a + b;
let sum: (x: number, y: number) => number;

// Valid assignment: parameters and return type match
sum = add;

let log = (message: string): void => console.log(message);
// Error: Type '(message: string) => void' is not assignable
// to type '(x: number, y: number) => number'.
```

```
// sum = log;
```

Here, sum can be assigned to add because their parameter types and return types are identical. Attempting to assign a function with incompatible types, such as log, results in an error, emphasizing the significance of matching function signatures.

Type coercion, by contrast, can be either implicit or explicit. Implicit coercion occurs when the language automatically converts one type to another, often when performing operations between mixed types. For example:

```
let result = "The answer is " + 42; // Implicitly coerced to string
console.log(result); // Output: "The answer is 42"

let product = "6" * 7; // Implicitly coerced to number
console.log(product); // Output: 42
```

In the above snippet, JavaScript's automatic type conversion seamlessly integrates with TypeScript, demonstrating how implicit coercion allows mixed-type expressions. However, implicit coercion can sometimes lead to unintended outcomes, as shown here:

```
let invalidResult = "5" - 3; // Naively assumed string concatenation
console.log(invalidResult); // Output: 2 (string "5" coerced to number)
```

To avoid confusion and enforce type safety, TypeScript supports explicit type coercion using type assertions. This transformation can be achieved using the as keyword or angle-bracket syntax. Example:

```
let inputValue: unknown = "123";
let numericValue: number = (inputValue as string).length;
// Alternatively, using angle-bracket syntax
// let numericValue: number = (<string>inputValue).length;
console.log(numericValue); // Output: 3
```

In this case, the unknown type variable inputValue is asserted as string before accessing its length property. Type assertions should be used cautiously to maintain type safety, especially when coerced types do not guarantee valid operations.

Further complexity arises when dealing with union types. By combining types, unions exhibit behaviors accommodating multiple forms:

```
type ID = number | string;
let userId: ID;

// Valid assignments
userId = 101;
userId = "A102";
```

```
// Operations requiring type narrowing or assertions
if (typeof userId === "string") {
    console.log(userId.toUpperCase());
} else {
    console.log(userId.toFixed(2));
}
```

This code snippet illustrates how TypeScript can handle a variable userId to accept either a number or a string, with narrowing performed using typeof checks to ensure correct methods are called on the variable.

Intersection types, which are used less frequently, combine multiple types into a single type that possesses all included types' properties:

```
interface Developer {
    name: string;
    code: () => void;
}

interface Manager {
    name: string;
    manage: () => void;
}

type TechLead = Developer & Manager;

let lead: TechLead = {
    name: "Eve",
    code: () => console.log("Coding"),
    manage: () => console.log("Managing"),
};

lead.code(); // Output: Coding
lead.manage(); // Output: Managing
```

Here, TechLead inherits properties from both Developer and Manager, requiring implementations for code and manage methods and showcasing the combined characteristics of types.

Finally, understanding how any and unknown types interact with type compatibility is paramount. While any circumvents type checking, unknown demands explicit assertions:

```
let flexible: any = 42;
flexible = "Now it's a string";
console.log(flexible); // Output: "Now it's a string"

let uncertain: unknown = { person: { name: "Jane" } };
if (typeof uncertain === "object" && uncertain !== null) {
    console.log((<any>uncertain).person.name); // Type assertion required
}
```

By leveraging structural typing, union and intersection types, and type safe coercion practices, TypeScript enforces robust type guarantees, enabling developers to write maintainable and error-resistant code.

Chapter 4

Functions and Modules

This chapter explores the definition and use of functions in TypeScript, including function types, type annotations, optional and default parameters, rest parameters, and the spread operator. It also covers advanced concepts such as function overloads, arrow functions, and function scope. Additionally, the chapter introduces modules, explaining how to import and export modules, re-export and create aggregate modules, and use dynamic import expressions to organize and manage code efficiently.

4.1 Basic Functions in TypeScript

Functions are fundamental components of any programming language, and in TypeScript, they are even more powerful due to the integration of strong typing. To define a basic function in TypeScript, we use the function keyword followed by a name, parameter list, and a return type. Here is an example of a simple function that adds two numbers:

```
function add(x: number, y: number): number {
    return x + y;
}
```

In this function, x and y are parameters annotated with the type number, and the function itself has a return type of number. This ensures that only numbers can be passed to the add function, and it will return a number.

To call this function, you simply use its name followed by arguments in parentheses:

```
let sum = add(5, 10);
console.log(sum); // Output: 15
```

The above code will output:

```
15
```

TypeScript also supports functions without parameters or return values. Consider a function that logs a message to the console:

```
function logMessage(): void {
    console.log("Hello, TypeScript!");
}
```

Here, the return type is void, indicating that the function does not return any value. When this function is called:

```
logMessage(); // Output: Hello, TypeScript!
```

The output will be:

```
Hello, TypeScript!
```

Another important aspect of functions in TypeScript is handling functions as first-class citizens. This means you can pass functions as arguments to other functions, return them from other functions, and assign them to variables. Consider this higher-order function that accepts a function as an argument:

```
function greet(name: string, callback: (msg: string) => void): void {
    callback(`Hello, ${name}`);
}
```

This greet function takes a string name and a callback function which takes a string and returns void. Here is how you can use it:

```
function logGreeting(message: string): void {
    console.log(message);
}

greet("World", logGreeting); // Output: Hello, World
```

The output will be:

```
Hello, World
```

Named functions aside, TypeScript also allows for anonymous functions, which can be defined without a name. These are particularly useful in situations where you need a function for a short duration or just once. For example, anonymous functions can be passed directly as arguments:

```
greet("Anonymous", function(msg: string): void {
    console.log(msg);
}); // Output: Hello, Anonymous
```

To manage typing more efficiently, it is advantageous to use defined function types. Consider the same higher-order function with a predefined type for the callback:

```
type GreetCallback = (msg: string) => void;

function greetTyped(name: string, callback: GreetCallback): void {
    callback(`Hello, ${name}`);
}
```

This approach improves code readability and reusability, making it easier to maintain as the codebase grows.

Additionally, TypeScript functions can have optional or default parameters. Optional parameters are denoted with a question mark (?) after the parameter name, whereas default parameters are assigned a default value:

```
function multiply(a: number, b: number = 2): number {
    return a * b;
}
```

In this example, b is a default parameter with a default value of 2. When calling this function, you can omit the second argument:

```
let result = multiply(5);
console.log(result); // Output: 10
```

The output will be:

```
10
```

Or provide it explicitly:

```
let explicitResult = multiply(5, 3);
console.log(explicitResult); // Output: 15
```

Here, the output will be:

```
15
```

TypeScript's function syntax is versatile and powerful. Through strict type annotations and advanced capabilities, it offers robust mechanisms to define, use, and manage functions more effectively. This foundation enables developers to write cleaner, safer, and more maintainable code.

4.2 Function Types and Type Annotations

TypeScript allows us to define and enforce the types of parameters and return values for functions through function types and type annotations. This enhances the code's readability and maintainability while reducing runtime errors.

Function types establish the type signature of a function, specifying the types of parameters it accepts and the type of value it returns. For instance, the type of a function that takes two numbers and returns a number can be defined as follows:

```
type Add = (a: number, b: number) => number;
```

In this example, Add is a function type indicating that any function conforming to this type must accept two arguments of type number and return a number.

Consider the following function that adds two numbers:

```
function add(a: number, b: number): number {
    return a + b;
}
```

We can assign this function to a variable of type Add:

```
const sum: Add = add;
```

This assignment is valid because add complies with the Add type signature. The type annotations (a: number, b: number): number explicitly specify the types of the parameters a and b, and the return type of the function.

Type annotations provide a clear contract regarding what types of arguments a function expects and what type it returns. If we attempt to pass arguments of incorrect types, TypeScript will raise a compile-time error:

```
sum('1', '2'); // Error: Argument of type 'string' is not assignable to parameter of type
      'number'
```

In some cases, it might be useful to define functions that accept parameters of various types. TypeScript supports this through union types and function overloads.

Union types allow parameters to accept multiple types. For instance, a function that logs its input may accept both numbers and strings:

```
function log(value: number | string): void {
    console.log(value);
}
```

In this example, value: number | string indicates that value can be either a number or a string. The return type of void signifies that the function does not return a value.

Function overloads provide another way to define multiple type signatures for a single function. It allows us to write multiple declarations for the same function name, each with different parameter and return types:

```
function combine(input1: number, input2: number): number;
function combine(input1: string, input2: string): string;
function combine(input1: any, input2: any): any {
    if (typeof input1 === 'number' && typeof input2 === 'number') {
        return input1 + input2;
    } else if (typeof input1 === 'string' && typeof input2 === 'string') {
        return input1 + input2;
    }
    throw new Error('Invalid input types');
}
```

This example illustrates function overloads where the combine function can take either two numbers and return a number or two strings and return a string. The third implementation provides the function body, using type guards to ensure that both arguments are of the same type and return the correct result.

Type annotations extend beyond parameters and return types. We can annotate the types of function expressions, arrow functions, and callback functions. Consider a function that accepts a callback function as an argument:

```
function process(data: number, callback: (value: number) => void): void {
    callback(data);
}

process(5, (value: number) => {
    console.log(value);
});
```

In this scenario, the callback parameter must be a function that accepts a single number and returns void. When process is called, the callback function will be executed with the provided data.

For more complex function types, it is possible to define custom types using the type alias. For instance, let's define a type for a function that receives an array and a predicate function, and returns a filtered array:

```
type Predicate<T> = (item: T) => boolean;

function filter<T>(array: T[], predicate: Predicate<T>): T[] {
    const result: T[] = [];
    for (const item of array) {
        if (predicate(item)) {
            result.push(item);
        }
    }
    return result;
}

const numbers: number[] = [1, 2, 3, 4, 5];
const evenNumbers: number[] = filter(numbers, (n: number) => n % 2 === 0);

console.log(evenNumbers);
```

Here, Predicate<T> defines a generic type for a function that takes a parameter of type T and returns boolean. The filter function utilizes this predicate type to filter elements of the provided array based on the predicate's logic, demonstrating effective use of generics and type annotations in function definitions.

Type annotations and function types are fundamental aspects of TypeScript, playing a crucial role in building robust and maintainable applications. By enforcing type constraints on function parameters and return values, they help prevent type-related errors, enhance code clarity, and facilitate development.

4.3 Optional and Default Parameters

In TypeScript, defining functions with optional and default parameters enhances flexibility and improves function usability by avoiding the need for multiple function overloads to accommodate varying numbers of arguments. This section delves into the mechanics, syntax, and practical applications of these parameter types.

TypeScript allows parameters to be optional by appending a question mark '¿ to the parameter name in the function definition. This feature means that calls to the function need not include a value for that parameter. Additionally, default parameters enable the assignment of default values to function parameters if no argument is supplied, thus ensuring that the function operates effectively in the absence of explicit inputs for those parameters.

Optional Parameters

To declare an optional parameter in TypeScript, append a '¿ to the parameter's name in the function signature. When a function is called without providing a value for an optional parameter, TypeScript assigns the parameter the value 'undefined'.

```
function buildName(firstName: string, lastName?: string): string {
    if (lastName) {
        return firstName + " " + lastName;
    } else {
        return firstName;
    }
}
```

In this example, lastName is an optional parameter. If lastName is not provided when calling the buildName function, it defaults to 'undefined', and the code inside the function accounts for such a scenario.

```
let result1 = buildName("John", "Doe"); // John Doe
let result2 = buildName("Jane"); // Jane
```

```
John Doe
Jane
```

Default Parameters

Default parameters allow function parameters to have a default value if no value or 'undefined' is passed. You can set a default value by assigning it directly in the function signature.

```
function greet(person: string, greeting: string = "Hello"): string {
    return greeting + ", " + person;
}
```

Here, the greeting parameter has a default value of "Hello". If greeting is omitted or given as 'undefined', it will automatically be assigned "Hello".

```
let greeting1 = greet("Alice"); // Hello, Alice
let greeting2 = greet("Bob", "Hi"); // Hi, Bob
let greeting3 = greet("Carol", undefined); // Hello, Carol
```

```
Hello, Alice
Hi, Bob
Hello, Carol
```

It is essential to note that optional parameters and default parameters interact predictably. If a parameter is both optional and has a default value, it will use the default value when not explicitly provided, like in the following example:

```
function assembleAddress(street: string, city: string = "Unknown City", country?:
```

```
    string): string {
  if (country) {
    return street + ", " + city + ", " + country;
  } else {
    return street + ", " + city;
  }
}
```

Depending on the arguments supplied, this function will behave accordingly by filling in the default value where necessary:

```
let address1 = assembleAddress("123 Main St");
// 123 Main St, Unknown City
let address2 = assembleAddress("123 Main St", "Springfield");
// 123 Main St, Springfield
let address3 = assembleAddress("123 Main St", "Springfield", "USA");
// 123 Main St, Springfield, USA
```

```
123 Main St, Unknown City
123 Main St, Springfield
123 Main St, Springfield, USA
```

Considerations must be given to the order of parameters. Optional parameters should follow required parameters to avoid ambiguity and compilation errors. Furthermore, if a sequence involves both default and optional parameters, the proper order must be maintained to ensure the proper application of default values.

The careful usage of optional and default parameters allows for more elegant and adaptable code, reducing redundancy and enhancing function flexibility. Proper implementation is crucial in writing comprehensive and maintainable TypeScript code.

4.4 Rest Parameters and the Spread Operator

Rest parameters and the spread operator are powerful features in TypeScript that allow functions to efficiently handle multiple arguments and operate on arrays. These features enable cleaner and more flexible code, improving both readability and functionality.

The *rest parameter* syntax allows a function to accept an indefinite number of arguments as an array. This is particularly useful when the exact number of arguments is not known upfront. The rest parameter syntax is denoted by three dots (...) followed by the name of the array representing the rest of the arguments.

Consider the following example that illustrates the use of rest parameters:

```
function sum(...numbers: number[]): number {
    return numbers.reduce((total, num) => total + num, 0);
}
```

In this example, the function sum accepts any number of number arguments. These arguments are automatically collected into an array named numbers, and the function computes their sum using the reduce method.

When calling the sum function, you can pass any number of arguments:

```
console.log(sum(1, 2, 3));
console.log(sum(10, 20, 30, 40, 50));
```

The outputs will be as follows:

```
6
150
```

The rest parameter must be the last parameter in the function's parameter list, as it collects all remaining arguments. Including parameters after the rest parameter will result in a syntax error.

The *spread operator*, also denoted by three dots (...), allows an iterable (like an array) to be expanded in contexts where multiple elements or arguments are expected. The spread operator can be used in function calls, array literals, and object literals.

For example, the spread operator can be used to pass array elements as individual arguments to a function:

```
const numbersArray: number[] = [1, 2, 3, 4, 5];
console.log(sum(...numbersArray)); // Output: 15
```

In this scenario, the array numbersArray is expanded into individual elements when passed to the sum function. The spread operator essentially spreads out the elements of the array as separate arguments.

The spread operator can also be used to create copies of arrays or concatenate arrays:

```
const array1: number[] = [1, 2, 3];
const array2: number[] = [4, 5, 6];
const combinedArray: number[] = [...array1, ...array2];
console.log(combinedArray); // Output: [1, 2, 3, 4, 5, 6]

const copiedArray: number[] = [...array1];
console.log(copiedArray); // Output: [1, 2, 3]
```

In these examples, the spread operator creates a new array, either by combining elements from array1 and array2 into combinedArray or by copying elements from array1 into copiedArray.

Additionally, you can use the spread operator to perform object spreading, which allows for copying properties from one object to another. This can be particularly useful in managing state and immutability in complex applications:

```
const obj1 = { a: 1, b: 2 };
const obj2 = { b: 3, c: 4 };
const combinedObj = { ...obj1, ...obj2 };
console.log(combinedObj); // Output: { a: 1, b: 3, c: 4 }

const copiedObj = { ...obj1 };
console.log(copiedObj); // Output: { a: 1, b: 2 }
```

Here, combinedObj is created by combining properties from obj1 and obj2. If there are overlapping properties, the latter object's properties overwrite the former's. The copiedObj example demonstrates how to create an exact copy of an existing object using the spread operator.

Both rest parameters and the spread operator simplify the handling of variable numbers of arguments and streamline array and object manipulations. These features enhance the expressiveness and flexibility of TypeScript, making it easier to write concise and maintainable code.

4.5 Function Overloads

TypeScript supports function overloading, a feature that allows a function to have multiple signatures. This capability is particularly useful in scenarios where a function needs to handle different types of input parameters and return varying types based on the input. Function overloading enhances code readability and ensures type safety.

Function overloading in TypeScript is implemented by defining multiple function signatures followed by a single implementation. The function signatures define the different permissible combinations of parameters and their types. The actual implementation must cover all the defined function signatures.

Consider the following example of an overloaded function to illustrate the concept.

```
function add(a: number, b: number): number;
function add(a: string, b: string): string;
function add(a: any, b: any): any {
```

```
    return a + b;
}
```

In this example, the add function has two distinct signatures:

- function add(a: number, b: number): number;
- function add(a: string, b: string): string;

Both signatures are followed by a single implementation that uses the any type to handle both cases. The implementation performs addition, whether the parameters are numbers or concatenation if they are strings. Below is an example of using the overloaded function:

```
console.log(add(1, 2)); // Output: 3
console.log(add("Hello, ", "World!")); // Output: Hello, World!
```

```
3
Hello, World!
```

It is crucial to ensure that the implementation is flexible enough to handle all the defined signatures. Any mismatch can lead to runtime errors or unexpected behavior.

The primary advantage of function overloading is the type-checking at compile time, which helps catch errors early. It also spares the user of the function from managing multiple function names for various parameter types. However, while function overloads provide flexibility, they must be used judiciously to avoid making code complex and harder to maintain.

Here is another example, this time demonstrating overloading with a class method. The same principles apply as with standalone functions:

```
class Calculator {
    add(a: number, b: number): number;
    add(a: string, b: string): string;
    add(a: any, b: any): any {
        return a + b;
    }
}

let calculator = new Calculator();
console.log(calculator.add(5, 10)); // Output: 15
console.log(calculator.add("Foo", "Bar")); // Output: FooBar
```

```
15
FooBar
```

In this example, the Calculator class has an overloaded add method. The usage is identical to the standalone function.

Function overloading can also be employed in situations where a function might accept a variable number of arguments. By providing multiple signatures, users can describe different acceptable combinations of arguments:

```
function concatenate(first: string, second: string): string;
function concatenate(first: string, second: string, third: string): string;
function concatenate(...args: string[]): string {
    return args.join(" ");
}

console.log(concatenate("Hello", "World")); // Output: Hello World
console.log(concatenate("TypeScript", "is", "great")); // Output: TypeScript is great
```

```
Hello World
TypeScript is great
```

This implementation of concatenate uses rest parameters (...args) to allow for a flexible number of string arguments. The different overloads specify the combinations of parameter counts that are permissible.

It is crucial to note that function overloading in TypeScript does not support multiple implementations. Only one implementation is allowed and must ensure that it accommodates each overloaded signature.

In essence, function overloading in TypeScript provides a robust mechanism that enhances type safety and flexibility, enabling developers to create interfaces that are intuitive to use and maintain.

4.6 Arrow Functions and Lexical 'this'

Arrow functions, introduced in ECMAScript 2015 (ES6), provide a concise syntax for writing function expressions in JavaScript and subsequently TypeScript. Arrow functions differ from regular functions in two main ways: their syntax and their handling of the this keyword.

An arrow function uses the following syntax:

```
const functionName = (parameters) => expression;
```

If the function body contains multiple statements, you use curly braces to group them. Otherwise, the expression's result is returned implicitly.

```
const add = (a: number, b: number): number => a + b;

const multiply = (a: number, b: number): number => {
    return a * b;
};
```

One of the arrow function's key characteristics is its lexical binding of this. Unlike regular functions, which have their this determined at call-time, arrow functions capture the this value of the enclosing context at the time they are defined. This can prevent many common mistakes when dealing with object-oriented programming and callbacks.

Consider the following example:

```
class Counter {
    count: number;

    constructor() {
        this.count = 0;
    }

    increment() {
        setTimeout(function() {
            this.count++;
            console.log(this.count);
        }, 1000);
    }
}

const counterInstance = new Counter();
counterInstance.increment(); // Outputs: NaN
```

In this code, setTimeout is a regular function, and within it, this does not refer to the instance of Counter as one might intuitively expect. Instead, this inside setTimeout refers to the global object (or undefined in strict mode), leading to an unexpected NaN result.

To fix this issue, you can use an arrow function, which retains the lexical this from increment's scope:

```
class Counter {
    count: number;

    constructor() {
        this.count = 0;
    }

    increment() {
        setTimeout(() => {
            this.count++;
            console.log(this.count);
        }, 1000);
    }
}

const counterInstance = new Counter();
counterInstance.increment(); // Outputs: 1
```

Here, the arrow function in setTimeout uses the this value of its enclosing method increment, allowing access to the instance properties correctly.

Arrow functions are particularly useful within methods that make use of asynchronous operations or event handling:

```
class Button {
    text: string;

    constructor(text: string) {
        this.text = text;
    }

    render() {
        const buttonElement = document.createElement('button');
        buttonElement.textContent = this.text;
        buttonElement.addEventListener('click', () => {
            console.log('Clicked button: ' + this.text);
        });
        document.body.appendChild(buttonElement);
    }
}

const myButton = new Button('Click Me');
myButton.render(); // Click event prints: 'Clicked button: Click Me'
```

In this example, the arrow function inside addEventListener ensures that this refers to the instance of the Button class, maintaining consistent access to the text property.

Despite their advantages, arrow functions are not suitable in all cases:

- Arrow functions cannot be used as constructors and will throw an error when invoked with the new keyword.
- They do not have their own arguments object, which may limit their use in functions requiring dynamic argument handling.
- In methods defined inside object literals, arrow functions do not have their own this.

Care must be taken to select the appropriate type of function depending on the context and required functionality.

4.7 Function Scope and Closures

Function scope and closures are fundamental concepts in TypeScript that dictate how variables are accessible within functions and how functions can remember the environment where they were created.

In TypeScript, like in JavaScript, the scope of a variable is determined by its location within the code structure. Variables declared within a function are local to that function and cannot be accessed from outside. Conversely, variables declared outside of a function can be accessed within that function if they fall within its outer scope.

To illustrate this, consider the following example:

```
function outerFunction() {
    let outerVariable = 'I am outside!';

    function innerFunction() {
        let innerVariable = 'I am inside!';
        console.log(outerVariable); // Accessible
        console.log(innerVariable); // Accessible
    }

    innerFunction();
    console.log(outerVariable); // Accessible
    // console.log(innerVariable); // Unaccessible
}

outerFunction();
```

In this example, outerFunction declares a variable outerVariable and defines an inner function innerFunction which in turn declares a variable innerVariable. The innerFunction can access both outerVariable and innerVariable, whereas outerFunction can only access outerVariable. The innerFunction's variable, innerVariable, is not accessible outside of innerFunction.

Closures are closely related to scopes. A closure gives a function access to all variables from its parent function, even after the parent function has finished executing. This is crucial for scenarios where a function needs to maintain state or when implementing function factories.

Let us restructure the above example to demonstrate closure:

```
function outerFunction() {
    let outerVariable = 'I am outside!';

    return function innerFunction() {
        let innerVariable = 'I am inside!';
        console.log(outerVariable); // Accessible within closure
    };
}

const closureFunction = outerFunction();
closureFunction(); // Executes innerFunction with access to outerVariable
```

In the modified example, outerFunction returns innerFunction. When closureFunction is called, it retains access to outerVariable due to the closure.

Closures provide the means for functions to retain reference to their surrounding state, which opens up vast opportunities in modular and functional programming. A practical use case is creating private variables or encapsulating functionality within modules.

Consider the following module that uses closures to encapsulate state:

```
function createCounter() {
    let count = 0;

    return {
        increment: function() {
            count++;
            console.log(`Count is now ${count}`);
        },
        decrement: function() {
            count--;
            console.log(`Count is now ${count}`);
        },
        getCount: function() {
            return count;
        }
    };
}

const counter = createCounter();
counter.increment(); // Output: Count is now 1
counter.increment(); // Output: Count is now 2
counter.decrement(); // Output: Count is now 1
console.log(counter.getCount()); // Output: 1
```

In this example, createCounter is a factory function that returns an object containing functions to manipulate the internal count variable. The functions returned by createCounter form closures that retain access to the count variable, even after createCounter has executed. This ensures count remains private to the module, effectively providing encapsulation.

Understanding scope and closures is not only fundamental for writing efficient TypeScript but also essential for mastering advanced programming concepts such as asynchronous programming, callback functions, and function currying.

4.8 Anonymous Functions and IIFE

Anonymous functions in TypeScript, as the name implies, are functions that do not have a name associated with them. They are often used where a function is required as a parameter or for short-lived use. A common scenario where anonymous functions are used includes array operations and event handlers. The basic syntax of an anonymous function involves omitting the function name while still defining the function body and parameters.

Consider the following example of an anonymous function used with the map method on an array:

```
let numbers: number[] = [1, 2, 3, 4, 5];
let squaredNumbers = numbers.map(function (num: number): number {
    return num * num;
});
console.log(squaredNumbers);
```

```
[1, 4, 9, 16, 25]
```

In this example, the anonymous function takes an element from the numbers array, squares it, and returns the result. The map method then constructs a new array squaredNumbers from the returned values.

Closely related to anonymous functions are Immediately Invoked Function Expressions (IIFE). An IIFE (pronounced "iffy") is a function that is executed as soon as it is defined. IIFEs are used to create a new scope, providing privacy for variables defined within the IIFE and preventing them from polluting the global scope.

The syntax for an IIFE involves wrapping the function definition inside parentheses and then immediately invoking it with a pair of trailing parentheses.

Here is an example of an IIFE:

```
(function() {
    let message: string = "Hello, IIFE!";
    console.log(message);
})();
```

```
Hello, IIFE!
```

In this example, the function is defined and immediately executed, printing "Hello, IIFE!" to the console. The variable message is scoped within the IIFE and is not accessible outside of it.

IIFEs are particularly useful in TypeScript to avoid variable collisions and maintain encapsulation. They can also be used to create module-like structures by exposing only selected parts to the outer scope.

For example:

```
let Counter = (function() {
    let count: number = 0;

    return {
        increment: function() {
            count++;
            return count;
```

```
    },
    getCount: function() {
      return count;
    }
  };
})();

console.log(Counter.increment()); // 1
console.log(Counter.getCount()); // 1
```

```
1
1
```

This example defines a Counter module using an IIFE. The count variable is private and can only be accessed via the publicly exposed methods increment and getCount. This pattern effectively hides the internal state and provides controlled access to the data.

Combining the power of anonymous functions and IIFEs can lead to clean, modular, and well-encapsulated code. When using IIFEs to create module-like structures, consider leveraging modern TypeScript modules for more robust and maintainable codebases. However, understanding and using IIFE effectively remains an essential part of mastering JavaScript and TypeScript.

4.9 Modules in TypeScript: An Introduction

Modules in TypeScript are a powerful mechanism to encapsulate and organize code. By structuring an application into smaller, self-contained modules, development becomes more manageable, enhances code reuse, and simplifies maintenance. TypeScript's module system adheres to the ECMAScript 2015 (ES6) standard, ensuring compatibility with modern JavaScript environments.

Modules are executed within their own scope, not in the global scope, which means that variables, functions, classes, etc., defined in a module are not visible outside the module unless they are explicitly exported. Conversely, other modules must import the exported elements to use them.

To define and use modules in TypeScript, we utilize two primary keywords: export and import.

export statements are used to authoritatively designate certain elements to be accessible outside the module.

```
export class User {
  constructor(public name: string) {}
```

```
}

export function greet(user: User) {
    return 'Hello, ${user.name}!';
}
```

In this example, the User class and greet function are exported from the module, making them available for import into other modules.

import statements allow you to use the exported features from another module.

```
import { User, greet } from './user';

const user = new User('Alice');
console.log(greet(user));
```

Here, the User class and greet function are imported from the user module, allowing for their instantiation and invocation.

For codebases with numerous elements, it's sometimes necessary to export or import everything from a module collectively.

```
export * from './user';
```

```
import * as UserModule from './user';

const user = new UserModule.User('Alice');
console.log(UserModule.greet(user));
```

Above, all the exports from user module are re-exported and then imported under the namespace UserModule.

Modules can also have a default export. A module can export one default element, which does not require curly braces when imported.

```
export default class User {
    constructor(public name: string) {}
}
```

```
import User from './user';

const user = new User('Alice');
```

The default export is especially useful when a module needs to provision a single primary object or function.

Modules in TypeScript can also be dynamic, which allows for importing modules only when they are required for execution, helping in optimizing loading time and conserving resources.

```
async function loadUserModule() {
```

```
    const module = await import('./user');
    const user = new module.User('Alice');
    console.log(module.greet(user));
}
```

The import() function returns a promise that resolves to the module, making it possible to load modules asynchronously.

Understanding how to create, export, and import modules efficiently enables developers to build more structured, maintainable, and scalable TypeScript applications. This seamless encapsulation and modularization underpin the development of robust software systems.

4.10 Importing and Exporting Modules

In TypeScript, modules play a crucial role in structuring large-scale applications by allowing developers to encapsulate code into smaller, reusable units. This section delves into the specifics of importing and exporting modules, which are essential for achieving modular and maintainable code in TypeScript.

Exporting Modules

To export a variable, function, class, or interface from a module so that it can be used in other files, TypeScript employs the export keyword. Here are various examples demonstrating different methods of exporting elements from a module:

```
export const PI = 3.14;

export function calculateArea(radius: number): number {
  return PI * radius * radius;
}

export class Circle {
  constructor(public radius: number) {}

  getArea(): number {
    return calculateArea(this.radius);
  }
}
```

Named exports allow multiple values to be exported from a single module. To import these exports, use the appropriate import statements.

```
import { PI, calculateArea, Circle } from './circleModule';

console.log(PI); // Output: 3.14
const area = calculateArea(5);
console.log(area); // Output: 78.5
```

```
const myCircle = new Circle(5);
console.log(myCircle.getArea()); // Output: 78.5
```

TypeScript also supports exporting elements under different names using the as keyword.

```
const name = 'John Doe';
function greet() {
  console.log('Hello, ' + name);
}

export { name as userName, greet as sayHello };
```

When importing these renamed exports, you need to use the new names:

```
import { userName, sayHello } from './userModule';

console.log(userName); // Output: John Doe
sayHello(); // Output: Hello, John Doe
```

Default Exports

A module can designate a single export as the default export using the default keyword. Default exports are useful when a module aims to export a single primary value or functionality.

```
export default class Rectangle {
  constructor(public width: number, public height: number) {}

  getArea(): number {
    return this.width * this.height;
  }
}
```

The import syntax for default exports is distinct; you do not use curly braces.

```
import Rectangle from './rectangleModule';

const myRectangle = new Rectangle(10, 20);
console.log(myRectangle.getArea()); // Output: 200
```

A module may combine default and named exports:

```
export const number = 42;
export default function square(x: number): number {
  return x * x;
}
```

```
import square, { number } from './mathModule';

console.log(square(3)); // Output: 9
console.log(number); // Output: 42
```

Re-exporting and Aggregate Modules

Re-exporting allows a module to pass through exports from another module, enabling the creation of aggregate modules. This is done using the export ... from syntax.

```
export { PI, calculateArea, Circle } from './circleModule';
export { default as Rectangle } from './rectangleModule';
```

These aggregate modules simplify importing from multiple modules into a single entry point.

```
import { PI, calculateArea, Circle, Rectangle } from './shapesModule';

console.log(PI); // Output: 3.14
const area = calculateArea(5);
console.log(area); // Output: 78.5
const myCircle = new Circle(5);
console.log(myCircle.getArea()); // Output: 78.5
const myRectangle = new Rectangle(10, 20);
console.log(myRectangle.getArea()); // Output: 200
```

Dynamic Import Expressions

Dynamic imports facilitate lazy loading of modules, thereby enhancing the performance of applications by loading code only when it is required.

```
async function loadCircleModule() {
  const circleModule = await import('./circleModule');
  const myCircle = new circleModule.Circle(5);
  console.log(myCircle.getArea());
}

loadCircleModule();
```

Dynamic imports return a promise that resolves to the module object, allowing its exports to be accessed only after the module has been loaded.

```
Output:
78.5
```

By mastering the import and export mechanisms within TypeScript, developers can effectively modularize their code, leading to well-organized and maintainable codebases. This empowers developers to manage dependencies cleanly and promote code reuse across different parts of an application.

4.11 Re-exporting and Aggregate Modules

In TypeScript, re-exporting and aggregate modules provide a means for better code organization and modular development. These techniques help streamline code maintenance by allowing developers to re-export components from other modules, thereby creating a more coherent and approachable structure. This section delves into the mechanisms and practical applications of re-exporting and aggregate modules.

Re-exporting allows a module to export functionalities (such as variables, functions, classes, or interfaces) that are imported from other modules. This can be particularly useful when you need to centralize exports, making it easier for other developers to consume functionality without concerning themselves with the underlying module structure.

Re-exporting Basics

Consider a scenario where you have two modules, moduleA.ts and moduleB.ts, each exporting different functionalities.

```
// moduleA.ts
export function functionA() {
    console.log("Function A from Module A");
}

export const constantA = 42;
```

```
// moduleB.ts
export function functionB() {
    console.log("Function B from Module B");
}

export class ClassB {
    greet() {
        console.log("Hello from Class B");
    }
}
```

To re-export these functionalities in another module, moduleC.ts, you can use the export keyword along with the from syntax:

```
// moduleC.ts
export { functionA, constantA } from './moduleA';
export { functionB, ClassB } from './moduleB';
```

By doing this, moduleC.ts now acts as a single point of export for components coming from moduleA.ts and moduleB.ts. Other modules can now import functionalities from moduleC.ts without needing to know their original source modules.

```
// anotherModule.ts
import { functionA, constantA, functionB, ClassB } from './moduleC';

functionA();
console.log(constantA);
functionB();
const instanceB = new ClassB();
instanceB.greet();
```

It is also possible to export all exported members from a module using the * syntax. This can simplify re-exporting when dealing with a large number of exports:

```
// moduleC.ts
export * from './moduleA';
export * from './moduleB';
```

Aggregate Modules

Aggregate modules combine multiple module exports into a single entity. This concept is highly beneficial when creating library packages where the end-user expects a single entry point to access all provided functionalities.

Consider a project structure where different modules group related functionalities:

```
// mathUtils.ts
export function add(a: number, b: number): number {
    return a + b;
}

export function subtract(a: number, b: number): number {
    return a - b;
}
```

```
// stringUtils.ts
export function toUpperCase(str: string): string {
    return str.toUpperCase();
}

export function toLowerCase(str: string): string {
    return str.toLowerCase();
}
```

An aggregate module, index.ts, can be created to provide a unified export interface:

```
// index.ts
export * from './mathUtils';
export * from './stringUtils';
```

Consumers of the package can simply import from the aggregate module:

```
// app.ts
import { add, subtract, toUpperCase, toLowerCase } from './index';

console.log(add(5, 3)); // Output: 8
console.log(subtract(5, 3)); // Output: 2
console.log(toUpperCase("hello")); // Output: HELLO
console.log(toLowerCase("WORLD")); // Output: world
```

It provides a streamlined approach for managing large projects and improves code maintainability by centralizing the export declarations. Moreover, when modules are added or removed, only the aggregate module may need updates, isolating the rest of the codebase from these changes.

In cases where naming conflicts arise due to re-exporting, it is possible to use aliasing:

```
// mathUtils.ts
export function add(a: number, b: number): number {
    return a + b;
}

export function multiply(a: number, b: number): number {
    return a * b;
}
```

```
// advancedMathUtils.ts
export function square(a: number): number {
    return a * a;
}

export function multiply(a: number, b: number): number {
    return a * b;
}
```

```
// index.ts
export { add, multiply as mathMultiply } from './mathUtils';
export { square, multiply as advancedMultiply } from './advancedMathUtils';
```

In this scenario, multiply functions from both mathUtils.ts and advancedMathUtils.ts are re-exported with aliases to resolve the naming conflict.

By understanding and employing re-exporting and aggregate modules, developers can achieve better modularization and maintainability in their TypeScript projects. These practices foster clean and understandable code structures, facilitating easier collaboration and scalability.

4.12 Dynamic Import Expressions

Dynamic import expressions in TypeScript offer a powerful mechanism to load modules asynchronously, a feature particularly advantageous in scenarios necessitating on-demand loading of code, such as in the case of large applications or deploying features contingent on user interaction. This section delineates the syntax, use cases, and considerations for dynamic import expressions, enriching one's expertise in efficient module management.

Dynamic imports are expressed using the import() function. Unlike static imports, which are hoisted and set up at the beginning of a module, dynamic imports return a Promise that resolves to the module and its exports. The import() function can be called at any point in the application's execution, thus enabling conditional loading.

```
async function loadModule() {
    const module = await import('./someModule');
    module.someFunction();
}

loadModule();
```

In this example, the loadModule function asynchronously loads the module specified by './someModule' and calls someFunction from the imported module. Note that dynamic imports inherently leverage JavaScript's promise-based syntax, hence why async/await is used for better readability and control flow.

Dynamic import expressions excel in cases where the full application functionality is not immediately necessary, thereby enhancing performance and user experience by minimizing the initial load time. Consider a scenario in which certain features are only activated upon user interaction:

```
document.getElementById('loadButton').addEventListener('click', async () => {
    const module = await import('./featureModule');
    module.initFeature();
});
```

Here, featureModule is loaded when the user clicks a button, as opposed to being bundled into the initial load. This lazy loading approach reduces the upfront cost of loading JavaScript resources.

Dynamic imports are also instrumental in code splitting, a technique that divides code into smaller bundles that can be loaded on-demand. This can be demonstrated within a routing context of a single-page application (SPA):

```
function loadRouteComponent(route: string) {
    switch(route) {
        case 'home':
            return import('./HomeComponent');
        case 'about':
            return import('./AboutComponent');
        default:
            return Promise.reject('Route not found');
    }
}

async function renderRoute(route: string) {
    try {
        const module = await loadRouteComponent(route);
        module.render();
    } catch (error) {
        console.error('Error loading route component:', error);
    }
}

window.addEventListener('hashchange', () => {
    const route = window.location.hash.slice(1);
    renderRoute(route);
});
```

In this implementation, loadRouteComponent dynamically imports the appropriate component based on the current route, permitting efficient modularization and potential reduction in the initial load payload.

Considerations for using dynamic imports include handling loading errors, as network issues or incorrect module paths can result in failed imports. The promise-based nature of dynamic imports allows error handling using try/catch blocks or Promise.then().catch() chains:

```
async function loadAndHandleError() {
    try {
        const module = await import('./potentialFailModule');
        module.someFunction();
    } catch (error) {
        console.error('Failed to load module:', error);
    }
}

loadAndHandleError();
```

It's critical to weigh the advantages of dynamic imports against complexities such as dependency management and potential impacts on runtime performance. If overused or misapplied, dynamic imports can lead to fragmentation of code, complicating debugging and tracing issues.

Utilization of dynamic import expressions necessitates familiarity with modern JavaScript features, particularly promises and the async/await syntax, which simplifies asynchronous operations into more readable code akin to synchronous structures.

Implementing dynamic imports can thus significantly optimize application performance through efficient resource management, on-demand loading, and facilitating advanced patterns such as lazy loading and code splitting, ultimately contributing to an improved user experience.

Chapter 5

Object-Oriented Programming in TypeScript

This chapter provides an in-depth introduction to object-oriented programming (OOP) in TypeScript, covering the creation and use of classes and objects, inheritance, and access modifiers such as public, private, and protected. It also explores advanced OOP features including readonly properties, static members, abstract classes, interfaces vs. abstract classes, polymorphism, method overriding, getters and setters, the role of the 'this' keyword, and the use of decorators and metadata reflection to enhance class functionality.

5.1 Introduction to Object-Oriented Programming (OOP)

Object-Oriented Programming (OOP) is a programming paradigm that uses objects—instances of classes—to structure software into manageable, modular pieces. It enables developers to create models based on the real world, contributing significantly to code reuse, maintainability, and scalability. In TypeScript, OOP extends the capabilities of JavaScript by introducing robust type-checking along with encapsulation, inheritance, and polymorphism.

A class in TypeScript serves as the blueprint for creating objects. It encapsulates data for the object and methods to manipulate that data. This encapsulation aligns well with the concept of data hiding, enabling developers to control how and where data is accessed or modified. This allows for more secure and predictable code.

To define a class in TypeScript, we use the class keyword followed by the class name. The following code snippet illustrates the basic syntax of a TypeScript class:

```
class Person {
    private name: string;
    private age: number;

    constructor(name: string, age: number) {
        this.name = name;
        this.age = age;
    }

    public getName(): string {
        return this.name;
    }

    public getAge(): number {
        return this.age;
    }

    public setName(name: string): void {
        this.name = name;
    }

    public setAge(age: number): void {
        this.age = age;
    }
}
```

In this example, the Person class has two private properties, name and age. These properties are assigned values via the constructor and can be accessed or modified using the public methods getName, getAge, setName, and setAge. Using private restricts direct access to these properties, enforcing encapsulation.

When instantiated, a class creates an object. For instance, we can create an instance of the Person class as follows:

```
let person1 = new Person('Alice', 30);
console.log(person1.getName()); // Output: Alice
console.log(person1.getAge()); // Output: 30
person1.setName('Bob');
console.log(person1.getName()); // Output: Bob
```

```
Output:
Alice
30
Bob
```

Encapsulation through property accessors and visibility modifiers (public, private, and protected) ensures that the state of an object can only be changed in controlled ways.

Inheritance is a core concept of OOP that allows a class to inherit properties and methods from another class. The class being inherited from is called the base class, parent class, or super class, and the class that inherits is called the derived class, child class, or subclass. This brings the principle of code reuse by enabling derived classes to use the properties and methods of their base classes.

In TypeScript, inheritance is implemented using the extends keyword as shown below:

```
class Employee extends Person {
    private employeeId: number;

    constructor(name: string, age: number, employeeId: number) {
        super(name, age);
        this.employeeId = employeeId;
    }

    public getEmployeeId(): number {
        return this.employeeId;
    }

    public setEmployeeId(employeeId: number): void {
        this.employeeId = employeeId;
    }
}
```

In the given example, the Employee class extends from Person, meaning it inherits the name and age properties, and the getName, getAge, setName, and setAge methods. The super keyword is used within the constructor of the Employee class to call the constructor of the Person class, ensuring that the properties name and age are properly initialized.

Polymorphism is another fundamental aspect of OOP that permits methods to do different things based on the object it is acting upon. In other words, the same method can have different implementations in different classes. This is achieved through method overriding, where a derived class provides a specific implementation for a method that is already defined in its base class.

Consider the following illustration:

```
class Manager extends Employee {
    private department: string;
```

```
    constructor(name: string, age: number, employeeId: number, department: string) {
        super(name, age, employeeId);
        this.department = department;
    }

    public getDetails(): string {
        return `${this.getName()} is a manager in the ${this.department} department.`;
    }
}

class Developer extends Employee {
    private programmingLanguage: string;

    constructor(name: string, age: number, employeeId: number, programmingLanguage:
        string) {
        super(name, age, employeeId);
        this.programmingLanguage = programmingLanguage;
    }

    public getDetails(): string {
        return `${this.getName()} is a developer who codes in ${this.
            programmingLanguage}.`;
    }
}

let manager = new Manager('Alice', 40, 1, 'HR');
let developer = new Developer('Bob', 25, 2, 'TypeScript');
console.log(manager.getDetails()); // Output: Alice is a manager in the HR department.

console.log(developer.getDetails()); // Output: Bob is a developer who codes in
    TypeScript.
```

```
Output:
Alice is a manager in the HR department.
Bob is a developer who codes in TypeScript.
```

In this example, both Manager and Developer classes extend the Employee class and provide their own implementation of the getDetails method, demonstrating polymorphism. The getDetails method behaves differently depending on the type of the object that invokes it.

Integrating these principles—encapsulation, inheritance, and polymorphism—enables TypeScript developers to write more modular, maintainable, and scalable applications. Transitioning to this paradigm might require initial effort, but its benefits in terms of robustness and clarity in project structure are undeniable. As we advance through this chapter, we will delve deeper into these principles, exploring various other features that TypeScript offers to facilitate effective use of OOP.

5.2 Classes and Objects

In TypeScript, classes form the foundational structure for object-oriented programming by providing a blueprint for creating objects. A class can encapsulate data for the object and methods to manipulate that data, following the key principles of OOP: encapsulation, inheritance, and polymorphism.

To define a class in TypeScript, use the class keyword followed by the class name. The body of the class is enclosed in curly braces {}. For example, consider a simple class Person:

```
class Person {
    // Properties
    name: string;
    age: number;

    // Constructor
    constructor(name: string, age: number) {
        this.name = name;
        this.age = age;
    }

    // Method
    greet() {
        console.log(`Hello, my name is ${this.name} and I am ${this.age} years old.`);
    }
}
```

In this example, the Person class has two properties, name and age, and a constructor that initializes these properties. The greet method outputs a greeting message using the class's properties.

To create an object, or an instance of a class, use the new keyword followed by the class name and the required parameters:

```
let person1 = new Person('John Doe', 30);
person1.greet();
```

When executed, this code will output:

```
Hello, my name is John Doe and I am 30 years old.
```

Classes can also have methods that perform operations related to the class's properties. These methods need to be defined within the class body and can be called on the object instances. Additionally, TypeScript supports access modifiers such as public, private, and protected to control the visibility of class members.

Public Access Modifier

By default, all members (properties and methods) of a TypeScript class are public. Public members can be accessed from anywhere:

```
class Car {
    public brand: string;

    constructor(brand: string) {
        this.brand = brand;
    }

    public drive() {
        console.log(`${this.brand} is driving.`);
    }
}

let car1 = new Car('Toyota');
car1.drive();
console.log(car1.brand);
```

This code will output:

```
Toyota is driving.
Toyota
```

Private Access Modifier

Private members are accessible only within the class where they are defined. Attempting to access these members from outside the class results in a compilation error:

```
class BankAccount {
    private balance: number;

    constructor(initialBalance: number) {
        this.balance = initialBalance;
    }

    public deposit(amount: number) {
        this.balance += amount;
        console.log(`Deposited: ${amount}. New balance: ${this.balance}`);
    }

    private showBalance() {
        console.log(`Balance: ${this.balance}`);
    }
}

let myAccount = new BankAccount(1000);
myAccount.deposit(500);
```

Access to balance and showBalance outside the class results in an error:

```
myAccount.balance; // Error: Property 'balance' is private and only accessible within
    class 'BankAccount'.
myAccount.showBalance(); // Error: Property 'showBalance' is private and only
    accessible within class 'BankAccount'.
```

Protected Access Modifier

Protected members behave similar to private members but are also accessible within derived classes (subclasses):

```
class Parent {
    protected message: string = 'Hello from Parent';

    protected showMessage() {
        console.log(this.message);
    }
}

class Child extends Parent {
    showParentMessage() {
        this.showMessage();
    }
}

let child = new Child();
child.showParentMessage(); // Accesses protected method from the derived class
```

This will output:

```
Hello from Parent
```

Constructor Overloading (optional)

TypeScript allows you to define constructors with different parameters, enabling the creation of objects in multiple ways:

```
class Book {
   title: string;
   author: string;
   pages?: number; // Optional property

   constructor(title: string, author: string, pages?: number) {
       this.title = title;
       this.author = author;
       if (pages) this.pages = pages;
   }

   getInfo() {
       console.log(`Title: ${this.title}, Author: ${this.author}, Pages: ${this.pages ? this.
             pages : 'Unknown'}`);
   }
}

let book1 = new Book("Book Title 1", "Author Name 1", 250);
let book2 = new Book("Book Title 2", "Author Name 2");

book1.getInfo(); // Output: Title: Book Title 1, Author: Author Name 1, Pages: 250
book2.getInfo(); // Output: Title: Book Title 2, Author: Author Name 2, Pages:
      Unknown
```

These features highlight how TypeScript supports the principles of object-oriented programming, making code organized, reusable, and easier to maintain.

5.3 Inheritance and Extending Classes

Inheritance is a fundamental principle of object-oriented programming that allows a class to inherit properties and methods from another class. In TypeScript, this is implemented using the extends keyword. By leveraging inheritance, developers can promote code reuse and establish a natural hierarchical relationship between base and derived classes.

Consider the following example where we define a base class Animal and a derived class Dog that extends Animal.

```
class Animal {
    name: string;

    constructor(name: string) {
        this.name = name;
    }

    move(distance: number = 0) {
        console.log(`${this.name} moved ${distance} meters.`);
    }
}

class Dog extends Animal {
    bark() {
        console.log('Woof! Woof!');
    }
}

let dog = new Dog('Rex');
dog.bark();
dog.move(10);
```

In this example, the Dog class inherits all properties and methods from the Animal class. Thus, an instance of Dog can both bark() (its own method) and move() (inherited from Animal). The output of this program would be:

```
Woof! Woof!
Rex moved 10 meters.
```

Additionally, derived classes can override methods of the base class. For instance, if a derived class needs to provide a specific implementation of a method, it can override the base class method:

```
class Snake extends Animal {
    move(distance: number = 5) {
        console.log('Slithering...');
        super.move(distance);
    }
}

let snake = new Snake('Sly');
snake.move();
```

In this case, the Snake class overrides the move() method. It first outputs "Slithering..." and then calls the move() method of the base class by using the super keyword. The super keyword is used within a derived class to reference its base class.

It's also important to understand the nuances of constructors in the context of inheritance. Specifically, if a derived class has a constructor, it must call super() to execute the constructor of the base class:

```
class Bird extends Animal {
    constructor(name: string, wingSpan: number) {
        super(name);
        this.wingSpan = wingSpan;
    }

    wingSpan: number;

    fly(distance: number = 0) {
        console.log(`${this.name}, with a wingspan of ${this.wingSpan} meters, flew ${
            distance} meters.`);
    }
}

let bird = new Bird('Eagle', 2);
bird.fly(100);
```

In this example, the Bird class extends Animal, and its constructor calls super(name) to ensure the name property is correctly initialized via the Animal constructor. This demonstrates how derived classes work and integrate with their base classes in TypeScript.

In addition to these basics, TypeScript also supports inheritance across multiple levels, allowing for complex object hierarchies. For example, you can have a FlyingBird class that inherits from Bird and adds new functionalities or overrides existing ones:

```
class FlyingBird extends Bird {
    constructor(name: string, wingSpan: number, maxAltitude: number) {
        super(name, wingSpan);
        this.maxAltitude = maxAltitude;
    }

    maxAltitude: number;

    fly(distance: number = 0, altitude: number = 0) {
        if (altitude <= this.maxAltitude) {
            console.log(`${this.name} is flying at an altitude of ${altitude} meters.`);
            super.fly(distance);
        } else {
            console.log(`${this.name} cannot fly above ${this.maxAltitude} meters.`);
        }
    }
}

let flyingBird = new FlyingBird('Hawk', 1.5, 3000);
flyingBird.fly(100, 2500);
```

```
flyingBird.fly(100, 3500);
```

The FlyingBird constructor calls super() to initialize properties from both its base classes, Animal and Bird. The fly() method in FlyingBird checks if the altitude is within limits before invoking the fly() method of the Bird class.

It's important to mention TypeScript features like visibility modifiers (e.g., public, private, protected) play a pivotal role in inheritance. For instance, a protected member of a base class can be accessed only within its class and derived classes:

```
class Base {
    protected x: number;

    constructor(x: number) {
        this.x = x;
    }
}

class Derived extends Base {
    show() {
        console.log(`Value of x is ${this.x}`);
    }
}

let derived = new Derived(10);
derived.show();
```

In this scenario, x is a protected member, and it's accessible within the Derived class but not outside of it, ensuring controlled access within an inheritance hierarchy.

5.4 Public, Private, and Protected Modifiers

TypeScript, being a statically typed superset of JavaScript, provides developers with the ability to define and enforce access control through modifiers. These modifiers determine the visibility and accessibility of class members (properties and methods). The three primary access modifiers in TypeScript are public, private, and protected.

Public members are accessible from any location within the program. By default, all members of a class in TypeScript are public, which means they can be accessed and modified freely.

Private members, on the other hand, are only accessible within the class that defines them. This restriction helps in encapsulating and safeguarding the internal state of objects.

Protected members share a middle ground between public and private. They can be accessed within the declaring class and its subclasses, but not outside of these classes.

Consider the following example to illustrate these modifiers:

```
class Animal {
    public name: string;
    private age: number;
    protected species: string;

    constructor(name: string, age: number, species: string) {
        this.name = name;
        this.age = age;
        this.species = species;
    }

    public getAge(): number {
        return this.age;
    }

    protected makeSound(): void {
        console.log(`${this.name} makes a sound.`);
    }
}

class Dog extends Animal {
    constructor(name: string, age: number, species: string) {
        super(name, age, species);
    }

    public bark(): void {
        console.log(`${this.name} barks.`);
        this.makeSound();
    }
}

const dog = new Dog('Rex', 5, 'Canine');
console.log(dog.name); // Rex
console.log(dog.getAge()); // 5
dog.bark(); // Rex barks. Rex makes a sound.

console.log(dog.age); // Error: Property 'age' is private and only accessible within class
      'Animal'.
console.log(dog.species); // Error: Property 'species' is protected and only accessible
      within class 'Animal' and its subclasses.
```

In this example, we define a class Animal with public, private, and protected members. The name property is public, the age property is private, and the species property is protected.

The Dog class extends Animal and has a bark method that demonstrates access to both public and protected members. Notice how the private age property cannot be accessed outside the Animal class, even though we created an instance of the Dog subclass.

To further illustrate the encapsulation and protection provided by these access modifiers, consider another example with more complex inheritance:

```
class Person {
    public name: string;
    private ssn: string;
    protected dateOfBirth: Date;

    constructor(name: string, ssn: string, dob: Date) {
        this.name = name;
        this.ssn = ssn;
        this.dateOfBirth = dob;
    }

    public getSsn(): string {
        return this.ssn;
    }
}

class Employee extends Person {
    protected employeeId: number;

    constructor(name: string, ssn: string, dob: Date, employeeId: number) {
        super(name, ssn, dob);
        this.employeeId = employeeId;
    }

    public getEmployeeInfo(): string {
        return `Employee ID: ${this.employeeId}, Name: ${this.name}, DOB: ${this.
            dateOfBirth.toDateString()}`;
    }
}

class Manager extends Employee {
    private department: string;

    constructor(name: string, ssn: string, dob: Date, employeeId: number, department:
        string) {
        super(name, ssn, dob, employeeId);
        this.department = department;
    }

    public getManagerInfo(): string {
        return `${this.getEmployeeInfo()}, Department: ${this.department}`;
    }
}

const manager = new Manager('Alice', '123-45-6789', new Date(1980, 1, 1), 101, '
    Engineering');
console.log(manager.getManagerInfo()); // Outputs: "Employee ID: 101, Name: Alice,
    DOB: Fri Feb 01 1980, Department: Engineering"

console.log(manager.ssn); // Error: Property 'ssn' is private and only accessible within
    class 'Person'.
console.log(manager.dateOfBirth); // Error: Property 'dateOfBirth' is protected and
    only accessible within class 'Person' and its subclasses.
console.log(manager.employeeId); // Error: Property 'employeeId' is protected and only
    accessible within class 'Employee' and its subclasses.
```

Here, three classes, Person, Employee, and Manager, are used to exhibit how public, private, and protected modifiers facilitate controlled access. The ssn is private and cannot be accessed outside the Person class. The dateOfBirth is protected and accessible within derived classes like Employee and Manager but not on an instance of Manager. The employeeId of Employee is also protected and only accessible within Employee and Manager.

With proper use of access modifiers, TypeScript enables robust encapsulation. These modifiers ensure that an object's internal states and behaviors are properly controlled, fostering a clear and maintainable structure that aligns with the principles of object-oriented programming.

5.5 Readonly Properties

Readonly properties in TypeScript offer a means to declare properties that cannot be modified after their initial assignment. This feature is of significant importance in enforcing immutability within object-oriented programming paradigms, ensuring that certain properties remain constant throughout the lifecycle of an object. By designating properties as readonly, developers can prevent accidental mutations which could introduce subtle bugs or inconsistent states.

The readonly modifier is applied at the point of property declaration within a class. This modifier ensures that the property is only assignable during either its initialization or within the constructor of the class. Attempts to reassign the value of a readonly property afterwards will result in a compilation error.

Consider the following example:

```
class Person {
  readonly name: string;
  readonly birthDate: Date;

  constructor(name: string, birthDate: Date) {
    this.name = name;
    this.birthDate = birthDate;
  }

  updateName(newName: string): void {
    // This will cause an error since 'name' is a readonly property
    // this.name = newName;
  }
}

const person = new Person('John Doe', new Date(1990, 1, 1));
console.log(person.name); // Outputs: John Doe
// person.name = 'Jane Doe'; // Error: Cannot assign to 'name' because it is a read-
    only property.
```

In this example, name and birthDate are declared as readonly properties. These properties can only be set once, during object instantiation through the constructor. Any attempt to reassign name or birthDate will raise a compile-time error, thus preserving their immutable nature post-initialization.

The immutability enforced by readonly properties is beneficial in contexts where data consistency and predictability are critical. Some common scenarios include:

- **Configuration Settings**: Once read and set, configuration values should not change to ensure consistent behavior of the application.
- **Mathematical Constants**: Properties representing constants such as π or e should remain unchanged after their initial definition.
- **Identifiers**: Unique identifiers such as User IDs or transaction IDs should not be modifiable once assigned.

It is important to note that readonly properties do not necessitate a primitive type. Complex types, such as objects or arrays, can also be declared as readonly, preventing reassignment, although the underlying data structure may still be mutable:

```
class Config {
  readonly settings: { [key: string]: string };

  constructor(initialSettings: { [key: string]: string }) {
    this.settings = initialSettings;
  }

  updateSetting(key: string, value: string): void {
    // This is allowed since we are not reassigning the 'settings' property
    this.settings[key] = value;
  }
}

const appConfig = new Config({ theme: 'dark', language: 'en' });
appConfig.settings['theme'] = 'light'; // This is allowed
// appConfig.settings = { theme: 'light' }; // Error: Cannot assign to 'settings' because
     it is a read-only property.
```

In this code, the settings property is declared as readonly. While direct reassignment of settings is prohibited, individual properties within the object can still be modified. This distinction highlights an essential aspect of the readonly modifier: it prevents reassignment of the property itself but does not necessarily imply full immutability of the property's contents, especially for non-primitive types.

For comprehensive immutability, where neither the property itself nor its content can be altered, developers may leverage the const assertion along with deep cloning or external libraries, such as Immutable.js, designed for immutable data structures.

By incorporating readonly properties into your TypeScript classes, you can safeguard critical properties from unintended modifications, promoting the development of robust and maintainable applications.

5.6 Static Members

Static members in TypeScript are properties and methods of a class that belong to the class itself rather than to any specific instance of the class. This means that they can be accessed without creating an instance of the class. To declare a static member, we use the static keyword.

Declaring Static Members

Static members are declared using the static keyword before the property or method definition. Here's a simple example illustrating how to define and access static members:

```
class MathUtils {
    static PI: number = 3.141592653589793;
    static E: number = 2.718281828459045;

    static areaOfCircle(radius: number): number {
        return this.PI * radius * radius;
    }

    static naturalLog(value: number): number {
        return Math.log(value) / Math.log(this.E);
    }
}

// Accessing static properties and methods
console.log(MathUtils.PI); // Output: 3.141592653589793
console.log(MathUtils.E); // Output: 2.718281828459045
console.log(MathUtils.areaOfCircle(10)); // Output: 314.1592653589793
console.log(MathUtils.naturalLog(7.389)); // Output: ~2 (approximately)
```

Static properties PI and E are class-level variables, and the methods areaOfCircle and naturalLog are class-level functions. Notice how we access them using the class name MathUtils without instantiating the class.

Usage Scenarios for Static Members

Static members are ideal for encapsulating utility functions or constants related to a class but not tied to any specific instance. Common situations where static members are used include:

- Defining constants (e.g., mathematical constants, configuration values).
- Creating utility or helper functions (e.g., conversion methods, validation functions).
- Maintaining a count of instances or applying a singleton pattern.

Instance vs. Static Context

Static members cannot be accessed from an instance of the class; they belong exclusively to the class itself. Conversely, static members cannot use this to access instance variables or instance methods. The following example demonstrates this distinction:

```
class Example {
    instanceVar: number;
    static staticVar: number = 10;

    constructor(instanceVar: number) {
        this.instanceVar = instanceVar;
    }

    instanceMethod(): string {
        return `Instance variable: ${this.instanceVar}`;
    }

    static staticMethod(): string {
        // Cannot use 'this.instanceVar', it's undefined in the static context
        return `Static variable: ${this.staticVar}`;
    }
}

const example = new Example(5);
console.log(example.instanceVar); // Output: 5
console.log(Example.staticVar); // Output: 10

console.log(example.instanceMethod()); // Output: Instance variable: 5
console.log(Example.staticMethod()); // Output: Static variable: 10
```

Here, Example.staticVar and Example.staticMethod are accessible through the class itself, not through an instance. Attempting to access this.instanceVar within a static method results in an error because this in a static context refers to the constructor function itself.

The Role of Static Initializers

TypeScript static initializers are expressions used to initialize static members. While the examples above use straightforward assignments for initialization, TypeScript also supports more complex expressions:

```
class ComputedStatic {
    static readonly startTime: Date = new Date();
    static readonly derivedValue: number = ComputedStatic.computeValue();

    private static computeValue(): number {
        return Math.floor(Math.random() * 1000);
    }
}

console.log(ComputedStatic.startTime);
console.log(ComputedStatic.derivedValue);
```

In this example, the static property derivedValue is initialized using the computeValue method at the time of class loading. Static initializers can be used to set up initial state based on computation or complex logic.

Static Members and Inheritance

Static members are inherited in TypeScript classes. Subclasses inherit static properties and methods from the parent class but cannot directly access instance members of the parent. Here is an example that illustrates inheritance of static members:

```
class Parent {
    static parentStaticProperty: string = 'ParentStatic';

    static parentStaticMethod(): string {
        return "This is a static method in the Parent class";
    }
}

class Child extends Parent {
}

console.log(Child.parentStaticProperty); // Output: ParentStatic
console.log(Child.parentStaticMethod()); // Output: This is a static method in the
    Parent class
```

The static property parentStaticProperty and the static method parentStaticMethod are available to the Child class, illustrating that static members are inherited.

To summarize, understanding how to efficiently utilize static members in TypeScript enhances the robustness and maintainability of your code by effectively managing class-level data and functionalities. Static members provide a mechanism to associate behavior and constants directly with the class, serving various architectural and design purposes in TypeScript development.

5.7 Abstract Classes and Methods

In TypeScript, abstract classes and methods provide a mechanism for defining classes that cannot be instantiated directly and methods that must be implemented by subclasses. An abstract class acts as a blueprint for other classes, enforcing a structure and contract that any derived class must adhere to. This concept is crucial in enforcing polymorphism and ensuring consistency throughout the code.

An abstract class is defined using the abstract keyword. Unlike regular classes, an abstract class may contain abstract methods, which are defined without implementation and must be implemented by any non-abstract subclass.

Consider the following example of an abstract class:

```
abstract class Animal {
  abstract makeSound(): void;

  move(): void {
    console.log('Moving along...');
  }
}
```

The Animal class above includes an abstract method makeSound that has no implementation. Non-abstract methods, like move, can still be defined and provide a default behavior that can be shared among subclasses.

A subclass must implement all abstract methods from its parent abstract class. Failing to do so will result in a compilation error. Below is an example of a subclass that correctly implements the makeSound method:

```
class Dog extends Animal {
  makeSound(): void {
    console.log('Woof! Woof!');
  }
}

let myDog = new Dog();
myDog.makeSound();
myDog.move();
```

Output:

```
Woof! Woof!
Moving along...
```

By inheriting from Animal, the Dog class authoritatively provides its version of makeSound. The non-abstract method move is inherited and can be used directly.

Abstract classes can also contain properties and constructors, allowing for shared state or initialization logic among subclasses. For example:

```
abstract class Employee {
  constructor(public name: string) {}

  abstract duties(): void;

  description(): string {
    return `${this.name} performs duties as per their role.`;
  }
}

class Developer extends Employee {
  duties(): void {
    console.log(`${this.name} writes and maintains code.`);
  }
}

class Manager extends Employee {
  duties(): void {
    console.log(`${this.name} manages team and projects.`);
  }
}

let dev = new Developer('Alice');
dev.duties();
console.log(dev.description());

let mgr = new Manager('Bob');
mgr.duties();
console.log(mgr.description());
```

Output:

```
Alice writes and maintains code.
Alice performs duties as per their role.
Bob manages team and projects.
Bob performs duties as per their role.
```

In the example above, the Employee class cannot be instantiated directly but serves as a foundation for the Developer and Manager classes, both of which provide concrete implementations of the duties method.

Abstract classes can also include a mix of properties and methods that must be shared across subclasses while still requiring subclasses to establish certain behaviors. Furthermore, TypeScript ensures type safety by enforcing the correct implementation of abstract methods in subclass definitions.

The following is an illustration of a scenario where subclasses derive from an abstract class and extend its capabilities:

```
abstract class Shape {
```

```
  constructor(public color: string) {}

  abstract area(): number;

  toString(): string {
    return `Shape with color: ${this.color}`;
  }
}

class Circle extends Shape {
  constructor(color: string, public radius: number) {
    super(color);
  }

  area(): number {
    return Math.PI * this.radius * this.radius;
  }
}

class Rectangle extends Shape {
  constructor(color: string, public width: number, public height: number) {
    super(color);
  }

  area(): number {
    return this.width * this.height;
  }
}

let circle = new Circle('red', 5);
console.log(circle.toString());
console.log(`Area of circle: ${circle.area()}`);

let rectangle = new Rectangle('blue', 4, 6);
console.log(rectangle.toString());
console.log(`Area of rectangle: ${rectangle.area()}`);
```

Output:

```
Shape with color: red
Area of circle: 78.53981633974483
Shape with color: blue
Area of rectangle: 24
```

In this illustration, the abstract class Shape establishes a structure that necessitates each subclass to provide an implementation for the area method while sharing common properties and methods like color and toString.

This ensures that every subclass maintains the integrity of the Shape contract, while still allowing for unique implementations of specific methods, thereby promoting code reuse and reducing redundancy. This structure enhances the robustness and maintainability of TypeScript applications.

5.8 Interfaces vs. Abstract Classes

In TypeScript, both interfaces and abstract classes serve the purpose of defining the structure of an object. They allow developers to describe what kinds of properties an object should have and the types of those properties, but there are significant differences in their use cases and functionalities. Understanding these differences is crucial for effectively programming in an object-oriented manner in TypeScript.

Interfaces in TypeScript are used to define the shape of an object. An interface can declare properties, methods, and events, but it does not provide any implementation. Interfaces are purely syntactic constructs used to ensure that an object adheres to a specific contract. When a class implements an interface, the class is obligated to provide concrete implementations for all the members defined in the interface. Here is an example of an interface:

```
interface Shape {
    area: number;
    getArea(): number;
}
```

This interface Shape ensures that any object or class that conforms to it will have an area property and a getArea method. To implement this interface in a class:

```
class Rectangle implements Shape {
    area: number;

    constructor(public width: number, public height: number) {
        this.area = width * height;
    }

    getArea(): number {
        return this.area;
    }
}
```

In this example, the Rectangle class implements the Shape interface. The Rectangle class has to provide an implementation for the area property and the getArea method. The presence of the implements keyword enforces that all the members of the interface are implemented in the class.

Abstract classes, on the other hand, can provide both a partial implementation and a contract. Abstract classes cannot be instantiated directly and must be extended by derived classes. An abstract class can have implemented methods, properties, and abstract methods, which must be implemented by subclasses. Here is an example of an abstract class:

```
abstract class Shape {
    // Notice that area is not defined here.
    abstract getArea(): number;

    printArea(): void {
        console.log(`Area: ${this.getArea()}`);
    }
}
```

In this example, the Shape class is abstract. It declares an abstract method getArea, which has no implementation, and a concrete method printArea that uses the getArea method. Subclasses of Shape are required to implement the getArea method:

```
class Circle extends Shape {
    constructor(public radius: number) {
        super();
    }

    getArea(): number {
        return Math.PI * this.radius * this.radius;
    }
}
```

The Circle class extends the Shape abstract class and provides a concrete implementation of the getArea method. The printArea method from the base Shape class can now be used with an instance of Circle:

```
const circle = new Circle(5);
circle.printArea(); // Outputs: Area: 78.53981633974483
```

Interfaces are flexible, as they can be used by any class regardless of where that class is in the inheritance hierarchy. Abstract classes are better suited for defining a common base class with some shared implementation details. When deciding whether to use an interface or an abstract class, consider the following factors:

- Use an interface if you need to define a contract that multiple, unrelated classes can implement.
- Use an abstract class if you want to share code among several closely related classes.
- An interface cannot contain any implementation, whereas an abstract class can.
- A class can implement multiple interfaces, but it can only extend

one class, abstract or not. This is because TypeScript does not allow multiple inheritance.

- Interfaces facilitate a more flexible and decoupled architecture because they are not tied to a class hierarchy.

- Abstract classes allow you to define protected members, which can only be accessed within the abstract class and its derived classes.

Interfaces are ideal for defining the structure of data objects and ensuring type-checking conformity across different parts of an application. Abstract classes, meanwhile, offer a way to defer implementation complexity until a subclass is created, while still allowing for some common behavior or state shared among the subclass instances.

Through proper use of interfaces and abstract classes, you can write more modular, understandable, and maintainable TypeScript code, leveraging the full power of TypeScript's type system while adhering to solid design principles.

5.9 Polymorphism and Method Overriding

Polymorphism is a foundational concept in object-oriented programming that allows objects of different types to be treated as objects of a common super type. This is accomplished through methods in different classes that implement the same interface or inherit from a common base class. The exact method that is invoked is determined at runtime, which is often referred to as dynamic binding or late binding.

In TypeScript, polymorphism is commonly achieved through method overriding, where a subclass provides a specific implementation of a method that is already defined in its superclass. This enables a child class to alter or extend the behavior of the parent class.

Here is a simple example to elucidate the concept of method overriding:

```
class Animal {
    makeSound(): void {
        console.log("Generic animal sound");
    }
}

class Dog extends Animal {
    makeSound(): void {
        console.log("Bark");
```

```
    }
}

class Cat extends Animal {
    makeSound(): void {
        console.log("Meow");
    }
}

const animals: Animal[] = [new Dog(), new Cat(), new Animal()];

for (const animal of animals) {
    animal.makeSound(); // Output: Bark, Meow, Generic animal sound
}
```

In this example, the Animal class has a makeSound method that is overridden by the Dog and Cat subclasses. When the makeSound method is called on an array of Animal objects, the correct subclass method is invoked, demonstrating polymorphism.

Polymorphism Through Interfaces

TypeScript provides another way to achieve polymorphism through interfaces. An interface can declare methods that must be implemented by any class that implements the interface. This technique ensures a consistent method signature across different classes implementing the interface, enabling polymorphic behavior.

```
interface Shape {
    area(): number;
}

class Rectangle implements Shape {
    constructor(private width: number, private height: number) {}

    area(): number {
        return this.width * this.height;
    }
}

class Circle implements Shape {
    constructor(private radius: number) {}

    area(): number {
        return Math.PI * this.radius * this.radius;
    }
}

const shapes: Shape[] = [new Rectangle(10, 20), new Circle(5)];

for (const shape of shapes) {
    console.log(shape.area()); // Output: 200, 78.53981633974483
}
```

In this example, both Rectangle and Circle classes implement the Shape interface, which declares an area method. Each class provides its own specific implementation of the area method. The array shapes contains objects of both Rectangle and Circle types, yet the correct area method is invoked for each shape instance.

Super Calls in Overriding Methods

In certain scenarios, it is necessary to call the original method from the base class while still providing additional functionality in the overriding method. This is achieved using the super keyword.

```
class Animal {
    makeSound(): void {
        console.log("Generic animal sound");
    }
}

class Dog extends Animal {
    makeSound(): void {
        super.makeSound();
        console.log("Bark");
    }
}

const myDog = new Dog();
myDog.makeSound(); // Output: Generic animal sound, Bark
```

In the above code, the Dog class overrides the makeSound method and also calls the makeSound method from its superclass (Animal) using the super.makeSound() call, adding its own message afterwards.

Method Overriding and Access Modifiers

When overriding methods, it's essential to respect the access modifiers (public, protected, private) defined in the base class. An overriding method must have the same or a more accessible access level than the method it overrides.

```
class Animal {
    protected makeSound(): void {
        console.log("Generic animal sound");
    }
}

class Dog extends Animal {
    public makeSound(): void {
        console.log("Bark");
    }
}
```

```
const myDog = new Dog();
myDog.makeSound(); // Output: Bark
```

Here, makeSound in Animal is marked as protected, but it is overridden as public in Dog. This follows the rule that the overriding method must have the same or a more accessible access level.

Understanding these concepts ensures that we can effectively utilize polymorphism and method overriding in TypeScript, fostering flexible and maintainable code.

5.10 Getters and Setters

Getters and setters in TypeScript encompass a pattern to encapsulate data within classes, promoting controlled access and modification of an object's properties. This encapsulation ensures that properties are not accidentally altered or accessed inappropriately, bolstering the integrity and reliability of the codebase.

In TypeScript, getters and setters are synthetic properties that behave like regular properties but are defined by special methods. The getter method allows for the retrieval of a property's value, while the setter method provides a means to update or set a property's value. These methods can include additional logic, ensuring that any constraints or requirements are met before altering the property.

Let's examine how to define and use getters and setters within a class.

```
class Person {
    private _name: string;
    private _age: number;

    constructor(name: string, age: number) {
        this._name = name;
        this._age = age;
    }

    // Getter for the _name property
    get name(): string {
        return this._name;
    }

    // Setter for the _name property
    set name(newName: string) {
        if (newName && newName.length > 0) {
            this._name = newName;
        } else {
            throw new Error('Invalid name');
        }
```

```
    }

    // Getter for the _age property
    get age(): number {
        return this._age;
    }

    // Setter for the _age property
    set age(newAge: number) {
        if (newAge >= 0 && newAge <= 150) {
            this._age = newAge;
        } else {
            throw new Error('Invalid age');
        }
    }
}

const person = new Person('Alice', 30);

console.log(person.name); // Output: Alice
person.name = 'Bob';
console.log(person.name); // Output: Bob

person.age = 32;
console.log(person.age); // Output: 32
// person.age = -5; // Uncommenting this line will throw an error: Invalid age
```

In the above example, the Person class has two private properties, _name and _age. By using private access modifiers, we ensure these properties cannot be accessed directly from outside the class, maintaining encapsulation.

The getter methods, name() and age(), provide read access to the properties and allow additional logic if needed. For instance, logging access or formatting returned values, such as transforming the _age property into a string with a unit suffix.

The setter methods, name() and age(), not only allow for setting the values of the properties but can also enforce constraints or validation logic. For example, the name property cannot be set to an empty string, and the age property must be within a plausible human lifespan.

The getters and setters are accessed like regular properties, while the class handles the internal logic which enforces the constraints:

```
Alice
Bob
32
```

This approach to property access offers a structured way to add logic around getting and setting operations without exposing the internal state directly. Now, to provide another illustrative example, consider a class representing a bank account, where encapsulation, validation, and control are paramount.

```
class BankAccount {
    private _balance: number;

    constructor(initialBalance: number) {
        if (initialBalance < 0) {
            throw new Error('Initial balance cannot be negative');
        }
        this._balance = initialBalance;
    }

    // Getter for the _balance property
    get balance(): number {
        return this._balance;
    }

    // Setter for the _balance property (simulating deposit and withdraw operations)
    set balance(amount: number) {
        if (amount < 0) {
            throw new Error('Balance cannot be negative');
        }
        this._balance = amount;
    }

    // Method to deposit money (utilizing the setter)
    deposit(amount: number) {
        if (amount <= 0) {
            throw new Error('Deposit amount must be positive');
        }
        this.balance += amount;
    }

    // Method to withdraw money (utilizing the setter)
    withdraw(amount: number) {
        if (amount <= 0) {
            throw new Error('Withdraw amount must be positive');
        }
        if (this._balance - amount < 0) {
            throw new Error('Insufficient funds');
        }
        this.balance -= amount;
    }
}
const account = new BankAccount(100);

console.log(account.balance); // Output: 100

account.deposit(50);
console.log(account.balance); // Output: 150

account.withdraw(30);
console.log(account.balance); // Output: 120

// account.withdraw(200); // Uncommenting this will throw an error: Insufficient funds
```

This example demonstrates how getters and setters can be used alongside other methods to encapsulate and safeguard the internal state of an entity.

The BankAccount class enforces rules for the balance property, ensuring it cannot be set to a negative value. The deposit and withdraw methods both utilize the setter method, reinforcing encapsulation and ensuring that only valid operations can alter the _balance property.

The encapsulation provided by getters and setters helps maintain the integrity of the object's state when subjected to various operations and potential misuse. Having validation logic encapsulated within these methods reduces redundancy and potential errors arising from improper direct property manipulations. This makes getters and setters in TypeScript essential for writing robust, maintainable, and secure code.

5.11 The 'this' Keyword in TypeScript

The this keyword is a crucial element in object-oriented programming, especially in TypeScript. It allows access to an object's properties and methods from within its own methods. Understanding how this behavior works in various contexts is essential for writing effective and bug-free TypeScript code.

The this keyword represents a special variable that stores the reference to the current object, the object that is executing the current function. In TypeScript, the way this behaves can change based on how and where it is used.

Firstly, consider a simple class example where this is used to access instance variables and methods within the same class:

```
class Person {
  name: string;
  age: number;

  constructor(name: string, age: number) {
    this.name = name;
    this.age = age;
  }

  greet() {
    console.log(`Hello, my name is ${this.name} and I am ${this.age} years old.`);
  }
}

const person1 = new Person("Alice", 30);
person1.greet();
```

The output of the above code will be:

```
Hello, my name is Alice and I am 30 years old.
```

In the greet method, this.name and this.age refer to the name and age properties of the Person instance that invokes the method.

A common pitfall in using this arises when methods are passed as callbacks, losing the context of their containing object. Here's an illustration of this issue:

```
class Counter {
  count: number = 0;

  increment() {
    this.count++;
    console.log(this.count);
  }
}

const counter = new Counter();
setTimeout(counter.increment, 1000);
```

The expected behavior is that the count property should increment and log 1 after 1 second. However, the output will result in an error since this no longer refers to the Counter instance. Instead, it points to the global object (or undefined in strict mode). To solve this, we can use the bind method or an arrow function.

The bind method creates a new function with this bound to the specified object:

```
setTimeout(counter.increment.bind(counter), 1000);
```

The output will now correctly be:

```
1
```

Alternatively, using an arrow function, which lexically binds this:

```
setTimeout(() => counter.increment(), 1000);
```

This will also result in the correct output of:

```
1
```

In TypeScript, this can also be explicitly typed to improve code readability and robustness. Consider a method that returns this for better method chaining:

```
class FluentCounter {
  count: number = 0;

  increment(): this {
    this.count++;
    return this;
  }

  decrement(): this {
    this.count--;
```

```
    return this;
  }

  print(): this {
    console.log(this.count);
    return this;
  }
}

const fluentCounter = new FluentCounter();
fluentCounter.increment().increment().decrement().print(); // Outputs: 1
```

Here, each method returns this, allowing successive calls to be chained together. Explicitly returning this ensures that the correct type is inferred across chained method calls.

When working within the context of a class hierarchy, the this keyword plays a vital role in maintaining the correct reference as methods are overridden in derived classes:

```
class Base {
  greet() {
    console.log("Hello from Base");
  }
}

class Derived extends Base {
  greet() {
    super.greet();
    console.log("Hello from Derived");
  }

  caller() {
    this.greet();
  }
}

const derivedInstance = new Derived();
derivedInstance.caller();
```

The output demonstrates:

```
Hello from Base
Hello from Derived
```

In this instance, this.greet() within caller() ensures that the overridden greet method in the Derived class is correctly called, showcasing how this allows methods to maintain proper context within class hierarchies.

Understanding the this keyword and its proper use is essential for mastering object-oriented programming in TypeScript. Properly managing this prevents common bugs and ensures that methods behave as expected across various contexts, such as callbacks and method chaining.

5.12 Decorators and Metadata Reflection

Decorators offer a way to add both annotations and a meta-programming syntax for class declarations and members. Decorators enable behaviors to be dynamically added to a class at runtime. They are a foundational feature in TypeScript, heavily inspired by similar patterns in other programming languages such as Python and Java.

To enable experimental support for decorators, you must set the experimentalDecorators compiler option to true in your tsconfig.json file:

```
{
  "compilerOptions": {
    "experimentalDecorators": true
  }
}
```

A decorator is a special kind of declaration that can be attached to a class, method, accessor, property, or parameter. Decorators use the form @expression, where expression evaluates to a function that will be called at runtime with information about the decorated declaration.

Class Decorators

A class decorator is applied to the constructor of the class and can be used to observe, modify, or replace a class definition. The class decorator is defined just before the class declaration, as shown in the example below:

```
function sealed(constructor: Function) {
    Object.seal(constructor);
    Object.seal(constructor.prototype);
}

@sealed
class Greeter {
    greeting: string;
    constructor(message: string) {
        this.greeting = message;
    }
    greet() {
        return `Hello, ${this.greeting}`;
    }
}
```

In this example, the sealed decorator ensures that both the constructor and its prototype are sealed, meaning that no new properties can be added to them.

Method Decorators

A method decorator is declared just before a method declaration. It is applied to the Property Descriptor for the method and can be used to observe, modify, or replace a method definition. Note that a method decorator cannot be used in a declaration file, in an abstract method, or when declaring a method in an interface.

```
function enumerable(value: boolean) {
    return function (target: any, propertyKey: string, descriptor: PropertyDescriptor) {
        descriptor.enumerable = value;
    };
}

class Greeter {
    greeting: string;
    constructor(message: string) {
        this.greeting = message;
    }

    @enumerable(false)
    greet() {
        return `Hello, ${this.greeting}`;
    }
}
```

In this scenario, the enumerable decorator configures whether a method appears in enumeration of the property on the prototype object.

Accessor Decorators

Accessor decorators are applied to the function that gets and sets a property. These decorators are essentially similar to method decorators but are applied to accessors. They can be used to observe, modify, or replace an accessor's definition. However, an accessor decorator cannot be applied to a property declaration.

```
function configurable(value: boolean) {
    return function (target: any, propertyKey: string, descriptor: PropertyDescriptor) {
        descriptor.configurable = value;
    };
}

class Point {
    private _x: number;
    private _y: number;

    constructor(x: number, y: number) {
        this._x = x;
        this._y = y;
    }

    @configurable(false)
    get x() {
        return this._x;
    }

    @configurable(false)
    get y() {
        return this._y;
```

```
    }
}
```

Here, the configurable decorator specifies whether the accessor's property descriptor can be changed and whether the property itself can be deleted.

Property Decorators

A property decorator can only be used to observe that a property of a specific name has been declared for a class. They are not applied to the property descriptor and, as such, cannot modify or replace a property definition.

```
function format(formatString: string) {
    return function (target: any, propertyKey: string) {
        let value: string;

        const getter = function () {
            return value;
        };

        const setter = function (newVal: string) {
            value = `${formatString} ${newVal}`;
        };

        Object.defineProperty(target, propertyKey, {
            get: getter,
            set: setter,
            enumerable: true,
            configurable: true,
        });
    };
}

class Person {
    @format('Mr.')
    name: string;

    constructor(name: string) {
        this.name = name;
    }
}

const person = new Person('John');
console.log(person.name);
```

In this example, the format decorator prefixes the value of the name property with "Mr."

Metadata Reflection API

TypeScript's decorators rely heavily on the metadata reflection API to allow for metadata to be attached to and reflected upon classes, methods, and parameters. This is facilitated through the reflect-metadata library. Firstly, you must install it via npm:

```
npm install reflect-metadata
```

Then you can use the metadata reflection API in conjunction with decorators.

```
import 'reflect-metadata';

const requiredMetadataKey = Symbol('required');

function required(target: Object, propertyKey: string | symbol, parameterIndex:
      number) {
   const existingRequiredParameters: number[] = Reflect.getOwnMetadata(
         requiredMetadataKey, target, propertyKey) || [];
   existingRequiredParameters.push(parameterIndex);
   Reflect.defineMetadata(requiredMetadataKey, existingRequiredParameters, target,
         propertyKey);
}

function validate(target: any, propertyName: string, descriptor:
      TypedPropertyDescriptor<Function>) {
   const method = descriptor.value;
   descriptor.value = function () {
      const requiredParameters: number[] = Reflect.getOwnMetadata(
            requiredMetadataKey, target, propertyName) || [];
      for (const parameterIndex of requiredParameters) {
         if (parameterIndex >= arguments.length || arguments[parameterIndex] ===
               undefined) {
            throw new Error('Missing required argument.');
         }
      }
      return method!.apply(this, arguments);
   };
}

class Greeter {
   greeting: string;

   constructor(message: string) {
      this.greeting = message;
   }

   @validate
   greet(@required name: string) {
      return `Hello, ${name} ${this.greeting}`;
   }
}

const greeter = new Greeter('world');
try {
   greeter.greet('John'); // Works fine
   greeter.greet(); // Throws an error
} catch (error) {
   console.error(error.message);
}
```

In this example, the `required` decorator marks the parameter as required, and the `validate` decorator ensures that all required parameters are present when the method is invoked. This demonstrates how the `reflect-metadata` library can be used to enhance the functionality of decorators, providing robust runtime type checking and metadata management capabilities.

Chapter 6

Interfaces and Type Aliases

This chapter covers the use and implementation of interfaces in TypeScript, including optional and read-only properties, function types, and indexable types. It also examines extending and overriding interfaces, and how intersection types can be utilized within interfaces. Additionally, the chapter introduces type aliases, explaining their syntax and use, differences from interfaces, and how they can be employed with union and intersection types and for defining function types, providing a comprehensive comparison and application of both interfaces and type aliases in TypeScript.

6.1 Introduction to Interfaces

In TypeScript, interfaces play a crucial role in defining the structure of an object. They provide a way to describe the shape of objects, ensuring that they adhere to a specific contract. This is essential for leveraging TypeScript's static typing capabilities, as it ensures that an object fits a particular structure, enhancing both code reliability and readability.

To define an interface in TypeScript, the interface keyword is used followed by the name of the interface. Inside the curly braces, you describe the properties and methods that the object should have. Consider the following example:

```
// Define an interface
interface Person {
    name: string;
    age: number;
}
```

In this example, the Person interface dictates that any object of type Person must have two properties: name, which is a string, and age, which is a number. If an object does not conform to this structure, TypeScript will throw a compile-time error.

To utilize this interface, you can implement it in a class or use it to type an object:

```
// Using the Person interface
let user: Person = {
    name: "John Doe",
    age: 30
};

// A class implementing the Person interface
class Employee implements Person {
    name: string;
    age: number;
    employeeId: number;

    constructor(name: string, age: number, employeeId: number) {
        this.name = name;
        this.age = age;
        this.employeeId = employeeId;
    }

    getDetails(): string {
        return `Name: ${this.name}, Age: ${this.age}, Employee ID: ${this.employeeId
            }`;
    }
}
```

In the above code snippet, user is an object typed as Person. Since it has both the name and age properties as defined in the Person interface, TypeScript does not produce any errors. The Employee class implements the Person interface and adds an additional property, employeeId, and a method, getDetails. The implementation of the Person interface ensures that the Employee class has at least the properties defined in Person.

Interfaces can also define methods alongside properties. This allows you to create a contract for methods that an implementing class must follow:

```
// Interface with a method
interface Movable {
    speed: number;
```

```
    move(): void;
}

// Class implementing the Movable interface
class Car implements Movable {
    speed: number;

    constructor(speed: number) {
        this.speed = speed;
    }

    move(): void {
        console.log(`The car is moving at ${this.speed} km/h`);
    }
}
```

In this example, the Movable interface requires that any implementing class has a speed property and a move() method. The Car class adheres to this contract by providing a concrete implementation of both the speed property and the move() method.

TypeScript interfaces are highly essential for defining the structure of complex objects. Custom types can be passed or returned in functions by ensuring a consistent structure through interfaces. They can be extended to create new interfaces while inheriting the existing properties and methods from the parent interface, facilitating reuse and modularity in code design.

Consider the scenario where we need to create an interface that extends another interface:

```
// Parent interface
interface Vehicle {
    name: string;
    speed: number;
}

// Child interface extending Vehicle
interface FourWheeler extends Vehicle {
    numberOfWheels: number;
}

let myCar: FourWheeler = {
    name: "Sedan",
    speed: 120,
    numberOfWheels: 4
};
```

Here, the FourWheeler interface extends the Vehicle interface, inheriting its properties (name and speed) and introducing a new property called numberOfWheels. The object myCar satisfies the structure defined by the FourWheeler interface, thereby confirming to TypeScript's type-checking mechanism.

Interfaces are pivotal in defining clear and enforceable contracts in your TypeScript code, leading to more predictable and error-resilient software development. The subsequent sections will delve deeper into various features of TypeScript interfaces, including optional properties, read-only properties, function types, indexable types, and more. These features enable developers to model complex types accurately, contributing significantly to robust and maintainable codebases.

6.2 Defining and Implementing Interfaces

Interfaces in TypeScript provide a powerful way to define the structure of objects, ensuring that they adhere to a specific shape. This is particularly useful for type-checking during development, which can prevent numerous runtime errors. To define an interface, the interface keyword is employed.

Consider the following example which defines a simple interface named Person:

```
interface Person {
    name: string;
    age: number;
}
```

This Person interface specifies that any object conforming to this type must have a name property with a string value and an age property with a number value.

To implement an interface in TypeScript, one simply ensures that an object adheres to the structure defined by the interface:

```
let employee: Person = {
    name: "John Doe",
    age: 30
};
```

Here, the employee object adheres to the Person interface, possessing both the name and age properties with the correct types.

Moreover, interfaces can also describe functions and their types. To illustrate, consider the following interface that represents a function:

```
interface Greet {
    (name: string): string;
}
```

This Greet interface specifies a function that takes a single string argument and returns a string. To implement this, a function must match the signature described by the interface:

```
let sayHello: Greet = function (name: string): string {
    return ‘Hello, ${name}‘;
};
```

Here, sayHello is a function that conforms to the Greet interface.

For more complex scenarios, interfaces can also dictate the structure of more complex objects such as functions that have properties. Consider the following compounded interface:

```
interface Counter {
    (start: number): string;
    interval: number;
    reset(): void;
}
```

This Counter interface specifies a function that takes a number and returns a string, includes an interval property of type number, and a reset method. Implementing this interface can be done as follows:

```
function getCounter(): Counter {
    let counter = <Counter>function (start: number) {
        // Implementation goes here.
        return ‘Counter started at ${start}‘;
    };
    counter.interval = 123;
    counter.reset = function () {
        // Implementation of reset.
    };
    return counter;
}

let c = getCounter();
c(10);
console.log(c.interval); // 123
c.reset();
```

In this example, the getCounter function returns an object that implements the Counter interface. The type assertion <Counter> helps in defining the object structure.

In addition to defining individual properties, interfaces can also be used to define arrays and their types. For instance:

```
interface StringArray {
    [index: number]: string;
}

let myArray: StringArray = ["Alice", "Bob"];
let secondItem: string = myArray[1];
```

The StringArray interface ensures that any object of this type must be indexed with a number and return a string. Thus, myArray conforms to this interface, ensuring type safety when accessing array elements.

Implementing interfaces enforces a contract within your code, ensuring adherence to a defined structure which is invaluable in maintaining consistency and avoiding common bugs. Understanding and leveraging interfaces appropriately can significantly enhance the robustness and reliability of TypeScript codebases.

6.3 Optional Properties in Interfaces

In TypeScript, interfaces can specify properties that are not mandatory. This allows objects of that interface type to have flexibility in the structure. Optional properties are particularly useful for defining patterns that support multiple configurations. By using a question mark (?) after the property name, you can denote an optional property in the interface.

The syntax for declaring an optional property in an interface is straightforward. Consider the following interface definition:

```
interface Person {
    name: string;
    age?: number;
}
```

In this example, the Person interface has two properties: name, which is required, and age, which is optional. An object conforming to the Person interface can include the age property, but it is not required. Here is how we can use this interface:

```
let person1: Person = {
    name: "Alice"
};

let person2: Person = {
    name: "Bob",
    age: 25
};
```

Both person1 and person2 are valid instances of the Person interface. The optional property age allows person1 to omit it, whereas person2 includes it.

Type Checking with Optional Properties

TypeScript's type checker respects optional properties and ensures that any object of the specified type conforms to the declared interface. If we try to violate this contract, TypeScript will produce an error:

```
let person3: Person = {
    age: 30
}; // Error: Property 'name' is missing in type '{ age: number; }' but required in type '
    Person'
```

In the above example, person3 lacks the required name property, thus TypeScript throws an error. The presence of optional properties does not diminish the necessity for required properties.

Functions with Optional Properties in Interfaces

When defining functions within interfaces that include optional properties, you can leverage these properties as part of the function's logic. Below is a practical example, showcasing a simple user greeting system:

```
interface Greeter {
    greet(person: Person): string;
}

class SimpleGreeter implements Greeter {
    greet(person: Person): string {
        if (person.age) {
            return `Hello ${person.name}, you are ${person.age} years old.`;
        }
        return `Hello ${person.name}`;
    }
}
```

In this example, SimpleGreeter implements the Greeter interface with the greet method. The method checks whether the age property is provided and returns a different string accordingly. This demonstrates how optional properties can be employed in method implementations to vary behavior.

```
Hello Alice
Hello Bob, you are 25 years old.
```

Optional Properties and Default Values

While TypeScript does not allow automatic assignment of default values to optional properties in interface definitions, default values can be assigned when objects are created or through class implementations. Consider the following example:

```
class DefaultPerson implements Person {
    name: string;
    age?: number;

    constructor(name: string, age?: number) {
        this.name = name;
        this.age = age !== undefined ? age : 18; // Default value of 18
    }
```

```
}
let person4: Person = new DefaultPerson("Charlie");
```

In this code, the DefaultPerson class implements the Person interface. The constructor function checks if age is provided; if not, it defaults to 18. Hence, person4 will have a default age of 18:

```
{
  name: "Charlie",
  age: 18
}
```

Considerations in Design

When designing interfaces with optional properties, it is crucial to consider scenarios where optional properties can lead to complexities or ambiguities in object handling. For instance, optional properties can lead to undefined values that require null checks or conditional logic. The use of TypeScript's Partial utility type can also be leveraged to make all properties in an interface optional, if needed:

```
interface Car {
    make: string;
    model: string;
    year: number;
}

type PartialCar = Partial<Car>;

let car1: PartialCar = {
    make: "Toyota"
};

let car2: PartialCar = {
    model: "Corolla",
    year: 2020
};
```

The Partial utility type transforms all properties of the Car interface into optional. This can facilitate scenarios where an object needs to be initialized with a subset of properties.

Optional properties in interfaces offer flexibility in defining types while preserving type safety. They enable developers to model real-world scenarios where certain attributes are not universally present. This helps in creating adaptable, maintainable types that ensure robust type checking and facilitate complex configurations across diverse use cases.

6.4 Read-only Properties in Interfaces

In TypeScript, interfaces play a crucial role by providing a means to define the structure of an object, ensuring that the object adheres to a specific contract. One of the valuable features of interfaces is the ability to declare properties as read-only. This ensures that the values of these properties cannot be altered once they are set. Read-only properties can be particularly useful in scenarios where integrity and immutability of the data must be preserved.

To declare a read-only property in an interface, the readonly modifier is used. The readonly modifier precedes the property name, indicating that the property can only be assigned a value during object initialization or within the constructor of a class implementing the interface. Any attempts to modify a read-only property after its initial assignment will result in a compile-time error.

Consider the following example:

```
interface Person {
  readonly id: number;
  name: string;
  age: number;
}

let person: Person = { id: 1, name: "Alice", age: 30 };

// The following line will cause a compile-time error
// person.id = 2;

person.name = "Bob"; // This is allowed
```

In this example, the id property of the Person interface is declared as read-only. As a result, any attempts to modify the id property after the object has been initialized will cause a compile-time error. On the other hand, properties name and age can be modified without any restriction.

Read-only properties are beneficial in various scenarios, such as defining constants or preserving the state of an object. They provide a mechanism to protect critical properties from being inadvertently changed, contributing to the predictability and reliability of the code.

When working with classes that implement interfaces, the readonly properties must be handled in a manner that respects their immutability. Attempting to modify a read-only property within a method of a class will similarly result in a compile-time error. Consider the following example:

```
class Employee implements Person {
  readonly id: number;
```

```
  name: string;
  age: number;

  constructor(id: number, name: string, age: number) {
    this.id = id;
    this.name = name;
    this.age = age;
  }

  changeName(newName: string): void {
    this.name = newName;
  }

  // The following method would cause a compile-time error
  // updateId(newId: number): void {
  // this.id = newId;
  // }
}

let employee = new Employee(1, "Alice", 30);
employee.changeName("Bob"); // Allowed
// employee.updateId(2); // Compile-time error
```

In this example, the Employee class implements the Person interface, where id is a read-only property. The class constructor assigns values to the properties, including the read-only id property. The method changeName attempts to modify the name property, which is allowed. However, a hypothetical method updateId that attempts to modify the id property would cause a compile-time error if uncommented, as it violates the read-only constraint.

It is also possible to combine read-only properties with optional properties. In such cases, the property must be assigned a value only once, if it is assigned at all. Consider the following example:

```
interface Vehicle {
  readonly vin?: string;
  make: string;
  model: string;
}

let vehicle: Vehicle = { make: "Toyota", model: "Corolla" };

// The following line will not cause an error
vehicle.vin = "1HGCM82633A123456";

// Once assigned, the following line will cause an error
// vehicle.vin = "5FNYF4H53DB012345";
```

In this example, the vin property of the Vehicle interface is both read-only and optional. It can be assigned a value once; any subsequent attempts to modify the vin property after its initial assignment will lead to a compile-time error.

By leveraging read-only properties in interfaces, developers can create more robust and maintainable TypeScript applications. This explicit enforcement of immutability at the type level enhances code safety, guarding against unintended side effects and ensuring that critical object properties remain consistent throughout the application lifecycle.

6.5 Function Types and Interfaces

In TypeScript, interfaces serve as an essential blueprint for structuring and enforcing the shape of data. This extends beyond just object types to also include defining function types. In this section, we will explore how interfaces can be used to define function types, why this is beneficial, and illustrate this with clear examples.

To begin, defining a function type within an interface can be done by specifying a call signature in the interface definition. A call signature describes the argument list and return type of a function. Consider the following example:

```
interface SearchFunction {
    (source: string, subString: string): boolean;
}
```

Here, SearchFunction is an interface that describes a function type. This interface ensures that any function conforming to SearchFunction must accept two parameters, both of which are strings, and must return a boolean value.

To implement this interface, we can assign a function to a variable of type SearchFunction. Observe the following example:

```
let mySearch: SearchFunction;
mySearch = function(source: string, subString: string): boolean {
    let result = source.includes(subString);
    return result;
};
```

In the above code, mySearch implicitly adheres to the SearchFunction interface because it matches the defined call signature. It accepts two string arguments and returns a boolean value. This ensures that any assignment to mySearch will follow the structure specified by the SearchFunction interface, leading to consistent and predictable behavior in code.

A key benefit of using interfaces to define function types is the clarity and type safety it provides. By explicitly outlining the types of functions, developers can avoid common pitfalls such as mismatched argument or return types, leading to fewer runtime errors.

Besides basic function types, interfaces can also support more complex configurations such as optional parameters and rest parameters. Optional parameters can be denoted in the call signature using a question mark (?) after the parameter name. Consider the following example:

```
interface FlexibleFunction {
    (arg1: string, arg2?: string): void;
}
```

In this example, FlexibleFunction describes a function that takes a mandatory arg1 parameter of type string and an optional arg2 parameter of type string, returning void. A function adhering to this interface can be implemented as follows:

```
let flexible: FlexibleFunction;
flexible = function(arg1: string, arg2?: string): void {
    if (arg2) {
        console.log(`${arg1}, ${arg2}`);
    } else {
        console.log(arg1);
    }
};
```

Another aspect that can be handled within interfaces is the use of rest parameters. Rest parameters allow a function to accept an indefinite number of arguments as an array. This can be specified in the call signature using the spread syntax (...). Examine the following example:

```
interface RestFunction {
    (firstArg: string, ...restArgs: number[]): void;
}
```

Here, RestFunction defines a function type where the first parameter is a string and the remaining parameters are an array of numbers. An implementation of such a function could look like this:

```
let handleRest: RestFunction;
handleRest = function(firstArg: string, ...restArgs: number[]): void {
    console.log(firstArg);
    for (let num of restArgs) {
        console.log(num);
    }
};
```

In conjunction with defining types for functions, interfaces can be extended to include properties, enabling a richer and more flexible design. For instance:

```
interface FunctionWithProps {
    (param: string): number;
```

```
    description: string;
}
```

The FunctionWithProps interface defines a call signature as well as a property named description. Here is an example of an object adhering to this interface:

```
let functionWithProps: FunctionWithProps;
functionWithProps = function(param: string): number {
    return param.length;
};
functionWithProps.description = "This function returns the length of a string.";
```

In this example, functionWithProps is a function that returns the length of a given string and also contains a property description that describes its purpose.

Using interfaces to define function types in TypeScript adds a substantial layer of type safety and can make code more maintainable and understandable. By leveraging call signatures, optional parameters, rest parameters, and even blending properties with functions, developers can construct comprehensive and type-safe function definitions that enhance code quality and developer experience.

6.6 Indexable Types and Interfaces

In TypeScript, indexable types are a powerful feature that allows defining the types for array-like objects. Index signatures can be used to describe the types of keys and values for objects accessed via indices. This concept is especially useful when dealing with data structures where the property names are not known in advance or when having dynamic keys is a necessity.

To define an indexable type using an interface, use the bracket notation ([]) within the interface definition. This interface specifies that any property accessed with an index will adhere to a certain type for both the key and the resulting value. Consider the following example:

```
interface StringArray {
    [index: number]: string;
}
```

In this interface, any time a StringArray is indexed with a number, it will return a string. Here is an example of how you can use this interface:

```
let myArray: StringArray;
```

```
myArray = ["Bob", "Alice", "Carol"];

let myStr: string = myArray[0]; // "Bob"
```

This demonstrates a common use case, where the indexable type is beneficial for arrays or collections of objects, ensuring type safety when accessing elements.

Further, you might sometimes encounter the need to index objects using strings, not just numbers. This can be achieved by using string index signatures:

```
interface NumberDictionary {
    [index: string]: number;
}
```

This interface can be used as follows:

```
let myDict: NumberDictionary;
myDict = {
    one: 1,
    two: 2,
    three: 3
};

let value: number = myDict["two"]; // 2
```

It is important to note that when a string index signature is used, all properties must conform to the type defined for the index signature. If an interface has both a string and a numeric index signature, the numeric index signature's type must be a subtype of the string index signature's type. This is due to JavaScript's handling of properties: while number indices are converted to strings, all number properties must also be accepted by the string indexer.

For instance:

```
interface MoreComplexArray {
    [index: number]: string;
    [index: string]: string | number;
}
```

In this example, any numeric index will return a string, while any string index will return a string or number. This ensures the types are consistent and compatible with JavaScript's property access semantics.

When defining indexable types, constraints such as optional properties can also be used to make interfaces more flexible. However, you must be cautious when combining these with index signatures to avoid contradictory or overlapping definitions.

Using indexable types with interfaces thus provides a robust way to handle dynamic property names and indices, ensuring type safety and consistency within your TypeScript code base. This mechanism not only aids in preventing errors but also enhances code readability and maintainability by clearly specifying allowed operations and their outcomes.

6.7 Extending and Overriding Interfaces

Interfaces in TypeScript provide a robust and flexible mechanism for structuring and enforcing types in your code. One of the significant advantages of interfaces is their extendibility. Extending an interface allows you to inherit properties and methods from another interface, facilitating a hierarchical and modular approach to type design. This capacity for extension paves the way for creating more complex and reusable type definitions without redundancy.

We begin by understanding the syntax for extending interfaces. Consider two interfaces, Person and Employee. The Person interface includes basic demographic information, while Employee extends Person to include professional details:

```
interface Person {
    name: string;
    age: number;
}

interface Employee extends Person {
    employeeId: number;
    department: string;
}
```

Here, the Employee interface inherits all the properties of the Person interface and adds employeeId and department. Any implementation of the Employee interface must satisfy all the properties defined in both Person and Employee.

Example Implementation:

```
const employee: Employee = {
    name: "Alice",
    age: 30,
    employeeId: 1234,
    department: "Engineering"
};
```

The object employee adheres to both the Person and Employee interfaces, demonstrating that the extension mechanism effectively merges properties from multiple interfaces.

Multiple Interface Inheritance:

TypeScript allows an interface to extend multiple interfaces, thus promoting a flexible composition of types. Here is an example where Employee extends both Person and another interface, Contactable:

```
interface Contactable {
    email: string;
    phoneNumber: string;
}

interface Employee extends Person, Contactable {
    employeeId: number;
    department: string;
}
```

In this case, Employee includes properties from Person and Contactable, alongside its specific properties:

```
const employee: Employee = {
    name: "Bob",
    age: 25,
    email: "bob@example.com",
    phoneNumber: "555-5555",
    employeeId: 5678,
    department: "Marketing"
};
```

This capability to inherit from multiple interfaces provides a powerful tool for creating intricate and comprehensive type structures.

Overriding Properties:

While TypeScript does not support overriding members in the classical sense found in object-oriented programming, you can redefine an interface in specific cases for particular needs. For instance, if you have a specialized case where an inherited property requires a reevaluation, you may declare another interface that redefines the extended properties:

```
interface DetailedPerson extends Person {
    age: string; // Override to string for specific use case
}
```

Now, DetailedPerson has a different definition for the age property than its base interface:

```
const person: DetailedPerson = {
    name: "Charlie",
    age: "Thirty"
};
```

Observe that the age property in DetailedPerson is now a string instead of a number, reflecting the specialized use case while still maintaining the overall structure provided by Person.

Combining Type Aliases and Interfaces:

TypeScript also allows the combination of type aliases with interfaces. A type alias can use the & operator to combine existing interfaces or other types:

```
type Admin = Person & Contactable & {
    role: string;
}

const admin: Admin = {
    name: "Dana",
    age: 40,
    email: "dana@example.com",
    phoneNumber: "777-7777",
    role: "Administrator"
};
```

Here, Admin is a type alias combining Person, Contactable, and an additional property role. The result is a composite type bringing together properties from several interfaces and custom additions.

By systematically utilizing these extending and overriding techniques, more elaborate and context-specific types can be created while promoting reusability, scalability, and maintainability within TypeScript codebases. The synergy of these capabilities underscores the robustness of TypeScript's type system, enabling developers to craft precise and reliable applications.

6.8 Intersection Types in Interfaces

In TypeScript, intersection types are utilized to combine multiple types into one. This becomes highly potent when working with interfaces, as it allows developers to build complex types by merging the characteristics of numerous interfaces. An intersection type, represented with the & operator, requires the resulting type to adhere to the properties and methods of all the intersected types.

Consider two basic interfaces, Person and Employee. Intersection types enable us to build a new type that encompasses the characteristics of both Person and Employee.

```
interface Person {
    name: string;
```

```
    age: number;
}

interface Employee {
    employeeId: number;
    department: string;
}
```

An intersection type combining Person and Employee can be defined as follows:

```
type PersonEmployee = Person & Employee;
```

The PersonEmployee type must now have all properties from both Person and Employee interfaces. Let's demonstrate this with an example:

```
let employee: PersonEmployee = {
    name: "John Doe",
    age: 30,
    employeeId: 123,
    department: "Engineering"
};
```

In the above code, the employee object respects the requirements of both Person and Employee interfaces. Any omission of a required property will result in a compilation error, ensuring type correctness.

Intersection types in interfaces are contextually significant when dealing with diverse data structures and polymorphism. For instance, consider a scenario where multiple behaviors must be enforced on an object. This can be achieved by intersecting corresponding interface types.

Let's extend our example by adding two more interfaces:

```
interface Manager {
    subordinates: number;
    departmentManaged: string;
}

interface Developer {
    languages: string[];
    yearsOfExperience: number;
}
```

We can now create an intersection type for a managerial developer:

```
type ManagerialDeveloper = Person & Employee & Manager & Developer;
```

An object of type ManagerialDeveloper must conform to all properties and methods defined in Person, Employee, Manager, and Developer interfaces:

```
let seniorDevManager: ManagerialDeveloper = {
    name: "Jane Doe",
    age: 40,
    employeeId: 456,
    department: "IT",
    subordinates: 10,
    departmentManaged: "Software Development",
    languages: ["TypeScript", "JavaScript", "Python"],
    yearsOfExperience: 15
};
```

The above usage of intersection types allows for a robust definition of objects that span multiple roles and responsibilities, providing clarity and type-safety in complex systems.

In practice, intersection types are a tool for ensuring that objects adhere to multiple contractual obligations. These are particularly helpful in scenarios where mixing properties and behaviors from various domains is necessary. For instance, in a software project, a team leader who also codes and manages various software components can be well-represented using intersection types that combine managerial and developer interfaces.

Algorithm 1: Merging Multiple Types through Intersection

Input: Object definitions abiding by multiple interfaces

Result: An object type that intersects attributes of the given interfaces

Function MergeTypes($type_1, type_2, \ldots, type_n$)**:**
  foreach *property* $p \in (type_1 \cup type_2 \cup \ldots \cup type_n)$ **do**
    $type_{result}[p] \leftarrow (type_1[p] \cap type_2[p] \cap \ldots \cap type_n[p])$;
  end
  return $type_{result}$;

Intersection types also offer a strong mechanism for composing new types from existing ones, fostering code reusability and enhancing maintainability. When designing libraries or frameworks, the use of intersection types can empower developers to enforce sophisticated type contracts without redundancy.

The integration of intersection types in TypeScript interfaces ensures that objects are obliged to maintain the structures and constraints catered by all the intersected types, promoting consistency and type integrity in program design.

6.9 Type Aliases: Basics and Syntax

In TypeScript, type aliases serve as a powerful tool allowing developers to create new names for existing types. This feature increases code readability and maintainability by providing meaningful names to complex types. A type alias can represent any type, including primitive types, union types, intersection types, tuples, and interfaces.

The syntax for declaring a type alias is straightforward. Type aliases are created using the type keyword followed by the alias name, an equals sign, and the type definition.

```
type UserID = number; // Alias for a number type
type UserName = string; // Alias for a string type
type UserLogin = { name: string, id: number }; // Alias for an object type
```

In the example above, UserID is an alias for the number type, UserName is an alias for the string type, and UserLogin is an alias for an object type with name and id properties. This reduces the complexity when these types are reused in multiple places within your code.

Type aliases can also represent union types. Union types allow for a variable to be one of several types. Consider the following example:

```
type Status = 'success' | 'error' | 'pending';
```

Here, Status is a type alias that can be either the string literal 'success', 'error', or 'pending'. Using such aliases improves code readability and enables TypeScript to perform correct type checking.

Intersection types can also be represented using type aliases. Intersection types combine multiple types into a single type that has all the properties of its constituent types.

```
type Person = { name: string };
type Contact = { email: string };
type Employee = Person & Contact;
```

In the above example, Person and Contact are simple object types, and Employee is an intersection type that includes all properties from both Person and Contact. Accordingly, an object of type Employee must possess both a name and an email property.

Type aliases are particularly useful in defining function types. TypeScript allows you to define function signatures using type aliases, making it easier to reuse and maintain function types.

```
type StringManipulator = (input: string) => string;
```

```
const toUpperCase: StringManipulator = (input) => input.toUpperCase();
const toLowerCase: StringManipulator = (input) => input.toLowerCase();
```

In this illustration, StringManipulator is a type alias for a function that takes a string as an input and returns a string. Two functions, toUpperCase and toLowerCase, are defined with the StringManipulator type, ensuring they adhere to the specified function signature.

Type aliases can further simplify the use of generic types. Generics are essential for creating flexible and reusable components. With type aliases, definitions can reference generic types, as shown below:

```
type Result<T> = { success: boolean, value: T };
```

Here, Result is a generic type alias where T represents a placeholder for any type. This generic alias can be utilized to type-safe responses that include a success boolean and a value of type T. For instance:

```
const resultString: Result<string> = { success: true, value: "Operation successful" };
const resultNumber: Result<number> = { success: false, value: 42 };
```

Both resultString and resultNumber align with the Result type alias, one holding a string and the other a number.

To ensure accurate type checking and enhance development experience, TypeScript's type aliases offer a versatile and clear method of defining types concisely. Utilizing type aliases can markedly improve code expressiveness, readability, and ease of maintenance.

6.10 Differences Between Type Aliases and Interfaces

Understanding the nuances between type aliases and interfaces in TypeScript is crucial for leveraging the full potential of the language. While they share similarities, they are not interchangeable and each has unique features.

At its core, an interface in TypeScript is used to define the structure of an object. It declares the properties, their types, and the functions an object must have. An interface ensures that objects adhere strictly to the specified contract. Below is an example of a basic interface:

```
interface Person {
    name: string;
```

```
    age: number;
    greet(): void;
}
```

In contrast, a type alias can alias any valid TypeScript type, including primitives, unions, intersections, tuples, and even interfaces. It essentially provides a name to a type but does not enforce nor create new structural contracts that objects must adhere to. Here is an example of a type alias:

```
type Person = {
    name: string;
    age: number;
    greet(): void;
};
```

Although the above examples of interface and type alias look similar, there are subtle differences:

1. Declaration Merging:

One of the key differences is that interfaces support declaration merging: if you define an interface with the same name multiple times, TypeScript will merge them into a single interface, whereas type aliases do not support this feature.

```
interface Vehicle {
    make: string;
}

interface Vehicle {
    model: string;
}

// Merging allows the interface to be:
const car: Vehicle = {
    make: 'Toyota',
    model: 'Corolla'
};
```

Attempting a similar approach with type aliases results in an error:

```
type Animal = {
    species: string;
};

type Animal = {
    habitat: string;
};

// Error: Duplicate identifier 'Animal'.
```

2. Extensibility and Compatibility:

Interfaces provide a straightforward mechanism to extend other interfaces using the extends keyword. This feature is particularly handy when building modular and reusable code.

```
interface Shape {
    color: string;
}

interface Square extends Shape {
    sideLength: number;
}

const square: Square = {
    color: 'blue',
    sideLength: 5
};
```

While type aliases cannot use extends directly, they can still achieve similar results using intersections.

```
type Shape = {
    color: string;
};

type Square = Shape & {
    sideLength: number;
};

const square: Square = {
    color: 'blue',
    sideLength: 5
};
```

3. Recursive Definitions:

Type aliases can define recursive types, quite useful for representing structures like trees or graphs. Interfaces have limited recursive capabilities due to their inability to reference themselves directly within their definition.

```
type Tree<T> = {
    value: T;
    left?: Tree<T>;
    right?: Tree<T>;
};
```

Implementing the same structure with interfaces requires more verbosity and sometimes indirect approaches to achieve recursion.

4. Union and Intersection Types:

Type aliases excel in creating complex types with union and intersection types. These capabilities extend the flexibility and utility in various programming scenarios, particularly in defining hybrids and complex data structures.

```
type Vehicle =
    | { type: 'car'; wheels: 4; make: string; }
    | { type: 'motorcycle'; wheels: 2; make: string; }
    | { type: 'bicycle'; wheels: 2; } ;
```

Interfaces do not inherently support union types; attempting to replicate such scenarios with interfaces can be cumbersome and less intuitive.

5. Simplicity in Usage:

Interfaces are generally preferred where a simpler, more declarative code style is beneficial. They provide clarity and are well-suited for defining object shapes and APIs. For example, when defining the structure of an HTTP response object:

```
interface HttpResponse {
    status: number;
    data: any;
    headers: object;
}
```

Deciding between an interface or type alias depends on the specific requirements of the code. While interfaces are beneficial for ensuring strict object shapes and leveraging declaration merging, type aliases offer versatility with unions, intersections, and the ability to define recursive structures.

Choosing the appropriate tool in TypeScript involves evaluating the features and constraints of interfaces and type aliases and considering the context of their usage. This understanding forms the foundation for crafting robust and maintainable TypeScript applications.

6.11 Union and Intersection Types with Type Aliases

In TypeScript, type aliases offer a versatile way of defining complex types using both union and intersection types. A type alias can simplify the manipulation and reuse of composite types, offering an advantage in managing and understanding code. This section explores the implementation and application of union and intersection types with type aliases, enhancing your TypeScript expertise with precise and unambiguous typing.

A *union type* represents a value that can belong to multiple possible types. Union types use the vertical bar | as a separator. For instance, consider a variable that can be either a string or a number. This is defined using a union type:

```
type StringOrNumber = string | number;
```

With the above type alias, a variable can be designated as a StringOrNumber, ensuring that it either holds a string or a number, but not other types. For example:

```
let value: StringOrNumber;

value = 'foo'; // valid
value = 123; // valid
value = true; // invalid
```

On the other hand, an *intersection type* merges multiple types into one. As a result, an intersection type must satisfy all constituent types concurrently. Intersection types use the ampersand & as a separator. Consider the necessity of defining a type that shares properties of two distinct interfaces:

```
interface Person {
  name: string;
  age: number;
}

interface Employee {
  employeeId: number;
  department: string;
}

type PersonEmployee = Person & Employee;
```

The PersonEmployee type combines the attributes of both Person and Employee, such that any variable of this type will need to have name, age, employeeId, and department properties:

```
const john: PersonEmployee = {
  name: 'John Doe',
  age: 30,
  employeeId: 12345,
  department: 'HR'
};
```

Integrating *union* and *intersection* types, type aliases enable sophisticated type definitions that maximize the expressive power of TypeScript. Consider a scenario where we need to model vehicles with a flexibility that certain properties might vary by vehicle type:

```
interface Car {
  type: 'car';
```

```
  make: string;
  model: string;
  numberOfDoors: number;
}

interface Truck {
  type: 'truck';
  make: string;
  model: string;
  towingCapacity: number;
}

type Vehicle = Car | Truck;
```

Here, the Vehicle type can either be a Car or a Truck, but not both simultaneously. A discriminated union is employed by defining a common property type which helps in distinguishing between different types within unions gracefully. For example:

```
function printVehicleInfo(vehicle: Vehicle) {
  if (vehicle.type === 'car') {
    console.log(`Car: ${vehicle.make} ${vehicle.model}, Doors: ${vehicle.
        numberOfDoors}`);
  } else if (vehicle.type === 'truck') {
    console.log(`Truck: ${vehicle.make} ${vehicle.model}, Towing Capacity: ${vehicle.
        towingCapacity}`);
  }
}

const myCar: Car = {
  type: 'car',
  make: 'Toyota',
  model: 'Corolla',
  numberOfDoors: 4
};

const myTruck: Truck = {
  type: 'truck',
  make: 'Ford',
  model: 'F-150',
  towingCapacity: 10000
};

printVehicleInfo(myCar); // Output : Car: Toyota Corolla, Doors: 4
printVehicleInfo(myTruck); // Output : Truck: Ford F-150, Towing Capacity: 10000
```

The expressiveness of TypeScript types can be further enhanced by leveraging intersection types within union types or vice versa, constructing robust and compound type definitions:

```
interface Electric {
  batteryCapacity: number;
}

type ElectricCar = Car & Electric;
type HybridVehicle = ElectricCar | Truck;
```

In HybridVehicle, a type is created which can be either an ElectricCar, satisfying both Car and Electric interfaces' contracts or a Truck. This facilitates succinct yet comprehensive type structures:

```
const tesla: ElectricCar = {
  type: 'car',
  make: 'Tesla',
  model: 'Model S',
  numberOfDoors: 4,
  batteryCapacity: 100
};

const hybridVehicles: HybridVehicle[] = [tesla, myTruck];
```

The correct integration and application of union and intersection types with type aliases greatly enrich TypeScript's type system, providing robust mechanisms to specify and enforce intricate type constraints.

6.12 Using Type Aliases for Function Types

In TypeScript, type aliases allow for the creation of new names for existing types. This is particularly useful when working with function types, as it can significantly enhance code readability and maintainability. A function type specifies the types of parameters and the return type of a function. Using type aliases to define function types simplifies repetitive type definitions and makes it easier to manage complex type definitions.

To illustrate the use of type aliases for function types, consider the following example where we define a type alias for a function that takes two numbers as arguments and returns a number:

```
type BinaryOperation = (x: number, y: number) => number;
```

In this example, BinaryOperation is a type alias for a function type that represents any function taking two arguments of type number and returning a number. This alias can now be used to declare variables of function types more succinctly:

```
let add: BinaryOperation = (x, y) => x + y;
let subtract: BinaryOperation = (x, y) => x - y;
let multiply: BinaryOperation = (x, y) => x * y;
```

Each variable add, subtract, and multiply is now declared with the type BinaryOperation. This approach provides a clear and concise way to specify that these variables are functions which conform to the defined function type.

Type aliases can also encapsulate function types with more complexity, including those with optional and rest parameters. Consider the following type alias for a function that has an optional second parameter and a rest parameter:

```
type FlexibleOperation = (x: number, y?: number, ...rest: number[]) => number;
```

This type defines a function that must take at least one number as a parameter, may take a second number, and can accept additional number arguments. An example of implementing this function type is shown below:

```
let flexibleAdd: FlexibleOperation = (x, y = 0, ...rest) => {
    return rest.reduce((acc, num) => acc + num, x + y);
};
```

Here, flexibleAdd adds the provided numbers together, initializing y to 0 if not provided, and summing up any additional numbers using the reduce function.

Using type aliases for function types is also beneficial when defining callback functions. Callbacks are functions passed as arguments to other functions and are often employed in asynchronous programming and event handling. For instance:

```
type Callback = (error: Error | null, result?: any) => void;

function asyncOperation(callback: Callback) {
    setTimeout(() => {
        const success = Math.random() > 0.5;
        if (success) {
            callback(null, 'Operation successful');
        } else {
            callback(new Error('Operation failed'));
        }
    }, 1000);
}

asyncOperation((error, result) => {
    if (error) {
        console.log('Error:', error.message);
    } else {
        console.log('Success:', result);
    }
});
```

In this scenario, Callback is a type alias for a function type that takes an Error | null as the first argument and an optional second argument of any type. The asyncOperation function utilizes this callback type, facilitating the handling of both success and error outcomes.

When working with higher-order functions—functions that take other functions as arguments or return functions as their result—the use of type aliases for function types can be extremely informative and streamline type declarations. For example:

```
type UnaryOperation = (x: number) => number;
type HigherOrderOperation = (op: UnaryOperation) => UnaryOperation;

let square: UnaryOperation = x => x * x;
let negate: UnaryOperation = x => -x;

let operateTwice: HigherOrderOperation = op => x => op(op(x));

console.log(operateTwice(square)(2)); // Output: 16
console.log(operateTwice(negate)(2)); // Output: 2
```

In this yet more complex example, UnaryOperation is a type alias for a function that takes a number and returns a number. HigherOrderOperation is a type alias for a function that takes a UnaryOperation as an argument and returns another UnaryOperation. The function operateTwice operates on the result of applying op to its input twice.

Type aliases are invaluable for managing more readable and maintainable code, particularly when dealing with intricate type definitions. By assigning meaningful names to function types, developers can reduce redundancy and focus on the logic and functionality of the code.

Chapter 7

Generics and Advanced Types

This chapter explores the concept of generics in TypeScript to create reusable and flexible components, covering generic functions, classes, interfaces, and type aliases. It delves into constraints in generics, the use of multiple type parameters, and advanced type inference techniques. Additionally, the chapter introduces advanced types such as mapped types, conditional types, utility types, discriminated unions, and recursive types, providing a thorough understanding of how to leverage generics and advanced typing mechanisms for robust and maintainable code.

7.1 Introduction to Generics

Generics are a powerful feature in TypeScript that allow developers to create code that is flexible, reusable, and type-safe. By allowing types to be passed as parameters to functions, classes, and interfaces, generics enable the creation of components that can work with a variety of data types without sacrificing type safety. This section provides a comprehensive introduction to generics, covering the basic concepts and illustrating their use through clear examples.

To begin with, consider a simple function that returns the first element of an array:

```
function getFirstElement(arr: any[]): any {
    return arr[0];
}
```

This function takes an array of any type and returns the first element. However, this approach lacks type safety, as it does not specify the type of the elements in the array, and the return type is any. This can lead to potential runtime errors and hinders the benefits of TypeScript's static type checking. Generics offer a solution to this problem by allowing us to specify a placeholder for the type that can be replaced with a specific type when the function is called.

To rewrite the getFirstElement function using generics, we define a type parameter T inside angle brackets < >:

```
function getFirstElement<T>(arr: T[]): T {
    return arr[0];
}
```

In this revised version, T represents a placeholder for the element type of the array. When the function is called, T is inferred based on the type of the elements in the array passed as an argument. Here is an example of how to use this generic function:

```
const numArray = [1, 2, 3];
const strArray = ['a', 'b', 'c'];

const firstNum = getFirstElement(numArray); // T is inferred as number
const firstStr = getFirstElement(strArray); // T is inferred as string
```

In these examples, TypeScript correctly infers that T is number for numArray and string for strArray, ensuring type safety and preserving the benefits of static type checking.

In addition to functions, generics can be applied to classes, interfaces, and type aliases. For example, consider a class that represents a generic stack:

```
class Stack<T> {
    private elements: T[] = [];

    push(element: T): void {
        this.elements.push(element);
    }

    pop(): T | undefined {
        return this.elements.pop();
    }

    peek(): T | undefined {
        return this.elements[this.elements.length - 1];
    }
```

```
    isEmpty(): boolean {
        return this.elements.length === 0;
    }
}
```

In this Stack class, T is a type parameter that allows the stack to hold elements of any specified type. When creating an instance of the Stack class, the type parameter T can be explicitly provided or inferred based on the usage:

```
const numberStack = new Stack<number>();
numberStack.push(1);
numberStack.push(2);
console.log(numberStack.pop()); // Output: 2

const stringStack = new Stack<string>();
stringStack.push('a');
stringStack.push('b');
console.log(stringStack.pop()); // Output: 'b'
```

This approach ensures that each stack instance is type-safe, accommodating different types of elements while maintaining the same stack operations.

Generics also extend to interfaces and type aliases, providing further flexibility and reusability in defining data structures. Here is an example of a generic interface for a key-value pair:

```
interface KeyValuePair<K, V> {
    key: K;
    value: V;
}

const numStrPair: KeyValuePair<number, string> = {
    key: 1,
    value: 'one'
};

const strNumPair: KeyValuePair<string, number> = {
    key: 'one',
    value: 1
};
```

In this KeyValuePair interface, K and V are type parameters representing the key and value types, respectively. The interface can then be used to create key-value pairs with different types of keys and values, while ensuring type safety.

By leveraging generics, TypeScript accommodates a wide range of programming paradigms, including functional and object-oriented programming. The typed abstractions provided by generics aid in constructing robust and maintainable code by ensuring type consistency across various parts of an application.

7.2 Generic Functions

Generic functions in TypeScript allow for the creation of functions that can work with different types without sacrificing type safety. These are highly useful for creating reusable and maintainable code. To define a generic function, type parameters are introduced, which can be used as placeholders for the types that will be passed into the function.

The basic syntax for a generic function involves placing the type parameter within angle brackets '<>' following the function name. The type parameter can then be used within the function signature and body.

```
function identity<T>(arg: T): T {
    return arg;
}
```

In this example, the function identity takes a parameter arg of type T and returns a value of the same type T. The type parameter T can be substituted with any type when the function is called.

To execute the identity function, the type argument can be specified explicitly or inferred by the compiler based on the function arguments.

```
// Explicit type argument
let output1 = identity<string>("myString");

// Type argument inferred
let output2 = identity("myString");
```

Both calls to the identity function are valid. In the first call, the type argument string is provided explicitly, while in the second call, the type argument is inferred to be string from the type of "myString".

Generic functions can also work with multiple type parameters by listing them within the angle brackets, separated by commas. This is particularly useful when the function operates on or returns multiple types.

```
function merge<U, V>(obj1: U, obj2: V): U & V {
    let result = <U & V>{};
    for (let id in obj1) {
        if ((<Object>obj1).hasOwnProperty(id)) {
            result[id] = (<any>obj1)[id];
        }
    }
    for (let id in obj2) {
        if ((<Object>obj2).hasOwnProperty(id)) {
            result[id] = (<any>obj2)[id];
        }
```

```
    }
    return result;
}
```

The merge function takes two parameters obj1 of type U and obj2 of type V, and returns a new object that combines the properties of both obj1 and obj2. The return type U & V is a combination of both types, using an intersection type.

TypeScript's type inference capabilities allow generic functions to be very flexible. However, certain constraints may be necessary to ensure that the generic types meet specific criteria. Constraints on generic type parameters are defined using the extends keyword.

```
function loggingIdentity<T extends { length: number }>(arg: T): T {
    console.log(arg.length);
    return arg;
}
```

In this modified identity function, the type parameter T is constrained to types that have a length property. This constraint ensures that any type used as T must have a length property, enabling the loggingIdentity function to safely access arg.length.

To illustrate the usage of loggingIdentity:

```
loggingIdentity("hello");
loggingIdentity([1, 2, 3, 4, 5]);
loggingIdentity({ length: 10, value: 3 });
```

All three calls to loggingIdentity are valid because the arguments have a length property. Attempting to call loggingIdentity with a type that lacks a length property would result in a compilation error.

TypeScript provides advanced type inference capabilities, which further enhance the flexibility and power of generic functions. The compiler can infer multiple type parameters and even their constraints in some complex scenarios, as demonstrated below.

```
function getProperty<T, K extends keyof T>(obj: T, key: K): T[K] {
    return obj[key];
}

let myObject = { name: "John", age: 25 };
let propertyName = getProperty(myObject, "name");
let propertyAge = getProperty(myObject, "age");
```

Here, the getProperty function takes an object obj of type T and a key key of type K, where K extends the keys of T. The return type is the type of the property at key key within the object obj. This leverages the keyof type operator, which returns a union of the keys of type T.

This comprehensive exploration of generic functions in TypeScript demonstrates how they enable the creation of flexible and reusable code, improving both the robustness and maintainability of TypeScript applications. Employing generic functions effectively requires understanding type parameters, constraints, and advanced type inference, all of which contribute to writing more versatile and type-safe code.

7.3 Generic Classes

In TypeScript, classes can be made generic such that they work with a variety of types while maintaining the structure and behavior defined by the class. This flexibility allows for designing components that are highly reusable and type-safe. A generic class is structured similarly to a generic function. The generic type parameters are placed within angle brackets <> following the class name, providing a means to define properties, methods, and constructors within the class that depend on the generic type.

Consider the following simple example of a generic class Box, which encapsulates a value of any type and provides methods for setting and retrieving the value:

```
class Box<T> {
    private value: T;

    constructor(value: T) {
        this.value = value;
    }

    getValue(): T {
        return this.value;
    }

    setValue(value: T): void {
        this.value = value;
    }
}
```

In this example, the Box class is generic over a type parameter T. This parameter can be any type, and the class stores a value of type T, which is set through the constructor and can be retrieved or updated using the provided methods.

To create instances of this generic class, we must specify the type parameter explicitly when instantiating the class:

```
let numberBox = new Box<number>(5);
console.log(numberBox.getValue()); // Outputs: 5

let stringBox = new Box<string>('Hello');
console.log(stringBox.getValue()); // Outputs: Hello
```

The above code snippet demonstrates creating instances of the Box class with the types number and string. The type safety of TypeScript ensures that only values of the specified type can be set or retrieved, thus preventing type errors.

Additionally, generic classes can have multiple type parameters to support more complex use cases. Consider the following example where the generic class Pair holds two values, each of possibly different types:

```
class Pair<T, U> {
    private first: T;
    private second: U;

    constructor(first: T, second: U) {
        this.first = first;
        this.second = second;
    }

    getFirst(): T {
        return this.first;
    }

    getSecond(): U {
        return this.second;
    }
}
```

In this Pair class, two type parameters, T and U, are defined. This allows the class to store and work with two different types. When creating instances of the Pair class, we need to specify both type parameters:

```
let pair = new Pair<number, string>(1, 'One');
console.log(pair.getFirst()); // Outputs: 1
console.log(pair.getSecond()); // Outputs: One
```

This example specifies that the first value is of type number and the second value is of type string. Again, TypeScript enforces type safety so that each value conforms to the specified types.

It is also possible to use constraints in generic classes to restrict the types that can be assigned to the generic type parameters. The following Container class requires that the type parameter T must extend the HasId interface:

```
interface HasId {
    id: number;
}
```

```
class Container<T extends HasId> {
    private items: T[] = [];

    addItem(item: T): void {
        this.items.push(item);
    }

    getItemById(id: number): T | undefined {
        return this.items.find(item => item.id === id);
    }
}
```

Here, the HasId interface defines a contract for objects that have an id property of type number. The Container class can only be instantiated with types that conform to the HasId interface. This allows the getItemById method to safely access the id property on items.

To use the Container class, define a type that extends HasId and create an instance of Container with that type:

```
interface Product extends HasId {
    name: string;
    price: number;
}

let productContainer = new Container<Product>();
productContainer.addItem({ id: 1, name: 'Laptop', price: 1000 });
productContainer.addItem({ id: 2, name: 'Phone', price: 500 });

let product = productContainer.getItemById(1);
console.log(product); // Outputs: { id: 1, name: 'Laptop', price: 1000 }
```

In this instance, Product extends HasId so that it can be used with the Container class. This ensures type safety and allows the getItemById method to access the id property without issues.

Generic classes in TypeScript provide a powerful mechanism for defining reusable and type-safe components that work with any type, or a restricted set of types using constraints. By leveraging generics, developers can create robust and maintainable code that can adapt to various type requirements while ensuring type correctness.

7.4 Generic Interfaces and Type Aliases

When working with TypeScript, creating reusable and flexible code is paramount. Generic interfaces and type aliases allow developers to define robust components that can adapt to different data types while maintaining type safety. These mechanisms provide a powerful means to express complex type relationships and to create abstractions that reduce redundancy and enhance maintainability.

Generic Interfaces allow us to define the shape of an object that can work with a variety of types without sacrificing the benefits of static type checking. For instance, consider a simple logging interface:

```
interface Logger<T> {
    log: (value: T) => void;
}
```

In this example, the interface Logger is generic over the type parameter T. This means Logger can be instantiated with different types, such as number, string, or a custom object. Here is how you would implement a logger for numbers:

```
class NumberLogger implements Logger<number> {
    log(value: number): void {
        console.log(`Number value: ${value}`);
    }
}
```

The NumberLogger class implements the Logger<number> interface by specifying number as the type parameter for T. This ensures that the log method only accepts number values while still adhering to the Logger interface.

Similarly, you can create a logger for strings:

```
class StringLogger implements Logger<string> {
    log(value: string): void {
        console.log(`String value: ${value}`);
    }
}
```

Generic Type Aliases provide an alternative way to define reusable and flexible types without the need for an overarching class or interface. Type aliases can be particularly useful for defining function signatures, complex object shapes, or even more advanced constructs like unions and intersections.

For example, you may want to define a generic type alias for a function that processes an array of any type:

```
type ArrayProcessor<T> = (items: T[]) => T[];
```

This alias ArrayProcessor defines a function type that takes an array of type T and returns an array of the same type. Here is how you can use it:

```
const processNumbers: ArrayProcessor<number> = (numbers) => {
```

```
    return numbers.map(num => num * 2);
};

const processStrings: ArrayProcessor<string> = (strings) => {
    return strings.map(str => str.toUpperCase());
};
```

Both processNumbers and processStrings adhere to the ArrayProcessor type alias, ensuring type safety and consistency while processing arrays of numbers and strings, respectively.

Moreover, generic type aliases can be leveraged to create more complex types, such as generic object shapes. Consider a type alias for a paginated response:

```
type PaginatedResponse<T> = {
    data: T[];
    page: number;
    totalPages: number;
};
```

The PaginatedResponse type alias encapsulates a generic response structure where data is an array of type T, and pagination information is included as well. This can be utilized in various scenarios, such as querying a database or fetching paginated data from an API:

```
const userResponse: PaginatedResponse<{ id: number; name: string; }> = {
    data: [{ id: 1, name: 'John' }, { id: 2, name: 'Jane' }],
    page: 1,
    totalPages: 2
};
```

Interoperability of Generic Interfaces and Type Aliases is another advantageous feature. Both can be combined to provide highly flexible and reusable type definitions. For instance, if there is a need to define a service that fetches data in a paginated manner, it can be done as follows:

```
interface FetchService<T> {
    fetch: (url: string) => Promise<PaginatedResponse<T>>;
}

class UserService implements FetchService<{ id: number; name: string; }> {
    async fetch(url: string): Promise<PaginatedResponse<{ id: number; name: string;
        }>> {
        const response = await fetch(url);
        const data = await response.json();
        return {
            data,
            page: 1,
            totalPages: 1
        };
    }
}
```

In this scenario, the UserService class implements the FetchService interface, which returns a PaginatedResponse with a specific shape. This design pattern ensures that different services can implement the same generic interface while working with different types of data.

Generic interfaces and type aliases form the backbone of TypeScript's capability to handle highly dynamic and type-safe code structures. By defining generic components that can adapt to varying types, it promotes code reusability and significantly enhances the maintainability of complex applications.

7.5 Constraints in Generics

In TypeScript, generics provide the flexibility to create components that can work with a variety of types. However, this flexibility can sometimes lead to scenarios where you would like to restrict the types that can be used with a generic. This is where constraints come into play. Constraints allow you to specify that a generic type must conform to a certain shape or behavior, providing more control over the types used in your generic components.

To illustrate the use of constraints, consider a simple function that returns the property of an object given the object and the property name as arguments. Without constraints, we might define such a function as follows:

```
function getProperty<T, K>(obj: T, key: K) {
    return obj[key];
}
```

This function, while generic, is too permissive. It allows the key parameter to be of any type, which may lead to errors if the key is not a valid property of obj. To restrict the key to be a property of obj, we can use a constraint:

```
function getProperty<T, K extends keyof T>(obj: T, key: K) {
    return obj[key];
}
```

In this updated function, the constraint K extends keyof T specifies that K must be a key of T. This ensures that key can only be a property name of the obj, thus providing type safety.

Benefits of Using Constraints

Using constraints in generics offers several advantages:

- **Type Safety**: Constraints ensure that the generic types meet certain criteria, preventing type-related runtime errors.
- **Enhanced Readability**: By specifying constraints, you communicate the intended usage of the generic to other developers, making the code more readable and maintainable.
- **Improved Tooling Support**: Constraints provide additional type information to TypeScript's type checker, improving development tools' ability to catch errors and offer relevant code suggestions.

Practical Examples of Constraints

Constraint to Object Types

Consider a function that merges two objects. We want to ensure that the function only accepts arguments that are objects. We can achieve this by constraining the generic type to an object type using extends.

```
function merge<T extends object, U extends object>(obj1: T, obj2: U): T & U {
    return { ...obj1, ...obj2 };
}

// Usage
const obj1 = { name: "Alice" };
const obj2 = { age: 30 };
const mergedObject = merge(obj1, obj2);
```

In this example, the merge function only accepts parameters that are objects, preventing misuse with non-object types.

Using Constraints with Interfaces

Constraints can also be applied using interfaces. Consider a generic class that manages a collection of items. We want to ensure that each item has a unique id property. By defining an interface for the constraint, we can enforce this structure:

```
interface Identifiable {
    id: number;
}

class ItemManager<T extends Identifiable> {
    private items: T[] = [];
```

```
    addItem(item: T): void {
        this.items.push(item);
    }

    getItem(id: number): T | undefined {
        return this.items.find(item => item.id === id);
    }
}

// Usage
const manager = new ItemManager<{ id: number; name: string }>();
manager.addItem({ id: 1, name: "Item 1" });
const item = manager.getItem(1);
```

In this example, the ItemManager class uses the Identifiable interface as a constraint, ensuring that the items managed by ItemManager have an id property.

Default Type Parameters

TypeScript also allows you to specify default types for generic type parameters with constraints. This can be useful to provide a default behavior while still allowing flexibility.

```
interface Response<T = string> {
    data: T;
    status: number;
}

function handleResponse<T>(response: Response<T>): T {
    return response.data;
}

// Usage
const response1: Response<number> = { data: 42, status: 200 };
const data1 = handleResponse(response1); // data1 is of type number

const response2: Response = { data: "Success", status: 200 };
const data2 = handleResponse(response2); // data2 is of type string (default)
```

In this case, the generic interface Response has a default type parameter string. If no type is specified for T, TypeScript uses string by default.

Conclusion

Constraints in generics are a powerful feature in TypeScript that ensure your generic components work with an expected set of types. By using constraints, you can enhance type safety, improve code readability, and leverage better tooling support. This allows the creation of more robust and maintainable TypeScript code.

7.6 Using Multiple Type Parameters

In TypeScript, the use of multiple type parameters significantly enhances the flexibility and reusability of generic components. This section explores how to define and utilize multiple type parameters in various contexts such as functions, interfaces, and classes. Multiple type parameters allow components to operate over more than one type of variable, thus broadening their applicability.

To illustrate the use of multiple type parameters in a function, we define a generic function that accepts two arguments of different types and returns a tuple containing both arguments. Consider the following example:

```
function pair<S, T>(first: S, second: T): [S, T] {
    return [first, second];
}

// Usage examples:
const stringNumberPair = pair<string, number>("Hello", 42);
const booleanArrayPair = pair<boolean, boolean[]>(true, [false, true, false]);

console.log(stringNumberPair); // Output: ['Hello', 42]
console.log(booleanArrayPair); // Output: [true, [false, true, false]]
```

In the above code, pair is a generic function with two type parameters S and T. It takes two arguments first of type S and second of type T, and returns a tuple [S, T]. The usage examples demonstrate how the function can accept various types of arguments and properly infer the types of the returned tuple.

Multiple type parameters can also be defined within classes, enabling more sophisticated type relationships. Consider a class that represents a simple key-value pair:

```
class KeyValuePair<K, V> {
    constructor(public key: K, public value: V) {}

    getKeyValuePair(): [K, V] {
        return [this.key, this.value];
    }
}

// Usage examples:
const numStrPair = new KeyValuePair<number, string>(1, "one");
const boolObjPair = new KeyValuePair<boolean, object>(true, { active: true });

console.log(numStrPair.getKeyValuePair()); // Output: [1, 'one']
console.log(boolObjPair.getKeyValuePair()); // Output: [true, { active: true }]
```

In this KeyValuePair class, K and V are type parameters indicating the types of the key and value, respectively. The constructor initializes the key and value properties, and the getKeyValuePair method returns a tuple containing the key-value pair.

Interfaces in TypeScript can also leverage multiple type parameters to define more complex and flexible type relationships. For example, an interface that defines a dictionary object can be defined as follows:

```
interface Dictionary<KEY, VALUE> {
    add(key: KEY, value: VALUE): void;
    get(key: KEY): VALUE | undefined;
}

// Implementation example:
class StringNumberDictionary implements Dictionary<string, number> {
    private data: { [key: string]: number } = {};

    add(key: string, value: number): void {
        this.data[key] = value;
    }

    get(key: string): number | undefined {
        return this.data[key];
    }
}

const dict = new StringNumberDictionary();
dict.add("one", 1);
console.log(dict.get("one")); // Output: 1
```

In this example, the Dictionary interface is defined with two type parameters, KEY and VALUE. The add method adds a key-value pair to the dictionary, and the get method retrieves the value associated with a given key. The StringNumberDictionary class implements the Dictionary interface with string as the key type and number as the value type.

Using multiple type parameters can also be combined with type constraints to impose limitations on the types that can be used. Type constraints are introduced using the extends keyword. Consider an interface that ensures the types used have certain properties:

```
interface NameValuePair<N extends string, V> {
    name: N;
    value: V;
}

function createNameValuePair<N extends string, V>(name: N, value: V):
        NameValuePair<N, V> {
    return { name, value };
}

// Usage example:
const nameValuePair = createNameValuePair("age", 30);
console.log(nameValuePair); // Output: { name: 'age', value: 30 }
```

In this case, N is constrained to be a string, ensuring that the name property of NameValuePair must always be a string while allowing the value property to be of any type.

To deepen the understanding, here is another example combining multiple type parameters with constraints to create a generic function that merges two objects while ensuring type safety:

```
function mergeObjects<A extends object, B extends object>(objA: A, objB: B): A & B
     {
   return { ...objA, ...objB };
}

// Usage examples:
const mergedObj = mergeObjects({ name: "Alice" }, { age: 25 });
console.log(mergedObj); // Output: { name: 'Alice', age: 25 }

const complexMerge = mergeObjects({ foo: "bar" }, { baz: [1, 2, 3] });
console.log(complexMerge); // Output: { foo: 'bar', baz: [1, 2, 3] }
```

The mergeObjects function takes two parameters objA and objB, both constrained to be objects, and returns a new object that is the combination of both input objects. The resultant type A & B represents the intersection type of A and B, ensuring that all properties from both objects are included in the resulting object with type safety.

This treatment of multiple type parameters builds upon the fundamental concepts examined earlier in the chapter, demonstrating their applicability in enhancing the type safety and reusability of generic components in TypeScript.

7.7 Advanced Type Inference

TypeScript's type inference capabilities are foundational in aiding developers to write robust and maintainable code by implicitly determining types and reducing the need for explicit type annotations. Advanced type inference extends beyond basic type deduction and encompasses several sophisticated mechanisms that enhance code expressiveness and safety. This section delves into these mechanisms, explaining their practical applications and nuances.

Inference in Generic Functions and Classes:

Type inference in the context of generics allows TypeScript to infer the type parameters passed to generic functions and classes. Consider the following generic function:

```
function identity<T>(arg: T): T {
    return arg;
}
```

When calling this function, TypeScript can infer the type T based on the argument provided:

```
let output = identity("myString"); // inferred type: string
```

Here, TypeScript infers the type parameter T as string. This type of inference is not limited to primitive types; it can also include complex types like objects and arrays.

Contextual Typing:

Contextual typing occurs when the type of an expression is inferred based on its context, such as the type expected by a function or a surrounding expression. It is especially useful in functions that take callbacks as arguments:

```
let numbers = [1, 2, 3];
numbers.forEach(num => console.log(num));
```

In the example above, TypeScript infers the type of num as number based on the type of the numbers array.

Return Type Inference:

TypeScript can often infer the return type of a function based on its implementation. Explicit return type annotations become optional unless necessary for clarity or complex scenarios:

```
function add(a: number, b: number) {
    return a + b;
}
```

Here, the return type is inferred as number.

Best Common Type:

When inferring the type of an array or similar structure, TypeScript uses the best common type algorithm to infer a single type that is compatible with all elements. Consider the following array:

```
let mixedArray = [1, "text", true];
```

TypeScript will infer the type of mixedArray as (string | number | boolean)[].

Advanced Contextual Types:

In more complex scenarios, TypeScript performs intricate inference to maintain type safety. For instance, when working with higher-order functions or conditional logic within callbacks:

```
function processInput(input: string | number) {
    if (typeof input === "string") {
        return input.toUpperCase();
    }
    return input.toFixed(2);
}
```

TypeScript infers the return type as string | string (since toFixed returns a string).

Type Guards and Control Flow Analysis:

Type guards enhance type inference within block scopes by refining types based on conditional checks:

```
function isString(x: any): x is string {
    return typeof x === "string";
}

function example(input: string | number) {
    if (isString(input)) {
        console.log(input.toUpperCase()); // input inferred as string
    } else {
        console.log(input.toFixed(2)); // input inferred as number
    }
}
```

Control Flow Analysis further enables TypeScript to refine types across different branches of code execution, ensuring that variables are accurately typed at every point.

Inference with Mapped and Conditional Types:

TypeScript's ability to infer types extends to mapped types and conditional types, allowing developers to define types dynamically based on other types. For instance, consider a utility type for making properties in an interface optional:

```
type Partial<T> = {
    [P in keyof T]?: T[P];
};

interface User {
    id: number;
    name: string;
}

type PartialUser = Partial<User>; // { id?: number; name?: string; }
```

Here, TypeScript correctly infers that PartialUser is an object type where all properties of User are optional.

Advanced type inference in TypeScript enhances code accuracy and developer efficiency by reducing the need for explicit type annotations. By understanding and applying these advanced inference techniques, developers can create more predictable and maintainable codebases.

7.8 Mapped Types

Mapped types in TypeScript provide a mechanism for transforming types. They enable the creation of new types based on an existing type, ensuring that repetitive tasks are minimized and that changes to a type's structure can propagate through the codebase automatically. This type of transformation is particularly useful for type manipulation and for generating new types that adapt to specific use cases without manual redefinition.

At the core of mapped types is the ability to take a type and systematically transform each of its properties according to a given operation. This section details the syntax and usage of mapped types, progressively building on foundational knowledge to explore more advanced applications.

Basic Syntax

The syntax of mapped types leverages TypeScript's ability to iterate over the properties of a given type. Here is the basic form:

```
type Readonly<T> = {
  readonly [P in keyof T]: T[P];
};
```

In this definition: - T represents a generic type parameter. - keyof T is an index type query that produces a union of string literal types, corresponding to the keys of T. - P in keyof T is a mapped type clause that iterates over each key P in the type T. - readonly is a modifier applied to each property P.

Thus, Readonly<T> transforms a type T into a new type where all of its properties are marked as readonly.

Practical Example

Consider an interface representing a person:

```
interface Person {
  name: string;
```

```
    age: number;
    address: string;
}
```

Using our previously defined Readonly mapped type, we can create a new type where all properties of Person are immutable:

```
type ReadonlyPerson = Readonly<Person>;

const person: ReadonlyPerson = {
    name: "Alice",
    age: 30,
    address: "123 Main St"
};

// The following assignment will produce an error
// because properties are read-only:
// person.age = 31;
```

This demonstrates how mapped types can enhance type safety by enforcing constraints on types.

Adding Modifiers

Mapped types can also be used to add or remove modifiers. For instance, the following mapped type removes the optional modifier from all properties:

```
type Required<T> = {
    [P in keyof T]-?: T[P];
};
```

Here, the -? modifier indicates that the optional flag should be removed from each property.

Combining Modifiers

Mapped types enable combining multiple operations. For example, to create a type with both read-only and required properties, we can combine both modifiers:

```
type ReadonlyRequired<T> = {
    readonly [P in keyof T]-?: T[P];
};
```

ReadonlyRequired<T> is a type transformation that enforces both immutability and non-nullability.

Advanced Usage

We can extend mapped types to perform more complex transformations. For instance, consider the following example where all properties are converted to functions returning their original values:

```
type Functions<T> = {
  [P in keyof T]: () => T[P];
};
```

Given a type Person, the Functions<Person> type would be:

```
type FunctionPerson = Functions<Person>;

const functionPerson: FunctionPerson = {
  name: () => "Alice",
  age: () => 30,
  address: () => "123 Main St"
};
```

Each property is now a function returning the appropriate value type.

Leveraging Conditional Types

Mapped types become even more powerful when combined with conditional types. As an example, we can conditionally transform types based on whether they extend a certain type:

```
type Nullable<T> = {
  [P in keyof T]: T[P] | null;
};
```

This transformation creates a new type where each property of T can also be null, adding flexibility to the type definitions.

Utility Mapped Types

TypeScript provides several built-in utility types that make use of mapped types. Some common examples include:

- Partial<T>: Makes all properties of T optional.
- Required<T>: Makes all properties of T required.
- Readonly<T>: Makes all properties of T read-only.
- Record<K, T>: Constructs an object type with keys of type K and values of type T.

These utilities rely on the same principles we have discussed, offering pre-defined, robust, and reusable transformations.

Conclusion through Code Integration

Learning to wield mapped types effectively allows for a significant reduction in repetitive code and increases type safety. By mastering these transformations, you can create types that adapt cohesively to changes within your codebase, enhancing both flexibility and maintainability. The following advanced concepts, such as conditional types, utility types, and recursive types, further extend this capability by providing more specific and powerful tools for type manipulation in TypeScript.

7.9 Conditional Types

Conditional types in TypeScript provide a powerful mechanism to express types that depend on a condition, enabling more precise type definitions. This flexibility is essential in creating type-safe, maintainable, and reusable code.

A conditional type selects one of two possible types based on a condition expressed as a type relationship test. The basic syntax is as follows:

```
T extends U ? X : Y
```

Here, T and U are types, and the expression evaluates to type X if T extends U, otherwise, it evaluates to type Y. This ternary-like syntax enables a broad range of type manipulations.

Consider a basic example where we define a type that strips away 'null' and 'undefined' from a type:

```
type NonNullable<T> = T extends null | undefined ? never : T;
```

For a given type T, if T is null or undefined, the result type is never. Otherwise, it results in T itself. The never type represents a type that never happens, effectively removing null and undefined from the resulting type.

When we test this with some types:

```
type T1 = NonNullable<string | number | undefined>; // string | number
type T2 = NonNullable<null | undefined>; // never
```

In T1, the undefined type is removed, resulting in string | number. In T2, both null and undefined result in never.

Conditional types are especially useful when dealing with types that change depending on certain conditions. Let's explore a more advanced scenario with generic types.

Imagine we want to create a type that transforms a union type into an intersection type. The following utility type UnionToIntersection achieves this:

```
type UnionToIntersection<U> =
    (U extends any ? (k: U) => void : never) extends (k: infer I) => void ? I :
        never;
```

This type transformation manipulates the union using conditional types to produce an intersection. To achieve this, it leverages two advanced TypeScript features: distribution of conditional types and infer keyword.

UnionToIntersection works in the following way:

- For each member of the union U, it creates a function type (k: U) => void.
- This utilizes the distributive nature of conditional types, breaking the union U into its members individually.
- Then, it creates an intersection out of these types through the infer I keyword.

When passed a union type, this utility type will create an intersection type. For example:

```
type U1 = UnionToIntersection<{ a: string } | { b: number }>; // {a: string} & {b
    : number}
```

In this example, the union type a: string | b: number is converted into the intersection a: string & b: number.

Conditional types can also be nested and combined with other TypeScript features like generics, mapped types, and utility types. Here's a more complex example, combining mapped types and conditional types to filter keys from an object type:

```
type FilterKeys<T, U> = {
    [K in keyof T]: T[K] extends U ? K : never
}[keyof T];
```

This type FilterKeys<T, U> creates a union of keys from T whose values are assignable to type U.

- It iterates over keys of T with a mapped type.
- For each key K, it checks if the corresponding value T[K] extends U.
- If T[K] extends U, it keeps K, otherwise, it results in never.

- Finally, it uses an index signature [keyof T] to create a union of the retained keys.

To illustrate this, let's filter keys from a type based on value type:

```
type Example = {
    name: string;
    age: number;
    active: boolean;
};

type StringKeys = FilterKeys<Example, string>; // 'name'
type NumberKeys = FilterKeys<Example, number>; // 'age'
type BooleanKeys = FilterKeys<Example, boolean>; // 'active'
```

In this example, FilterKeys<Example, string> extracts only the string keys from the Example type, resulting in 'name'.

Mastering conditional types significantly enhances the ability to work with complex type transformations, ensuring precise type safety and expressiveness in TypeScript code.

7.10 Utility Types

Utility types in TypeScript provide built-in type manipulation capabilities that enable developers to transform existing types into new ones. These utilities can simplify common type transformations, leading to more maintainable and readable code. This section discusses some of the most commonly used utility types: Partial<T>, Required<T>, Readonly<T>, Pick<T, K>, Omit<T, K>, Record<K, T>, and ReturnType<T>.

To illustrate these utility types, consider the following interface representing an essential user object:

```
interface User {
  id: number;
  name: string;
  age?: number;
  email: string;
}
```

Partial<T> The Partial<T> type constructs a type with all properties of T set to be optional. This utility is particularly useful when creating functions that update some properties of an object without requiring all properties to be present.

```
type PartialUser = Partial<User>;
```

In this example, PartialUser can be used as a type where id, name, age, and email are all optional:

```
const updateUser: PartialUser = {
  name: 'Alice',
};
```

Required<T> Conversely, the Required<T> type constructs a type where all properties of T are mandatory. This can be used to ensure that an object is fully defined.

```
type RequiredUser = Required<User>;
```

Here, RequiredUser expects all properties to be specified:

```
const newUser: RequiredUser = {
  id: 1,
  name: 'Bob',
  age: 25,
  email: 'bob@example.com',
};
```

Readonly<T> The Readonly<T> type constructs a type with all properties of T set to be read-only. This utility ensures that once an object is created, its properties cannot be modified.

```
type ReadonlyUser = Readonly<User>;
```

This would enforce read-only properties, preventing reassignment:

```
const user: ReadonlyUser = {
  id: 2,
  name: 'Charlie',
  age: 30,
  email: 'charlie@example.com',
};

// This assignment will cause a TypeScript error
// user.name = 'Charles';
```

Pick<T, K> The Pick<T, K> type allows selecting a subset of properties from a type T. The selected properties are specified by the union type K.

```
type UserContactInfo = Pick<User, 'name' | 'email'>;
```

Here, UserContactInfo includes only name and email properties:

```
const contactInfo: UserContactInfo = {
  name: 'David',
  email: 'david@example.com',
};
```

Omit<T, K> The Omit<T, K> type constructs a type by removing properties K from T. This utility is the inverse of Pick.

```
type UserWithoutEmail = Omit<User, 'email'>;
```

In this case, the UserWithoutEmail type includes all properties except email:

```
const userWithoutEmail: UserWithoutEmail = {
  id: 3,
  name: 'Eve',
  age: 28,
};
```

Record<K, T> The Record<K, T> type constructs a type with a set of properties K of type T. This utility is often used to create dictionary-like structures where the keys and values are of specific types.

```
type UserDictionary = Record<string, User>;
```

Here, UserDictionary represents an object where keys are strings, and values are of type User:

```
const users: UserDictionary = {
  alice: { id: 4, name: 'Alice', email: 'alice@example.com' },
  bob: { id: 5, name: 'Bob', email: 'bob@example.com', age: 32 },
};
```

ReturnType<T> The ReturnType<T> type constructs a type by extracting the return type of a function type T. This utility is useful for obtaining the return type of function expressions and function declarations.

```
function getUser(): User {
  return { id: 6, name: 'Frank', email: 'frank@example.com' };
}

type GetUserReturnType = ReturnType<typeof getUser>;
```

Here, GetUserReturnType is inferred to be of type User:

```
const user: GetUserReturnType = getUser();
```

Utility types provide concise ways to manipulate types, enabling developers to write more expressive and maintainable TypeScript code. Their judicious use can significantly streamline type management in complex applications.

7.11 Discriminated Unions

Discriminated unions, also known as tagged unions or algebraic data types, are a powerful feature in TypeScript that allows you to create a type that can be one of several different types while providing a way to distinguish between them using a common property. This construct is particularly useful for defining types that can represent a finite set of distinct cases, each with their own structure and semantics.

To define discriminated unions in TypeScript, we leverage type aliases and interfaces. The common property that acts as the discriminant must have a literal type, and each member of the union must have a unique value for this common property. Let's consider an example involving shapes.

```
interface Circle {
  kind: 'circle';
  radius: number;
}

interface Square {
  kind: 'square';
  sideLength: number;
}

interface Rectangle {
  kind: 'rectangle';
  width: number;
  height: number;
}

type Shape = Circle | Square | Rectangle;
```

In this example, we define three interfaces: Circle, Square, and Rectangle. Each interface has a kind property that acts as the discriminant, with a literal type unique to each shape. The union type Shape can be any one of these interfaces.

When working with discriminated unions, you can use conditional checks on the discriminant property to determine the exact type of the union member. Here's how you can write a function to calculate the area of a Shape:

```
function getArea(shape: Shape): number {
  switch (shape.kind) {
    case 'circle':
      return Math.PI * Math.pow(shape.radius, 2);
    case 'square':
      return Math.pow(shape.sideLength, 2);
    case 'rectangle':
      return shape.width * shape.height;
    default:
      throw new Error('Unknown shape!');
  }
}
```

In this function, the switch statement checks the kind property of the shape argument. TypeScript's type inference system is able to narrow the type of shape within each case block based on the kind property. This ensures that properties specific to each shape type can be accessed safely.

Using discriminated unions not only makes it easy to handle different cases but also enhances type safety by ensuring that each possible case is handled explicitly. This can help prevent bugs due to unhandled cases, especially when the set of possible types evolves over time.

Let's explore another example to illustrate the advantages of discriminated unions in the context of a state management scenario. Consider an application that tracks the status of a network request:

```
interface LoadingState {
  state: 'loading';
}

interface SuccessState<T> {
  state: 'success';
  data: T;
}

interface ErrorState {
  state: 'error';
  error: string;
}

type RequestState<T> = LoadingState | SuccessState<T> | ErrorState;
```

In this example, we define three interfaces to represent different states of a network request: LoadingState, SuccessState, and ErrorState. Each interface has a state property with a unique literal type that acts as the discriminant. The union type RequestState<T> can be any one of these states, with the SuccessState allowing for a generic type T to represent the data returned by a successful request.

Here is a function that handles different request states and performs appropriate actions:

```
function handleRequestState<T>(state: RequestState<T>): void {
  switch (state.state) {
    case 'loading':
      console.log('Loading...');
      break;
    case 'success':
      console.log('Data:', state.data);
      break;
    case 'error':
      console.error('Error:', state.error);
      break;
    default:
      throw new Error('Unknown state!');
  }
}
```

In this function, the switch statement checks the state property of the state argument. Depending on the value of state.state, the function takes different actions. TypeScript's type narrowing ensures that within each case block, the type of state is appropriately refined, allowing access to properties specific to each state type.

Discriminated unions provide a clear and type-safe way to handle multiple related types and their specific properties. They enable developers to write more maintainable and error-resistant code by making sure that all possible cases are explicitly handled.

In practice, discriminated unions are used in various scenarios such as state management, error handling, and representing complex data structures that can be one of several types.

7.12 Recursive Types

Recursive types in TypeScript enable us to define types that reference themselves. This is particularly useful in various data structures like linked lists, trees, and graphs, where a type can nest within itself. Understanding recursive types is essential for grasping more complex type relationships and ensuring type safety in scenarios involving nested or hierarchical data.

To begin, consider the definition of a simple recursive type for a linked list. A linked list is a data structure where each element points to the next element in the list. In TypeScript, we can define such a structure using a recursive type definition:

```
type LinkedList<T> = {
    value: T;
    next: LinkedList<T> | null;
};
```

Here, LinkedList<T> is a generic type that holds a value of type T and a next property that can either be another LinkedList<T> or null, indicating the end of the list.

Similarly, recursive types are instrumental in defining tree structures. Consider a binary tree, where each node has at most two children:

```
type BinaryTree<T> = {
    value: T;
    left: BinaryTree<T> | null;
    right: BinaryTree<T> | null;
};
```

In the above example, BinaryTree<T> is a generic type that includes a value of type T and two children, left and right, each of which can either be another BinaryTree<T> or null.

Another practical use of recursive types is in the representation of JSON structures in TypeScript. JSON objects can contain other JSON objects, arrays of JSON objects, or simple values. We can define a recursive type to represent a JSON value:

```
type JSONValue =
    | string
    | number
    | boolean
    | null
    | JSONArray
    | JSONObject;

interface JSONArray extends Array<JSONValue> {}

interface JSONObject {
    [key: string]: JSONValue;
}
```

Here, JSONValue is a union type that can be any of the basic JSON data types: string, number, boolean, null, or recursively, an JSONArray or JSONObject. The JSONArray type extends the Array interface to hold JSONValue elements, while JSONObject is an indexed type that holds JSONValue properties.

```
{
  "name": "John",
  "age": 30,
  "isStudent": false,
  "courses": ["Math", "Science"],
  "address": {
    "street": "123 Main St",
    "city": "Anytown"
  }
}
```

To type the above JSON structure, TypeScript leverages the recursively defined JSONValue type, ensuring type safety and consistent validation across all elements.

Recursive types can also intersect with other advanced TypeScript features, such as conditional types, to create more flexible and powerful type definitions. For instance, to implement a deep read-only transformation for any nested object structure, we can define:

```
type DeepReadonly<T> =
  T extends object
  ? { readonly [K in keyof T]: DeepReadonly<T[K]> }
  : T;
```

In this example, DeepReadonly<T> is a recursive conditional type. If T extends object, each property of T is recursively transformed into a read-only version; otherwise, the type remains unchanged. This approach ensures that deeply nested properties are correctly marked as read-only, adhering to immutability practices.

Recursive types are a powerful feature in TypeScript, allowing for complex, self-referential type definitions that are essential in many programming contexts. Understanding and utilizing recursive types can significantly enhance the robustness and maintainability of TypeScript code, especially when dealing with intricate data structures.

Chapter 8

Error Handling and Exceptions

This chapter examines the mechanisms for error handling and exception management in TypeScript, highlighting differences from JavaScript. Topics include the use of the try-catch statement, creating and handling custom errors, error propagation, and best practices for error handling. Additionally, the chapter covers debugging techniques, using TypeScript's strict mode to prevent errors, handling errors when working with external libraries, and managing errors in asynchronous code, ensuring robust and resilient applications.

8.1 Introduction to Error Handling

Error handling is a critical aspect of software development, ensuring that applications can gracefully handle unexpected conditions and continue to operate or fail gracefully, providing meaningful feedback to the user. In TypeScript, similar to JavaScript, error handling is primarily managed via the try-catch statement, but with additional type-checking advantages inherent to TypeScript.

Errors can be categorized into three primary types: Syntax Errors, Runtime Errors, and Logical Errors. Syntax errors are predominantly caught during the compilation phase in TypeScript due to its static type-checking feature, reducing the likelihood of running into such issues during execution.

Runtime errors occur while the program is executing and can result from various causes, such as invalid operations, file-not-found exceptions, or null reference exceptions. Logical errors, the most insidious type, do not generate explicit errors but result in incorrect program behavior. These are typically identified through thorough testing and debugging processes.

An efficient error handling strategy in TypeScript involves anticipating potential problems and using error handling constructs to manage them. One of the fundamental constructs for this purpose is the try-catch-finally statement. The syntax is as follows:

```
try {
    // Code that might throw an error
} catch (error) {
    // Code to handle the error
} finally {
    // Code that will run regardless of whether an error occurred
}
```

In the try block, you place code that might throw an error. The catch block contains the code to handle the error. The finally block is optional and will execute regardless of whether an error was thrown, making it an ideal place for cleanup code.

When an error occurs inside a try block, control is immediately transferred to the catch block. If the error object is needed for further processes, it can be accessed within the catch block. For instance:

```
try {
    let jsonResponse = JSON.parse(someInvalidJsonString);
} catch (error) {
    if (error instanceof SyntaxError) {
        console.error("JSON Parsing Error: ", error.message);
    } else {
        console.error("General Error: ", error.message);
    }
}
```

Here, the instanceof operator is used to differentiate between a SyntaxError and a general error. This level of specificity is good practice as it allows for tailored error handling.

Custom error handling becomes powerful when combined with the ability to throw errors intentionally using the throw statement. This can be useful in functions where certain conditions are expected:

```
function validateAge(age: number) {
```

```
    if (age < 0 || age > 150) {
        throw new RangeError("Invalid age value.");
    }
}

try {
    validateAge(-5);
} catch (error) {
    console.error(error.message);
}
```

In this example, a RangeError is thrown if the age is out of a realistic range. This practice ensures that errors are caught early, maintaining the integrity and robustness of the application.

TypeScript's strict type-checking aids significantly in reducing runtime errors by catching potential issues at compile-time. For instance, TypeScript can enforce the type of the error object within the catch block to ensure that it is always of a specific type, promoting more predictable error handling. Consider the following:

```
try {
    throw new Error('Something went wrong');
} catch (error: unknown) {
    if (error instanceof Error) {
        console.error(error.message);
    }
}
```

Here, error is typed as unknown, a safer initial type, and then narrowed down using a type guard.

With the power of static type-checking, developers are encouraged to define more precise error types and handle them accordingly. Custom error classes can also be designed, inheriting from the built-in Error class to capture more specific error conditions:

```
class InvalidInputError extends Error {
    constructor(message: string) {
        super(message);
        this.name = "InvalidInputError";
    }
}

try {
    throw new InvalidInputError('This is an invalid input.');
} catch (error: unknown) {
    if (error instanceof InvalidInputError) {
        console.error("Custom Error: ", error.message);
    }
}
```

By defining custom error types, applications can be more expressive and precise in their error handling.

Proper integration of error handling in TypeScript not only ensures the application's robustness and resilience but also enhances the developer's ability to debug and maintain code effectively. The forthcoming sections will delve deeper into the nuances of error handling, including error propagation, custom error creation, and best practices for handling errors in asynchronous operations. The goal is to build a comprehensive understanding that leverages TypeScript's unique strengths for robust and resilient application development.

8.2 JavaScript and TypeScript Error Handling Differences

Error handling is an essential aspect of any programming language as it determines how efficiently a program can handle unexpected situations. JavaScript, as a dynamically typed language, has a different approach to error handling compared to TypeScript, which introduces static typing on top of JavaScript. Understanding these differences is crucial for taking full advantage of TypeScript's capabilities.

JavaScript uses the try-catch mechanism for error handling. This method catches exceptions thrown by the code within the try block and allows for custom handling in the catch block. The syntax is straightforward and effective for synchronous code:

```
try {
  // Code that may throw an error
  riskyFunction();
} catch (error) {
  console.error('An error occurred:', error.message);
}
```

In JavaScript, error is an object that holds information about the error, such as the message and stack trace. However, because JavaScript is dynamically typed, the type of error is not enforced. This can lead to scenarios where non-error objects might be thrown, making error handling inconsistent.

TypeScript inherits the try-catch mechanism from JavaScript but adds the advantage of static type-checking. In TypeScript, we can leverage types to ensure more structured and predictable error handling. By defining error types explicitly, TypeScript allows developers to catch and handle specific types of errors more effectively.

Firstly, let's examine how a TypeScript error handling block mirrors

JavaScript syntax:

```
try {
  // Code that may throw an error
  riskyFunction();
} catch (error) {
  console.error('An error occurred:', (error as Error).message);
}
```

In this example, error as Error is a TypeScript type assertion. This informs the TypeScript compiler to treat error as an instance of the standard Error object, enabling better type safety.

Moreover, TypeScript allows the creation of custom error classes which can be tailored to handle specific error types. This can be particularly useful for large applications where different modules may need to throw and handle distinct error types:

```
class CustomError extends Error {
  constructor(message: string) {
    super(message);
    this.name = 'CustomError';
  }
}

try {
  // Code that may throw an error
  throw new CustomError('This is a custom error');
} catch (error) {
  if (error instanceof CustomError) {
    console.error('Custom error occurred:', error.message);
  } else {
    console.error('An unexpected error occurred:', (error as Error).message);
  }
}
```

In this snippet, CustomError is a subclass of the built-in Error class. By checking error instanceof CustomError, the code can distinguish between different types of errors and handle them accordingly. This type of granularity is harder to achieve in vanilla JavaScript due to its lack of static typing.

Another key difference is how TypeScript interfaces with external libraries. JavaScript relies on runtime checks and has a more forgiving error handling culture. On the other hand, TypeScript's type system ensures that errors can be caught at compile time, reducing the likelihood of runtime errors.

Consider a common scenario interfacing with a third-party library:

```
const result = thirdPartyLibraryFunction();
if (result.error) {
  console.error('An error occurred:', result.error.message);
}
```

In JavaScript, this kind of error handling relies on runtime type checking. However, TypeScript leverages its type definitions to handle errors more robustly:

```
interface Result {
  data?: any;
  error?: Error;
}

const result: Result = thirdPartyLibraryFunction();
if (result.error) {
  console.error('An error occurred:', result.error.message);
} else {
  console.log('Data received:', result.data);
}
```

By defining an interface Result, TypeScript ensures that the result object conforms to a predictable structure. This predictability enhances the reliability of error handling and contributes to more maintainable code.

Furthermore, TypeScript's strict mode enforces robust error handling practices by preventing operations that could lead to runtime errors. For example, accessing a property on undefined or null values is a common source of errors in JavaScript. TypeScript mitigates this with strict null checks:

```
let value: string | null = getValue();
if (value) {
  console.log(value.trim());
} else {
  console.error('Value is null or undefined');
}
```

In this code, getValue returns a string or null. The strict null check ensures that value is not null before calling a method on it, thereby reducing the risk of runtime errors. JavaScript would only raise such issues at runtime, whereas TypeScript catches them at compile time.

Overall, while JavaScript and TypeScript share foundational error handling mechanisms, TypeScript's enhancements such as static typing, custom error classes, and compile-time checks offer a more structured and robust approach to managing errors. This leads to more predictable and maintainable code, especially in large-scale applications.

8.3 The try-catch Statement

The try-catch statement is a fundamental construct for error handling in TypeScript, providing a structured approach to manage runtime exceptions. By using try-catch, developers can segregate normal execution flow from error handling, ensuring that unexpected conditions do not cause the program to terminate abruptly.

The try block contains code that may result in an exception. If an exception is thrown within the try block, control is immediately transferred to the corresponding catch block. Each catch block can specify an error object that contains information about the error.

The basic syntax of a try-catch statement in TypeScript is as follows:

```
try {
    // Code that may throw an error
} catch (error) {
    // Code to handle the error
    console.error(error);
}
```

Consider the following example, which demonstrates the usage of a try-catch statement in a TypeScript program:

- A function, divideNumbers, is defined to perform division of two numbers.
- Within the function, a check is performed to prevent division by zero, throwing a custom error if the divisor is zero.
- The function invocation is wrapped in a try-catch block to catch and handle any errors.

```
function divideNumbers(numerator: number, denominator: number): number {
    if (denominator === 0) {
        throw new Error("Division by zero is not allowed.");
    }
    return numerator / denominator;
}

try {
    let result = divideNumbers(10, 0);
    console.log("Result: ", result);
} catch (error) {
    console.error("An error occurred:", error.message);
}
```

In this example:

- The function divideNumbers checks if the denominator equals zero. If true, it throws an Error object with a descriptive message.
- The try block calls divideNumbers with arguments that lead to a division by zero.
- The catch block captures the resulting error and logs an informative message to the console using error.message.

The catch block not only captures the error but can also be utilized to perform other operations such as logging the error details to files, notifying stakeholders via alerts, or even attempting a recovery process.

In addition to the simple try-catch, TypeScript also permits a finally block, which executes regardless of whether an error was thrown or caught. This is particularly useful for cleanup activities such as closing file handles or releasing resources.

The syntax incorporating the finally block is shown below:

```
try {
    // Code that may throw an error
} catch (error) {
    // Code to handle the error
    console.error(error);
} finally {
    // Code that executes regardless of an error being thrown
    console.log("Execution of try-catch-finally completed.");
}
```

For a comprehensive example, assume we expand the previous function to include resource management:

```
function divideNumbers(numerator: number, denominator: number): number {
    if (denominator === 0) {
        throw new Error("Division by zero is not allowed.");
    }
    return numerator / denominator;
}

try {
    console.log("Attempting division...");

    let result = divideNumbers(10, 0);
    console.log("Result: ", result);

} catch (error) {
    console.error("An error occurred: ", error.message);

} finally {
    console.log("Execution of division process completed.");
}
```

In this script:

- The finally block logs an informational message to indicate the end of the error handling process.
- The finally block will execute irrespective of the success or failure of the division operation.

It is important to note that handling exceptions appropriately is crucial in maintaining the stability and predictability of an application. Negligence in managing exceptions can lead to undetermined states, security vulnerabilities, and poor user experiences. The try-catch statement is a powerful tool that, when used judiciously, can significantly enhance the robustness of TypeScript applications.

8.4 Error Objects and Error Types

Error handling in TypeScript is deeply intertwined with the concept of Error objects. These objects serve as the cornerstone for conveying error-related information. TypeScript, inheriting this concept from JavaScript, allows developers to create, manipulate, and enhance error objects to improve debugging and reliability.

An Error object is instantiated using the Error constructor, which can be extended to build custom error objects. This section delves into the structure of Error objects, various built-in error types, and practical ways to utilize these objects for effective error handling.

Error objects encapsulate several properties:

- message: A string describing the error.
- name: The name of the error, typically matching the constructor name.
- stack: A string providing a stack trace at the point where the error was instantiated.

To create a standard Error object in TypeScript, you can use the following code:

```
const error = new Error("An unexpected error occurred");
console.log(error.message); // Output: An unexpected error occurred
console.log(error.name); // Output: Error
console.log(error.stack); // Output: Stack trace information
```

Besides the standard Error type, TypeScript also supports several built-in error types derived from the Error object. Some of the most commonly used are:

- EvalError: Indicates an error in the eval() function.
- RangeError: Signals an error when a value is not within the set or range of allowable values.
- ReferenceError: Occurs when de-referenced variables are not found.
- SyntaxError: Represents errors in code syntax.
- TypeError: Indicates a mismatch of data types or incompatible operations.
- URIError: Triggers errors related to malformed URIs.

Each of these error types inherits from the base Error class, facilitating specific error handling protocols. Below are examples demonstrating how to create and manage different error types:

EvalError Example

```
try {
    eval("invalid code");
} catch (e) {
    if (e instanceof EvalError) {
        console.error("An EvalError occurred");
    }
}
```

RangeError Example

```
function checkNumber(n: number) {
    if (n > 100) {
        throw new RangeError("The number exceeds the allowed range");
    }
}

try {
    checkNumber(200);
} catch (e) {
    if (e instanceof RangeError) {
        console.error(e.message); // Output: The number exceeds the allowed range
    }
}
```

ReferenceError Example

```
try {
    console.log(nonExistentVariable);
} catch (e) {
    if (e instanceof ReferenceError) {
        console.error("A ReferenceError occurred");
    }
}
```

SyntaxError Example

```
try {
    JSON.parse("{bad json}");
} catch (e) {
    if (e instanceof SyntaxError) {
        console.error("A SyntaxError occurred");
    }
}
```

TypeError Example

```
try {
    null.someMethod();
} catch (e) {
    if (e instanceof TypeError) {
        console.error("A TypeError occurred");
    }
}
```

URIError Example

```
try {
    decodeURIComponent("%");
} catch (e) {
    if (e instanceof URIError) {
        console.error("A URIError occurred");
    }
}
```

Creating and handling custom errors enhances a program's readability and robustness. By extending the Error class, developers can create domain-specific error types with customized properties and messages. Here is an example of a custom error class:

```
class ValidationError extends Error {
    constructor(public field: string, message: string) {
        super(message);
        this.name = "ValidationError";
    }
}

try {
    throw new ValidationError("email", "Invalid email address");
} catch (e) {
    if (e instanceof ValidationError) {
        console.error(`Validation error on field ${e.field}: ${e.message}`);
    }
}
```

ValidationError not only includes the error message but also which field caused the error, providing more context for debugging.

Error objects are fundamental to effective error handling in TypeScript, offering a structured and extensible approach to managing exceptions. Understanding both built-in and custom error types is crucial for writing robust and maintainable code.

8.5 Custom Errors

Custom errors play a critical role in creating robust applications by providing specific and meaningful feedback about what went wrong, thus making it easier to debug and maintain the code base. While TypeScript leverages JavaScript's inherent error-handling capabilities, it also offers the ability to define custom error types that can be used to signal application-specific error conditions.

To create a custom error in TypeScript, we extend the built-in Error class. This allows the new error to inherit properties and methods of the native Error object, ensuring compatibility with the existing error-handling mechanisms.

Here is an example of defining a custom error type called ValidationError.

```
class ValidationError extends Error {
    constructor(message: string) {
        super(message); // (1) Call the constructor of the parent class (Error)
        this.name = 'ValidationError'; // (2) Assign a name to the error
    }
}
```

In this example, the ValidationError class extends the Error class. The super method call (1) invokes the constructor of the parent class, passing the error message. This ensures that properties like message and stack are correctly initialized. We also set the name property (2) to differentiate this custom error from other errors.

To use this custom error type, we can create an instance of ValidationError and throw it when needed.

```
function validateUserInput(input: string) {
    if (input.length < 5) {
        throw new ValidationError('Input must be at least 5 characters long.');
    }
```

```
    // Further validation logic...
}

try {
    validateUserInput('abc');
} catch (error) {
    if (error instanceof ValidationError) {
        console.error(error.message); // Output: Input must be at least 5 characters
            long.
    } else {
        console.error('An unexpected error occurred');
    }
}
```

In the validateUserInput function, we check the length of the input. If the input does not meet the criteria, we throw a ValidationError with a specified message.

When this function is called within a try-catch block, we catch the error and check if it is an instance of ValidationError. This specific instance check enables handling of different types of errors distinctly, providing meaningful responses based on the error type.

Furthermore, extending the concept of custom errors can be critical for building an application with multiple layers and complex logic. Consider the following example of extending the base custom error for more specific error conditions:

```
class DatabaseError extends Error {
    constructor(message: string) {
        super(message);
        this.name = 'DatabaseError';
    }
}

class ConnectionError extends DatabaseError {
    constructor(message: string) {
        super(message);
        this.name = 'ConnectionError';
    }
}

class QueryError extends DatabaseError {
    constructor(message: string) {
        super(message);
        this.name = 'QueryError';
    }
}
```

In this code snippet, we define a base custom error DatabaseError then extend it into two more specific error types: ConnectionError and QueryError. This hierarchical structure allows for very precise error signaling relevant to the application's different domains.

Handling these hierarchical errors follows the same pattern:

```
try {
    // Some database logic...
    throw new ConnectionError('Failed to connect to database.');
} catch (error) {
    if (error instanceof ConnectionError) {
        console.error('Database connection issue:', error.message);
    } else if (error instanceof QueryError) {
        console.error('Database query issue:', error.message);
    } else if (error instanceof DatabaseError) {
        console.error('General database error:', error.message);
    } else {
        console.error('An unexpected error occurred');
    }
}
```

In this handler, we check for the most specific error types first and handle them accordingly. This approach not only ensures that the error-handling logic is specific and detailed but also that the broader error conditions can be handled appropriately.

When defining custom errors, it's also essential to maintain consistency and clarity in the error messages, ensuring that they are descriptive and facilitate easier debugging and problem resolution.

By leveraging custom errors, developers can create a more controlled and defined error-handling strategy that aligns closely with the application's logic and requirements, thus making the application more robust and easier to maintain.

8.6 Throwing Errors

TypeScript, like JavaScript, provides a mechanism to throw errors using the throw statement. This statement is used to indicate that an error or exceptional condition has occurred. When an error is thrown, the normal flow of program execution is interrupted, and control is transferred to the nearest catch block that can handle the error. If no such block exists, the error propagates up the call stack and eventually results in an unhandled exception.

The following example demonstrates the basic usage of the throw statement:

```
function riskyOperation() {
    let success = Math.random() > 0.5;
    if (!success) {
        throw new Error("The operation failed");
    }
    return "Operation succeeded";
}
```

```
try {
    console.log(riskyOperation());
} catch (error) {
    console.error(error.message);
}
```

In this example, the function riskyOperation may either succeed or fail, determined by a random boolean value. If the operation fails, an Error object is thrown. The calling code uses a try-catch block to handle the potential error. If the error is thrown, the catch block logs the error message to the console.

The throw statement can be used to throw any expression, not just Error objects. It's common to throw instances of built-in error types like RangeError, ReferenceError, SyntaxError, and TypeError. You can also throw custom error objects, which will be covered in the section on custom errors.

```
function checkAge(age: number) {
    if (age < 0) {
        throw new RangeError("Age cannot be negative");
    }
    if (typeof age !== "number") {
        throw new TypeError("Age must be a number");
    }
    return age;
}

try {
    console.log(checkAge(-1));
} catch (error) {
    console.error(error.message);
}
```

Here, the checkAge function performs two validations on the input age parameter. It throws a RangeError if the age is negative and a TypeError if the age is not a number. The try-catch block handles any errors thrown by checkAge and logs the error messages accordingly.

Throwing custom errors allows you to provide more context and specific information about the exceptional conditions that occur in your application. A custom error is typically a subclass of the built-in Error class.

```
class ValidationError extends Error {
    constructor(message: string) {
        super(message);
        this.name = "ValidationError";
    }
}

function validateUserInput(input: string) {
    if (input.trim() === "") {
        throw new ValidationError("Input cannot be empty");
```

```
    }
    return input;
}

try {
    console.log(validateUserInput(" "));
} catch (error) {
    if (error instanceof ValidationError) {
        console.error("Validation failed: " + error.message);
    } else {
        console.error("An unexpected error occurred: " + error.message);
    }
}
```

In this example, a ValidationError class is defined, extending the built-in Error class. The validateUserInput function throws a ValidationError if the input string is empty after trimming whitespace. The calling code checks if the error is an instance of ValidationError and handles it accordingly. This pattern allows different types of errors to be distinguished and handled in a more granular manner.

Throwing errors in asynchronous code, particularly in functions that return promises, requires careful consideration. Unhandled promise rejections can lead to issues that are difficult to trace and debug.

```
async function fetchData(url: string) {
    let response = await fetch(url);
    if (!response.ok) {
        throw new Error(`HTTP error! status: ${response.status}`);
    }
    return await response.json();
}

fetchData("https://example.com/data")
    .then(data => {
        console.log("Data fetched successfully:", data);
    })
    .catch(error => {
        console.error("Failed to fetch data:", error.message);
    });
```

In this asynchronous example, the fetchData function performs an HTTP request using the fetch API. If the response is not ok, an Error is thrown with a message containing the HTTP status. The caller of fetchData handles any errors by attaching a catch method to the promise returned by the function.

To ensure robust error handling in asynchronous code, always provide catch handlers when working with promises, and use try-catch blocks within async functions whenever possible.

8.7 Error Propagation and Handling

Error propagation and handling play an essential role in developing resilient TypeScript applications. Propagating errors ensures that when an error occurs in one part of a program, proper notification mechanisms exist to inform other parts, allowing for appropriate handling or recovery measures.

In TypeScript, error propagation typically involves re-throwing errors to higher levels in the call stack until a suitable handler is found. This process aligns closely with error propagation mechanisms in JavaScript but benefits from TypeScript's type system to add type safety and predictability.

The following example demonstrates how an error propagates through nested function calls:

```
function levelOne(): void {
    try {
        levelTwo();
    } catch (error) {
        console.error("An error occurred in levelOne: ", error);
    }
}

function levelTwo(): void {
    levelThree();
}

function levelThree(): void {
    throw new Error("An unexpected error in levelThree");
}

levelOne();
```

When levelThree() throws an error, it propagates up to levelTwo(), and since levelTwo() does not have a catch block, it continues to propagate until levelOne(), where it is caught and logged.

```
An error occurred in levelOne: Error: An unexpected error in levelThree
```

Key concepts involved in error propagation and handling include:

- try-catch blocks
- throw statements
- Call stack unwinding

To improve error propagation strategies, developers should be familiar with these concepts and tailor error-handling mechanisms to specific contexts.

Usage of try-catch-finally

The try-catch-finally statement is a structured way to manage exceptions, ensuring necessary cleanup actions regardless of whether an error occurred. The finally block executes after the try and catch blocks, offering a reliable approach to release resources or perform other completion tasks.

Example:

```
function processFile(fileName: string): void {
    let fileHandle: FileHandle | null = null;
    try {
        fileHandle = openFile(fileName);
        const data = fileHandle.read();
        processData(data);
    } catch (error) {
        console.error("An error occurred:", error);
    } finally {
        if (fileHandle) {
            fileHandle.close();
        }
    }
}
```

In this snippet, the finally block ensures the file is closed irrespective of an error being thrown, maintaining resource integrity.

Error Propagation Best Practices

- Ensure every asynchronous function has appropriate error handling.
- Utilize try-catch blocks judiciously. Overusing them can degrade readability and performance.
- Contextualize errors with additional information to aid troubleshooting.
- Avoid catching generic errors unless re-throwing or logging them with additional context.
- Combine type guards with instanceof checks to handle specific error types gracefully.

Transforming low-level errors into domain-specific errors can provide more actionable context. For instance:

```
class DatabaseError extends Error {
    constructor(message: string) {
        super(message);
        this.name = "DatabaseError";
    }
}

class ValidationError extends Error {
    constructor(message: string) {
        super(message);
        this.name = "ValidationError";
    }
}
```

```
function queryDatabase(query: string): void {
    try {
        const result = executeQuery(query);
        processResult(result);
    } catch (error) {
        if (error instanceof ConnectionError) {
            throw new DatabaseError("Failed to connect to the database");
        } else if (error instanceof SyntaxError) {
            throw new DatabaseError("Query syntax is incorrect");
        } else {
            throw error;
        }
    }
}
```

This approach helps aggregate and transform technical errors into logical ones, aligning with the business context and making code easier to debug and maintain.

Developers should apply consistent error-handling patterns across the codebase. For asynchronous code, using async/await combined with try-catch enhances readability and error management:

```
async function fetchData(url: string): Promise<Response> {
    try {
        const response = await fetch(url);
        if (!response.ok) {
            throw new Error(`HTTP error! status: ${response.status}`);
        }
        return response;
    } catch (error) {
        console.error("Fetch error:", error);
        throw error; // Propagate the error further
    }
}
```

Properly propagating and handling errors ensures robustness, by managing faults gracefully at the correct abstraction level, leading to more reliable TypeScript applications.

8.8 Best Practices in Error Handling

Effective error handling is critical in the development of robust TypeScript applications. Proper techniques ensure that code can gracefully manage unexpected situations, provide meaningful feedback, and maintain the application's stability. Several best practices guide the implementation of error handling in TypeScript.

- **Use try-catch Sparingly**
  Placing try-catch blocks around code segments can prevent unforeseen exceptions from crashing the application. However, overuse can lead to code clutter and reduce readability. It is essential to localize error handling to areas where exceptions are anticipated and where recovery is possible. For instance, IO operations and network requests are prime candidates for try-catch constructs.

```
try {
    const response = await fetchData();
    processResponse(response);
} catch (error) {
    handleError(error);
}
```

- **Provide Meaningful Error Messages**
  Error messages should be clear, informative, and assist debugging. Avoid generic messages like "An error occurred." Instead, provide context that can help identify the issue and its source. This may include indicating the function where the error happened and relevant variable values.

```
if (!data) {
    throw new Error("Data not found in function processData");
}
```

- **Use Custom Error Types**
  Creating custom error types aids in distinguishing between different error conditions. This practice involves extending the base Error class to create specific errors relevant to the application's domain.

```
class ValidationError extends Error {
    constructor(message: string) {
        super(message);
        this.name = "ValidationError";
    }
}
```

```
throw new ValidationError("Invalid input data");
```

- **Leverage TypeScript's Strict Mode**
TypeScript's strict mode can catch potential issues at compile time before they reach runtime. Enabling strict mode through the tsconfig.json file includes settings such as strictNullChecks and noImplicitAny, which help prevent null or undefined errors and demand explicit typing, respectively.

```
// tsconfig.json
{
    "compilerOptions": {
        "strict": true
    }
}
```

- **Centralize Error Handling**
Centralizing error handling, especially for asynchronous operations, can simplify maintaining and updating code. Using middleware in frameworks like Express or services in Angular to manage errors centrally is a robust approach.

```
// Express.js middleware example
app.use((err, req, res, next) => {
    console.error(err.stack);
    res.status(500).send('Something broke!');
});
```

- **Avoid Catching Code Errors**
Logical errors or bugs should be detected via testing and debugging rather than try-catch blocks. Error handling via try-catch should be reserved for handling exceptional conditions and runtime errors.

```
// Instead of using try-catch to handle a null pointer exception
if (!data) {
    console.error("Data should not be null");
    return;
}
```

- **Ensure Resource Cleanup**
Use the finally clause to release resources regardless of whether an error occurred. This guarantees that files, network connections, or other resources do not remain open, leading to potential memory leaks or other issues.

```
try {
    const connection = openConnection();
```

```
    // Perform operations
} catch (error) {
    console.error("Operation failed", error);
} finally {
    closeConnection();
}
```

- **Implement Comprehensive Logging**
  Logging helps monitor the application's behavior and diagnose issues. Integrate robust logging mechanisms to track errors, including structured logging to capture detailed error contexts and stack traces.

```
logger.error(`Error in processData: ${error.message}`, { stack: error.stack });
```

- **Gracefully Handle Promise Rejections**
  Unhandled promise rejections can cause application crashes. Ensure that all promises are properly handled using catch statements or with the async/await syntax enclosed within try-catch blocks.

```
fetchData()
    .then(data => processData(data))
    .catch(error => handleError(error));
```

8.9 Debugging TypeScript Code

Effective debugging is essential in TypeScript to identify and fix errors promptly. This section explores various debugging techniques tailored for TypeScript, from utilizing built-in tools to leveraging TypeScript's advanced features.

To debug TypeScript, developers often employ tools and methodologies specific to the language:

- Integrated Development Environments (IDEs) and editors with debugging support.
- Source maps for interpreting compiled JavaScript back to TypeScript.
- Logging mechanisms.
- Conditional breakpoints and watches.

- Debugger statements.

Using IDEs and Editors

Modern IDEs such as Visual Studio Code (VS Code), WebStorm, and others provide comprehensive debugging support for TypeScript. Here, the emphasis is on VS Code due to its popularity and robust support for TypeScript debugging.

In VS Code, set up debugging by creating a launch.json configuration file. This file resides within the .vscode directory. Below is an example configuration:

```
{
    "version": "0.2.0",
    "configurations": [
        {
            "type": "node",
            "request": "launch",
            "name": "Launch Program",
            "skipFiles": ["<node_internals>/**"],
            "program": "${workspaceFolder}/app.ts",
            "preLaunchTask": "tsc: build - tsconfig.json",
            "sourceMaps": true,
            "outFiles": ["${workspaceFolder}/dist/**/*.js"]
        }
    ]
}
```

This configuration specifies the node type, uses the launch request type, and identifies app.ts as the entry point for debugging. It also includes source maps for accurate TypeScript debugging and instructs the debugger to build the TypeScript code using tsconfig.json prior to launching.

Source Maps

Source maps are essential for debugging TypeScript since the actual execution occurs in JavaScript. TypeScript can generate these maps, preserving the mapping between the TypeScript code and the transpiled JavaScript. Enable source maps by configuring the tsconfig.json file:

```
{
    "compilerOptions": {
        "sourceMap": true
    }
}
```

When a source map is generated, it links the compiled JavaScript back to the original TypeScript, making the debugging process more intuitive. This feature acknowledges TypeScript's typing and structure during breakpoints and step-through debugging sessions.

Logging Mechanisms

Logging functions as a straightforward mechanism for debugging TypeScript. The console.log function displays variable values or execution paths. However, efficiently using logging involves strategic placement and sufficient detail to capture the program's state without cluttering the output. Example usage can be seen below:

```
function calculateArea(radius: number): number {
    console.log(`Input radius: ${radius}`); // Log input
    const area = Math.PI * radius * radius;
    console.log(`Computed area: ${area}`); // Log output
    return area;
}
```

The above example logs the function's input and calculated area, aiding in tracing the function's execution at critical points.

Conditional Breakpoints and Watches

Advanced debugging involves setting conditional breakpoints and watches. Conditional breakpoints pause execution only when specific conditions are met. In VS Code, set a conditional breakpoint by right-clicking the breakpoint icon in the left gutter and entering the condition:

```
radius > 5
```

Watches allow monitoring variables and expressions at runtime. In VS Code, add watches via the "Run and Debug" view, ensuring continuous insight into variable states.

Debugger Statements

Strategically use debugger statements within the TypeScript code to invoke breakpoints programmatically:

```
function calculateArea(radius: number): number {
    debugger; // Trigger breakpoint
    const area = Math.PI * radius * radius;
    return area;
```

```
}
```

Upon execution, the debugger halts at the debugger statement, permitting inspection of the call stack and variables' current values.

Common Issues and Solutions

Debugging TypeScript often exposes common issues such as mismatched types, uninitialized variables, or incorrect function signatures. Relying on TypeScript's type system significantly minimizes such issues, as types are verified at compile time. When encountering a runtime error, re-examine type declarations and ensure accurate initialization and usage.

For instance, uninitialized variables might result in a TypeError:

```
let uninitializedVar: number;
console.log(uninitializedVar.toFixed(2)); // Throws TypeError
```

Prevent such issues by initializing variables with default values if applicable:

```
let initializedVar: number = 0;
console.log(initializedVar.toFixed(2)); // Outputs: 0.00
```

Equipping yourself with these debugging tools and techniques enhances error detection and resolution, fostering robust and error-free TypeScript applications.

8.10 Using TypeScript's Strict Mode for Error Prevention

TypeScript's strict mode serves as a powerful tool for preventing errors and enhancing code reliability. When enabled, strict mode enforces a set of stringent rules that catch common programming errors and ensure that all variables are explicitly typed and initialized.

To enable strict mode, modify the tsconfig.json file. The relevant configuration is:

```
{
  "compilerOptions": {
    "strict": true
  }
}
```

Activating strict mode encompasses several compiler options including:

- strictNullChecks
- noImplicitAny
- strictBindCallApply
- strictFunctionTypes
- strictPropertyInitialization
- noImplicitThis
- alwaysStrict

We will delve into each of these options to understand their roles in error prevention within TypeScript.

strictNullChecks eliminates the pervasive issue of null and undefined type errors by disallowing them as valid values unless explicitly declared. This ensures that variables are always initialized appropriately:

```
let name: string;
name = null; // Error: Type 'null' is not assignable to type 'string'
```

Conversely, with strictNullChecks enabled, you must specify that a variable can hold null or undefined:

```
let name: string | null;
name = null; // Valid
```

Next, noImplicitAny forces the developer to explicitly annotate types, preventing unintentional type inference to any:

```
function add(a, b) {
  return a + b; // Error: Parameter 'a' implicitly has an 'any' type
}
```

By declaring parameter types, the function becomes safer and clearer:

```
function add(a: number, b: number): number {
  return a + b; // Valid
}
```

The strictBindCallApply option tightens checks on the methods bind, call, and apply, ensuring type safety when manipulating the context of this:

```
let foo = function(x: number, y: number): void { };
let bar = foo.bind(null, "5"); // Error: Argument of type '"5"' is not assignable to
      parameter of type 'number'
```

strictFunctionTypes opts for a more conservative variable relation checking methodology to prevent function assignments with incompatible types, reducing errors during function assignments:

```
type Greet = (message: string) => void;
let greet: Greet;
greet = (message: number) => console.log(message); // Error: Cannot assign a '
      number' to a 'string'
```

Property initialization issues are addressed with the strictPropertyInitialization option, ensuring that all declared properties within a class are correctly initialized before usage:

```
class User {
  name: string; // Error: Property 'name' has no initializer and is not definitely
        assigned in the constructor
}
```

This issue is remedied using definite assignment assertions or initializing properties in the constructor:

```
class User {
  name!: string; // Definite assignment assertion
  constructor() {
    this.name = "John Doe"; // Initialization
  }
}
```

The noImplicitThis option prevents this from being assigned the any type within functions, ensuring that you explicitly type this:

```
function f() {
  this.x = 10; // Error: 'this' implicitly has type 'any' because it does not have a type
        annotation
}
```

Incorrectly annotated this must be fixed by specifying its type:

```
function f(this: { x: number }) {
  this.x = 10; // Valid
}
```

Lastly, alwaysStrict applies use strict directive globally, enabling strict mode in all JavaScript files, which catches potential silent errors and ensures that the entire codebase adheres to a rigorous interpretation and execution of the ECMAScript standard.

8.11 Working with External Libraries and Error Handling

When integrating external libraries within a TypeScript project, error handling becomes more critical and intricate. External libraries, often written in JavaScript, may not enforce TypeScript's type safety and can introduce runtime errors that are harder to trace. This section explores strategies and best practices for handling errors stemming from such libraries, ensuring your TypeScript applications remain robust and resilient.

Firstly, it is crucial to understand the type definitions of the libraries being used. TypeScript provides the capability to install type definitions via DefinitelyTyped, where the type definitions are hosted. Such type definitions assist the TypeScript compiler in type-checking code that interacts with these libraries.

Consider a sample scenario where we integrate Lodash, a popular JavaScript utility library, into a TypeScript project:

```
import _ from 'lodash';

const data: any[] = [1, 2, 3, 'four', 5];

// Using Lodash function to sum array elements
const sum = _.sum(data);
console.log(sum);
```

In this example, importing Lodash and calling the _.sum function results in a type error because the array data contains a string. This leads to runtime errors as _.sum expects an array of numbers. Here, the importance of proper type definition and checking comes into play.

To safely handle such errors, follow these practices:

- **Install and Use Type Definitions:** Ensure type definitions for third-party libraries are installed. For Lodash, install the corresponding types:

```
npm install --save @types/lodash
```

- **Explicit Type Checking:** Validate and sanitize inputs before passing them to external library functions.

```
const data: (number | string)[] = [1, 2, 3, 'four', 5];
const numericData = data.filter((item): item is number => typeof item === '
    number');
```

```
const sum = _.sum(numericData);
console.log(sum); // Output: 11
```

- **Error Handling with Try-Catch:** Wrap potentially error-prone library calls with try-catch blocks.

```
try {
    const data: any[] = [1, 2, 3, 'four', 5];
    const sum = _.sum(data);
    console.log(sum);
} catch (error) {
    console.error('Error calculating sum:', error);
}
```

In addition to these practices, handling errors effectively when the library functions return promises is essential. Libraries often return promises, especially those interacting with asynchronous operations such as network requests.

Let's examine an example using the Axios library for HTTP requests:

```
import axios from 'axios';

async function fetchData(url: string): Promise<void> {
    try {
        const response = await axios.get(url);
        console.log('Data:', response.data);
    } catch (error) {
        console.error('Error fetching data:', error);
    }
}

fetchData('https://api.example.com/data');
```

In this example, the `fetchData` function utilizes the Axios library to make an HTTP GET request. The `try-catch` block ensures any network or transformation-related errors are caught and logged.

There are scenarios where errors from external libraries propagate further in the application. For instance, when building larger applications with multiple services relying on external libraries, error handling should be centralized to ensure consistency and effectiveness.

A centralized error handling mechanism can be implemented using custom error classes and a global error handler:

```
class ExternalLibraryError extends Error {
    constructor(message: string) {
        super(message);
        this.name = 'ExternalLibraryError';
    }
}
```

```
function globalErrorHandler(error: Error): void {
    if (error instanceof ExternalLibraryError) {
        console.error('Handled ExternalLibraryError:', error.message);
    } else {
        console.error('Unhandled error:', error.message);
    }
}

async function fetchData(url: string): Promise<void> {
    try {
        const response = await axios.get(url);
        console.log('Data:', response.data);
    } catch (error) {
        throw new ExternalLibraryError('Failed to fetch data from external API: ' +
                error.message);
    }
}

fetchData('https://api.example.com/data')
    .catch(globalErrorHandler);
```

In this implementation, the 'ExternalLibraryError' class encapsulates errors specific to external libraries, allowing the global error handler to react appropriately.

Another vital aspect is leveraging TypeScript's type assertions and guards, ensuring library functions' return values conform to expected types:

```
import axios, { AxiosResponse } from 'axios';

interface ApiResponse {
    id: number;
    data: string;
}

async function fetchData(url: string): Promise<void> {
    try {
        const response: AxiosResponse<ApiResponse> = await axios.get(url);
        if (isApiResponse(response.data)) {
            console.log('Data:', response.data);
        } else {
            throw new ExternalLibraryError('Invalid response format');
        }
    } catch (error) {
        globalErrorHandler(error);
    }
}

function isApiResponse(data: any): data is ApiResponse {
    return data && typeof data.id === 'number' && typeof data.data === 'string';
}

fetchData('https://api.example.com/data');
```

The sample above defines the 'ApiResponse' interface and a type guard 'isApiResponse' to ensure the response object matches the expected structure before processing.

Ultimately, handling errors when working with external libraries in TypeScript necessitates meticulous type-checking, proper sanitization of inputs and outputs, and centralized error handling. By applying these principles, developers can mitigate risks and maintain the stability and reliability of their applications.

8.12 Error Handling in Asynchronous Code

Error handling in asynchronous code poses unique challenges. TypeScript provides robust mechanisms to manage these errors, drawing from its close ties with JavaScript's event-driven nature.

Asynchronous operations, typically facilitated by promises, the async/await syntax, and callback functions, require a distinct approach to error handling compared to synchronous code. Understanding these methods ensures that your application remains responsive and resilient.

Promises and Error Handling

Promises represent eventual completion or failure of asynchronous operations. They can be in one of three states: pending, fulfilled, or rejected. Handling promise rejections is crucial to prevent application crashes and ensure errors do not go unhandled.

Here's an example of error handling using promises:

```
function fetchData(url: string): Promise<Response> {
    return fetch(url)
        .then(response => {
            if (!response.ok) {
                throw new Error('Network response was not ok');
            }
            return response;
        })
        .catch(error => {
            console.error('There has been a problem with your fetch operation:', error);
            throw error; // Re-throw the error to propagate it if necessary
        });
}
```

In this example, if the fetch operation fails, the error is caught by the catch block, logged to the console, and then re-thrown to allow further handling upstream.

Async/Await and Try/Catch

The async/await syntax provides a more concise way to work with asynchronous code, making it easier to read and maintain. Error handling in async/await mimics synchronous try/catch blocks.

Here's the equivalent of the previous example using async/await:

```
async function fetchData(url: string): Promise<Response> {
    try {
        const response = await fetch(url);
        if (!response.ok) {
            throw new Error('Network response was not ok');
        }
        return response;
    } catch (error) {
        console.error('There has been a problem with your fetch operation:', error);
        throw error; // Re-throw the error to propagate it if necessary
    }
}
```

Here, any errors that occur within the try block will be caught by the catch block, logged, and re-thrown if required.

Error Handling with Multiple Asynchronous Operations

When dealing with multiple asynchronous operations, it's essential to manage potential errors across all operations. Below is an example showcasing how to handle errors when performing multiple independent asynchronous tasks:

```
async function performMultipleRequests(urls: string[]): Promise<void> {
    try {
        const requests = urls.map(async url => {
            const response = await fetch(url);
            if (!response.ok) {
                throw new Error(`Failed to fetch from ${url}`);
            }
            return response;
        });

        const results = await Promise.all(requests);
        console.log('All requests successful:', results);
    } catch (error) {
        console.error('One or more requests failed:', error);
    }
}
```

In this example, Promise.all is used to execute multiple fetch operations concurrently. If any promise is rejected, the catch block handles the error.

Handling Errors in Event Listeners

Handling errors within event listeners also requires careful consideration. Event listeners often operate asynchronously, responding to user input or other events.

```
document.getElementById('myButton')?.addEventListener('click', async () => {
    try {
        const response = await fetchData('https://api.example.com/data');
        console.log('Data fetched successfully:', response);
    } catch (error) {
        console.error('Error occurred while fetching data:', error);
    }
});
```

In this code, an event listener on a button handles potential errors that may occur during the fetchData operation.

Uncaught Promise Rejections

An important aspect of error handling in asynchronous code is managing uncaught promise rejections. Beginning with Node.js 15, and similarly in browsers, unhandled promise rejections may terminate the process or trigger warnings.

To centrally handle unhandled rejections, you can listen to the unhandledrejection event:

```
window.addEventListener('unhandledrejection', event => {
    console.error('Unhandled promise rejection:', event.reason);
    // Perform any cleanup or logging needed
});
```

For Node.js environments, process events can be used:

```
process.on('unhandledRejection', (reason, promise) => {
    console.error('Unhandled promise rejection:', reason);
    // Perform any cleanup or logging needed
});
```

Effective error handling in asynchronous code ensures that your application behaves predictably and remains robust even when confronted with unexpected conditions.

Chapter 9

Asynchronous Programming

This chapter addresses asynchronous programming in TypeScript, beginning with callbacks and higher-order functions. It covers promises, including their syntax and chaining, and introduces async and await for simplifying asynchronous code. Topics include error handling in asynchronous contexts, parallel and sequential execution, async iterators, and working with the Fetch API. The chapter also discusses consuming third-party asynchronous libraries, concurrency patterns, and best practices for writing efficient and maintainable asynchronous code.

9.1 Introduction to Asynchronous Programming

Asynchronous programming allows a program to operate efficiently by executing potentially blocking operations, such as network requests, file system interactions, or lengthy computations, without interrupting the overall flow of application execution. This concept becomes critical in modern applications, where responsiveness and performance are paramount.

JavaScript, and by extension TypeScript, is inherently asynchronous. The event-driven nature of JavaScript manifests in features like callback functions, promises, and the async/await syntax. These constructs enable developers to manage asynchronous operations effectively.

In a synchronous execution model, operations are performed sequentially, each one waiting for the previous one to complete before starting. This model is straightforward but can cause issues in scenarios that require non-blocking operations. For instance, a network request to fetch data from a server may take an indeterminate amount of time, and a synchronous model would cause the entire program to wait, leading to a poor user experience.

Asynchronous programming decouples the execution of potentially blocking operations from the main control flow, allowing the program to continue executing other tasks while waiting for the asynchronous operation to complete. When the asynchronous operation finishes, it typically triggers some form of notification mechanism, such as a callback or promise resolution, to process the result.

Consider the following TypeScript code snippet demonstrating a synchronous HTTP request using the fetch API:

```
function fetchDataSync() {
  const response = fetch('https://api.example.com/data').then(response => {
    return response.json();
  });
  console.log(response);
}
```

In this synchronous model, console.log(response) will not execute until the fetch request is complete, causing the program to wait.

Asynchronous programming provides mechanisms to avoid such blocking behavior. Initially, JavaScript used callback functions. Callbacks are functions passed as arguments to other functions and invoked when an asynchronous operation completes. Here's an example of using a callback to handle an asynchronous HTTP request:

```
function fetchDataWithCallback(url: string, callback: (data: any) => void) {
  fetch(url)
    .then(response => response.json())
    .then(data => callback(data))
    .catch(error => console.error('Error:', error));
}

fetchDataWithCallback('https://api.example.com/data', data => {
  console.log(data);
});
```

In the code above, the fetchDataWithCallback function performs a fetch operation and uses a callback to handle the fetched data once it is available. The console.log(data) statement runs only after the fetch operation completes without blocking other parts of the program.

Although callbacks are useful, they can lead to deeply nested structures known as "callback hell," making the code difficult to read and maintain. To mitigate these issues, JavaScript introduced promises. A promise represents an operation that hasn't completed yet but is expected to in the future. A promise can be in one of three states: pending, fulfilled, or rejected.

The following is an example of using promises to handle an asynchronous operation:

```
function fetchDataWithPromise(url: string): Promise<any> {
  return fetch(url).then(response => response.json());
}

fetchDataWithPromise('https://api.example.com/data')
  .then(data => {
    console.log(data);
  })
  .catch(error => {
    console.error('Error:', error);
  });
```

In this model, the fetchDataWithPromise function returns a promise, and the caller can handle the resolution or rejection using then and catch methods. This decouples the management of the asynchronous operation from the operation itself, allowing for chaining and more sophisticated error handling.

Despite their advantages, promises can still be slightly cumbersome for complex sequences of asynchronous operations. Therefore, TypeScript, building on ECMAScript 2017 (ES8), adopted the async and await syntax to streamline asynchronous code further.

The async keyword designates a function as asynchronous, allowing the use of the await keyword within it. The await keyword pauses the execution of the async function until the awaited promise resolves, simplifying asynchronous code to appear more like synchronous code.

An example using async and await:

```
async function fetchDataAsync(url: string): Promise<void> {
  try {
    const response = await fetch(url);
    const data = await response.json();
    console.log(data);
  } catch (error) {
    console.error('Error:', error);
  }
```

```
}
fetchDataAsync('https://api.example.com/data');
```

This snippet demonstrates an improved readability and maintainability. The async function fetches data and waits for each asynchronous operation to complete in a sequence without deeply nested callbacks or chaining multiple then calls.

Understanding asynchronous programming principles and mastering various approaches, from callbacks to async/await, is foundational for developing efficient and responsive TypeScript applications. Equipped with these concepts, developers can handle real-world asynchronous tasks, ensuring applications remain performant and user-friendly.

9.2 Callbacks and Higher-Order Functions

Asynchronous programming in TypeScript often utilizes callbacks and higher-order functions to manage operations that do not complete immediately. This section delves into these concepts, providing a foundational understanding necessary for more advanced topics in asynchronous programming.

A callback is a function passed as an argument to another function that is invoked inside the outer function to complete some form of routine or action. Here's a simple example of a synchronous callback:

```
// A synchronous callback example
function greet(name: string, callback: (message: string) => void) {
    const message = `Hello, ${name}`;
    callback(message);
}

function displayMessage(message: string) {
    console.log(message);
}

greet('Alice', displayMessage);
```

```
Hello, Alice
```

In this example, greet takes a name and a callback. The callback is executed within greet, showcasing a basic callback pattern. However, real-world scenarios typically involve asynchronous callbacks, commonly encountered with I/O operations like reading files, network requests, or database operations.

```
// An asynchronous callback example with setTimeout
```

```
function fetchData(callback: (data: string) => void) {
    setTimeout(() => {
        callback('Data fetched after delay');
    }, 2000);
}

function processData(data: string) {
    console.log(data);
}

fetchData(processData);
```

```
Data fetched after delay
```

In fetchData, setTimeout simulates an asynchronous operation, invoking callback after two seconds. This pattern is prevalent in Node.js, especially when dealing with file systems, HTTP operations, and more. Here's an example using Node.js fs module:

```
import * as fs from 'fs';

// Asynchronous readFile operation with a callback
fs.readFile('example.txt', 'utf8', (err, data) => {
    if (err) {
        console.error('Error reading file:', err);
        return;
    }
    console.log('File content:', data);
});
```

```
File content: (Content of example.txt)
```

The callback function provided to fs.readFile handles the file reading operation's result, processing the data if the operation is successful or handling errors if it's not.

A higher-order function is a function that takes one or more functions as arguments or returns a function as a result. Higher-order functions are fundamental to functional programming and enable powerful abstraction mechanisms.

Creating higher-order functions can simplify asynchronous programming in specific scenarios. Here, higher-order functions can accept callbacks and provide utilities for managing these callbacks more effectively:

```
// Higher-order function example
function calculate(a: number, b: number, operation: (x: number, y: number) =>
      number): number {
    return operation(a, b);
}

const add = (x: number, y: number) => x + y;
const subtract = (x: number, y: number) => x - y;
```

```
console.log(calculate(5, 3, add)); // Outputs 8
console.log(calculate(5, 3, subtract)); // Outputs 2
```

Here, calculate is a higher-order function taking an operation callback, abstracting away the operations to perform on the provided numbers.

In asynchronous programming, higher-order functions can manage asynchronous control flows. Consider the following example, which demonstrates a higher-order function handling asynchronous tasks sequentially:

```
function doTask(taskName: string, duration: number, callback: (result: string) => void)
    {
    setTimeout(() => {
        callback(`Task ${taskName} completed`);
    }, duration);
}

function doTasksSequentially(tasks: Array<{name: string, duration: number}>,
      finalCallback: () => void) {
    let index = 0;

    function nextTask() {
        if (index < tasks.length) {
            doTask(tasks[index].name, tasks[index].duration, (result) => {
                console.log(result);
                index++;
                nextTask();
            });
        } else {
            finalCallback();
        }
    }

    nextTask();
}

const tasks = [
    {name: 'A', duration: 1000},
    {name: 'B', duration: 2000},
    {name: 'C', duration: 1500}
];

doTasksSequentially(tasks, () => {
    console.log('All tasks completed');
});
```

```
Task A completed
Task B completed
Task C completed
All tasks completed
```

The doTasksSequentially function orchestrates a series of asynchronous tasks, ensuring they execute in sequence by recursively invoking the nextTask function. This technique is foundational to more sophisticated control flow libraries, paving the way for understanding Promises and async/await constructs.

Callbacks and higher-order functions are essential in managing asynchronous programming, enabling developers to build flexible, maintainable code that handles asynchronous operations effectively. Understanding these foundational concepts prepares you for more advanced mechanisms in TypeScript.

9.3 Promises: Basics and Syntax

In this section, we delve into the concept of promises in TypeScript, elucidating their basic structure and syntax. Promises provide a more manageable and cleaner approach to handling asynchronous operations compared to traditional callback functions. This section will walk through the creation and consumption of promises, explaining the core concepts along the way.

A promise in TypeScript is an object that represents the eventual completion (or failure) of an asynchronous operation and its resulting value. A promise has three states: pending, fulfilled, and rejected. Initially, a promise is in the pending state. It transitions to fulfilled if the asynchronous operation completes successfully or to rejected if it fails. The state of the promise can be observed and acted upon using the then() and catch() methods.

To create a promise, the Promise constructor is used. The constructor accepts a function, called the *executor*, which takes two arguments: resolve and reject. The resolve function is called when the asynchronous operation completes successfully, passing the result as an argument. The reject function is called when the operation fails, passing the error as an argument.

Here is an example of creating a simple promise:

```
const myPromise = new Promise<number>((resolve, reject) => {
  const success = true; // Simulate success or failure
  if (success) {
    resolve(42); // Operation succeeded, returning result 42
  } else {
    reject(new Error('Failed operation')); // Operation failed, returning error
  }
});
```

In this example, myPromise is a promise that is resolved with the value 42 if success is true, and is rejected with an error message if success is false.

To consume promises, we use the then() and catch() methods. The then() method takes two callback functions: one for handling the resolved value and one for handling the rejection reason (optional). The catch() method is a shortcut for .then(null, rejectionCallback).

Here is an example of consuming the myPromise created above:

```
myPromise.then((value) => {
  console.log(`Promise resolved with value: ${value}`);
}).catch((error) => {
  console.error(`Promise rejected with error: ${error.message}`);
});
```

In this example, if myPromise is resolved, the first callback in then() logs the resolved value. If myPromise is rejected, the catch() method logs the error message.

Promises can be chained, allowing for sequential execution of asynchronous operations. Each then() call returns a new promise, enabling further chaining. This is particularly useful for operations that depend on the result of the previous operation.

Consider the following example:

```
const fetchData = new Promise<string>((resolve, reject) => {
  setTimeout(() => { resolve('Data received'); }, 1000); // Simulate async operation
});

fetchData.then((data) => {
  console.log(data); // Logs: Data received
  return 'Processing data';
}).then((processedData) => {
  console.log(processedData); // Logs: Processing data
  return 'Data processed';
}).then((finalData) => {
  console.log(finalData); // Logs: Data processed
}).catch((error) => {
  console.error(error.message);
});
```

The above example demonstrates chaining multiple then() calls. Each then() method returns a new promise, which allows the next then() method to handle its resolved value. If any of the operations fail, the catch() method ensures proper error handling.

Promises also have methods for handling multiple asynchronous operations. The Promise.all() method takes an array of promises and returns a single promise that resolves when all the promises in the array resolve. The resolved value is an array of values from the resolved promises. If any of the promises in the array reject, the returned promise is immediately rejected with the reason from the first rejected promise.

Here is an example using Promise.all():

```
const promise1 = new Promise<number>((resolve) => setTimeout(() => resolve(1),
    1000));
const promise2 = new Promise<number>((resolve) => setTimeout(() => resolve(2),
    2000));
const promise3 = new Promise<number>((resolve) => setTimeout(() => resolve(3),
    3000));

Promise.all([promise1, promise2, promise3]).then((values) => {
  console.log(values); // Logs: [1, 2, 3]
}).catch((error) => {
  console.error(`One of the promises failed: ${error.message}`);
});
```

In this example, promise1, promise2, and promise3 resolve after 1, 2, and 3 seconds, respectively. The Promise.all() method ensures that the then() block executes only when all promises have resolved, logging the array [1, 2, 3].

Additionally, Promise.race() method can be used to return a promise that resolves or rejects as soon as one of the promises in the array resolves or rejects. It is practical when the timing of the first resolved promise matters more than waiting for all to complete.

Consider this example:

```
const fastPromise = new Promise<number>((resolve) => setTimeout(() => resolve(1),
    1000));
const slowPromise = new Promise<number>((resolve) => setTimeout(() => resolve
    (2), 3000));

Promise.race([fastPromise, slowPromise]).then((value) => {
  console.log(value); // Logs: 1
}).catch((error) => {
  console.error(`A promise failed: ${error.message}`);
});
```

In this illustration, fastPromise resolves in 1 second while slowPromise resolves in 3 seconds. The Promise.race() method resolves immediately with the value from fastPromise, logging 1.

Understanding these concepts of promises lays a strong foundation for writing asynchronous code in TypeScript in a clean and manageable way, avoiding the pitfalls of nested callbacks, commonly referred to as "callback hell." The next sections will build on this understanding, exploring advanced promise usage, error handling, and integrating promises with async and await.

9.4 Chaining Promises

Chaining promises is a technique in TypeScript that allows for executing asynchronous operations in a sequence. This methodology ensures that each subsequent operation starts only after the previous one has successfully completed, allowing for a clean and readable flow of asynchronous tasks.

In TypeScript, chaining promises is achieved using the then method, which is available on every promise. Each then method returns a new promise, enabling the chaining of further then methods. This approach can be elegantly integrated to handle complex asynchronous flows.

First, let's consider a straightforward example of promise chaining in TypeScript:

```
function firstAsyncOperation(): Promise<number> {
    return new Promise((resolve, reject) => {
        setTimeout(() => {
            console.log("First operation completed.");
            resolve(1);
        }, 1000);
    });
}

function secondAsyncOperation(input: number): Promise<number> {
    return new Promise((resolve, reject) => {
        setTimeout(() => {
            console.log("Second operation completed.");
            resolve(input + 1);
        }, 1000);
    });
}

firstAsyncOperation().then(result => {
    return secondAsyncOperation(result);
}).then(finalResult => {
    console.log("Final result:", finalResult);
});
```

In this example, we have two asynchronous functions, firstAsyncOperation and secondAsyncOperation. The firstAsyncOperation resolves after one second, logging a message and returning the value 1. This result is then passed to the secondAsyncOperation, which resolves after another second. The final result of 2 is logged to the console.

Promise chaining provides an efficient way to handle a series of dependent asynchronous operations while avoiding callback hell. This technique is particularly beneficial when the output of one asynchronous operation serves as the input for the next.

One key aspect of promise chaining is error propagation. If any promise in the chain fails, control is immediately transferred to the nearest catch method. Here's an enhanced version of the previous example with error handling:

```
function firstAsyncOperation(): Promise<number> {
    return new Promise((resolve, reject) => {
        setTimeout(() => {
            console.log("First operation completed.");
            resolve(1);
        }, 1000);
    });
}

function secondAsyncOperation(input: number): Promise<number> {
    return new Promise((resolve, reject) => {
        setTimeout(() => {
            console.log("Second operation completed.");
            if (input > 1) {
                reject(new Error("Input must not be greater than 1"));
            } else {
                resolve(input + 1);
            }
        }, 1000);
    });
}

firstAsyncOperation().then(result => {
    return secondAsyncOperation(result);
}).then(finalResult => {
    console.log("Final result:", finalResult);
}).catch(error => {
    console.error("Error encountered:", error.message);
});
```

In this code, the secondAsyncOperation may reject if the input is greater than 1, in which case the catch block captures and logs the error message.

Another power of promise chaining is its capability to handle sequences of promises that depend on both previous results and new data. For example, fetching multiple resources in sequence:

```
function fetchResourceA(): Promise<string> {
    return new Promise((resolve, reject) => {
        setTimeout(() => {
            console.log("Fetched resource A");
            resolve("Data from A");
        }, 1000);
    });
}

function fetchResourceB(): Promise<string> {
    return new Promise((resolve, reject) => {
        setTimeout(() => {
            console.log("Fetched resource B");
            resolve("Data from B");
        }, 1000);
    });
}
```

```
fetchResourceA().then(dataA => {
    console.log(dataA);
    return fetchResourceB();
}).then(dataB => {
    console.log(dataB);
});
```

In this situation, fetchResourceA and fetchResourceB are executed in sequence, with dataA and dataB printed in the order they are resolved.

Chaining promises also simplifies managing multiple asynchronous operations that can be run concurrently using Promise.all. Each promise runs independently, and once they all resolve, the results are handled together:

```
function fetchResourceA(): Promise<string> {
    return new Promise((resolve, reject) => {
        setTimeout(() => {
            console.log("Fetched resource A");
            resolve("Data from A");
        }, 1000);
    });
}

function fetchResourceB(): Promise<string> {
    return new Promise((resolve, reject) => {
        setTimeout(() => {
            console.log("Fetched resource B");
            resolve("Data from B");
        }, 1000);
    });
}

Promise.all([fetchResourceA(), fetchResourceB()]).then(results => {
    console.log("All resources fetched:");
    results.forEach((data, index) => {
        console.log(`Resource ${index + 1}: ${data}`);
    });
}).catch(error => {
    console.error("Error fetching resources:", error.message);
});
```

Here, fetchResourceA and fetchResourceB are executed concurrently, and their results are processed once all promises have resolved.

Incorporating promise chaining in TypeScript results in more maintainable and comprehensible asynchronous code. It enables handling sequences, dependencies, and concurrent operations with ease, fostering a robust approach to modern asynchronous programming.

9.5 Async and Await: Simplifying Asynchronous Code

Asynchronous code in TypeScript is significantly simplified through the use of async functions and the await keyword. These additions provide a way to write asynchronous code that appears synchronous, making it easier to understand, maintain, and reason about.

async functions enable you to write functions that return promises but look like they contain synchronous code. By prepending the async keyword before a function, the function automatically returns a promise, and within this function, you can use the await keyword.

The await keyword can only be used inside async functions, and it pauses the execution of the function until the Promise settles. It effectively replaces the .then() and .catch() methods used with promises, leading to cleaner and more concise code.

To illustrate, consider the following example:

```
function fetchData(url: string): Promise<any> {
    return fetch(url)
        .then(response => response.json())
        .catch(error => console.log(error));
}
```

This promise-based function can be rewritten using async and await:

```
async function fetchData(url: string): Promise<any> {
    try {
        const response = await fetch(url);
        const data = await response.json();
        return data;
    } catch (error) {
        console.log(error);
    }
}
```

This change allows for a more linear flow of execution and simplifies error handling through the use of try...catch blocks.

Detailed Breakdown

1. **Async Functions**:

A function is marked as async by prefixing it with the async keyword. This makes the function automatically return a Promise, even if it does not explicitly do so.

```
async function exampleFunction() {
    return 123;
```

```
}
```

In the example above, exampleFunction() returns a promise that resolves to the value 123. Even though the return type appears to be a number, it is wrapped in a Promise due to the async keyword.

2. **The Await Expression**:

The await keyword is used to pause the execution of an async function until a Promise is resolved. It can only be used inside async functions. Here's an example:

```
async function getNumber(): Promise<number> {
    return 42;
}

async function getResult() {
    let num = await getNumber();
    console.log(num); // Output: 42
}
```

Inside getResult(), the execution will be paused at the await getNumber() line until getNumber()'s promise resolves. Once resolved, its result is assigned to num and the function proceeds with the next line, logging the number.

3. **Handling Asynchronous Loops**:

Consider a scenario where you need to fetch data from multiple URLs sequentially. Using async and await, you can perform these operations in a straightforward manner:

```
const urls = ['url1', 'url2', 'url3'];

async function processUrls(urls: string[]) {
    for (const url of urls) {
        const data = await fetchData(url);
        console.log(data);
    }
}

async function fetchData(url: string): Promise<any> {
    try {
        const response = await fetch(url);
        const data = await response.json();
        return data;
    } catch (error) {
        console.log(error);
    }
}

processUrls(urls);
```

This example demonstrates how to loop through an array of URLs and fetch data sequentially using async and await.

Performance Considerations

While async and await greatly simplify the syntax of asynchronous operations, it is important to be aware of potential performance implications. For tasks that can be executed concurrently, running them sequentially as shown in the previous example might not be optimal.

To execute multiple asynchronous operations concurrently, Promise.all() can be used in conjunction with async and await:

```
async function processUrlsConcurrently(urls: string[]) {
    const promises = urls.map(url => fetchData(url));
    const results = await Promise.all(promises);
    results.forEach(data => console.log(data));
}
```

In this enhanced example, Promise.all(promises) will wait until all promises in the array promises are resolved, which will be significantly faster than processing each URL sequentially.

Error Handling

One of the most beneficial aspects of combining async and await with try...catch blocks is the enhanced error handling. For instance:

```
async function processUrlsWithErrorHandling(urls: string[]) {
    for (const url of urls) {
        try {
            const data = await fetchData(url);
            console.log(data);
        } catch (error) {
            console.error(`Failed to fetch data from ${url}:`, error);
        }
    }
}
```

By wrapping the await fetchData(url) call within a try...catch block, any errors thrown by fetchData() will be caught and can be handled appropriately. This localized error handling enables more robust and maintainable asynchronous functions.

9.6 Error Handling in Asynchronous Code

Error handling in asynchronous programming is crucial for building robust applications. Given that asynchronous operations, such as API calls, file I/O, and timers, can fail, it's important to handle errors gracefully to maintain the reliability and stability of the application. In this section, we will explore various methods for handling errors in asynchronous TypeScript code, focusing on callbacks, promises, and async/await.

Consider the following general strategies for handling errors in asynchronous code:

- Using error-first callbacks
- Handling errors in promises using catch
- Employing try/catch blocks with async/await
- Advanced techniques like Promise.all, Promise.race, and custom error handling middleware

We will begin by examining how errors are managed using callbacks.

```
function readFile(filePath: string, callback: (error: Error | null, data?: string) => void)
    {
    setTimeout(() => {
        // Simulate reading a file
        const error = new Error("File not found");
        callback(error, null);
    }, 1000);
}

readFile("/path/to/file", (error, data) => {
    if (error) {
        console.error("An error occurred:", error.message);
    } else {
        console.log("File contents:", data);
    }
});
```

In this example, the callback function takes an error parameter as its first argument, which is null if no error occurred. This pattern is known as the error-first callback. The error can be checked and handled inside the callback function, ensuring that the error is caught and managed appropriately.

Next, let's consider how errors can be handled using promises. Promises provide a cleaner way to handle asynchronous operations compared to callbacks. Errors in promises can be handled with the catch method.

```
function readFile(filePath: string): Promise<string> {
    return new Promise<string>((resolve, reject) => {
        setTimeout(() => {
            // Simulate reading a file
            const error = new Error("File not found");
            reject(error);
```

```
        }, 1000);
    });
}

readFile("/path/to/file")
    .then(data => {
        console.log("File contents:", data);
    })
    .catch(error => {
        console.error("An error occurred:", error.message);
    });
```

In the example above, the promise is rejected with an error if the file read operation fails. The .catch method is used to catch and handle this error, simplifying the error handling process compared to callbacks.

With the introduction of async/await, asynchronous code becomes even more readable and maintainable. Errors in async functions can be handled using try/catch blocks, much like synchronous code.

```
async function readFile(filePath: string): Promise<string> {
    return new Promise<string>((resolve, reject) => {
        setTimeout(() => {
            // Simulate reading a file
            const error = new Error("File not found");
            reject(error);
        }, 1000);
    });
}

async function main() {
    try {
        const data = await readFile("/path/to/file");
        console.log("File contents:", data);
    } catch (error) {
        console.error("An error occurred:", error.message);
    }
}

main();
```

In this example, the try/catch block is used to handle errors that may occur when calling the readFile function. This approach is often preferred due to its synchronous-like style and simplicity.

Let's consider some advanced error handling techniques. One common pattern is using Promise.all to handle multiple asynchronous operations simultaneously. If any of the promises in the array are rejected, the entire Promise.all call is rejected.

```
const promise1 = Promise.resolve("Result 1");
const promise2 = Promise.reject(new Error("Error in promise2"));
const promise3 = Promise.resolve("Result 3");

Promise.all([promise1, promise2, promise3])
    .then(results => {
```

```
        console.log("All promises resolved:", results);
    })
    .catch(error => {
        console.error("One or more promises were rejected:", error.message);
    });
```

In this example, promise2 is rejected, causing the Promise.all call to be rejected. The catch method handles the error, enabling developers to respond appropriately to the failure of any promise in the group.

Another pattern, Promise.race, can be used to handle errors when you are interested in the first promise that settles (either resolves or rejects).

```
const slowPromise = new Promise((resolve) => {
    setTimeout(() => {
        resolve("Slow promise resolved");
    }, 2000);
});

const fastPromise = new Promise((resolve, reject) => {
    setTimeout(() => {
        reject(new Error("Fast promise rejected"));
    }, 1000);
});

Promise.race([slowPromise, fastPromise])
    .then(result => {
        console.log("Race won by:", result);
    })
    .catch(error => {
        console.error("Race error:", error.message);
    });
```

In this example, Promise.race is used to wait for the first promise to settle. Since fastPromise is rejected first, the catch method is triggered to handle the error.

Finally, creating custom error handling middleware for promises can further enhance error handling in complex applications. This middleware can centralize error handling, making the code more maintainable and consistent.

```
function handlePromiseError(promise: Promise<any>): Promise<any> {
    return promise.catch(error => {
        // Custom error handling logic
        console.error("Custom error handler:", error.message);
        // Optionally rethrow the error or return a default value
        throw error; // Or return a default value, e.g.,: return Promise.resolve("default
            value");
    });
}

const promise = new Promise((resolve, reject) => {
    reject(new Error("Promise rejected"));
});
```

```
handlePromiseError(promise)
    .then(data => {
        console.log("Promise resolved:", data);
    })
    .catch(error => {
        console.error("Handled error:", error.message);
    });
```

In this final example, handlePromiseError is a middleware function that adds custom error handling to promises. This centralizes error logging and handling logic, making it easier to maintain and update.

Effective error handling in asynchronous code is essential for building reliable and maintainable applications. Understanding and applying these techniques ensures that your application can respond gracefully to failures, improving both user experience and overall application stability.

9.7 Parallel and Sequential Execution

In TypeScript, and JavaScript in general, understanding the distinction between parallel and sequential execution of asynchronous tasks is crucial for writing efficient code. The Event Loop is a core part of how JavaScript manages asynchronous operations, but it's important to note that JavaScript is single-threaded. This means that true parallel execution, as seen in multi-threaded environments, isn't directly possible within the main thread. However, with features such as Promises, async/await, and Web Workers, we can simulate parallelism and efficiently manage sequential tasks.

Sequential Execution:

Sequential execution, as the name implies, involves executing tasks one after another. This can be achieved using async/await which makes asynchronous code appear synchronous and easier to follow.

Consider the following example where three asynchronous functions need to be executed in sequence:

```
async function taskOne(): Promise<void> {
  console.log("Task One starting");
  return new Promise((resolve) => setTimeout(() => {
    console.log("Task One completed");
    resolve();
  }, 1000));
}

async function taskTwo(): Promise<void> {
```

```
  console.log("Task Two starting");
  return new Promise((resolve) => setTimeout(() => {
    console.log("Task Two completed");
    resolve();
  }, 1000));
}

async function taskThree(): Promise<void> {
  console.log("Task Three starting");
  return new Promise((resolve) => setTimeout(() => {
    console.log("Task Three completed");
    resolve();
  }, 1000));
}

async function executeSequentially(): Promise<void> {
  await taskOne();
  await taskTwo();
  await taskThree();
}

executeSequentially();
```

The output of this code will demonstrate the sequential nature of the execution:

```
Task One starting
Task One completed
Task Two starting
Task Two completed
Task Three starting
Task Three completed
```

Here, each task starts only after the previous task has completed, ensuring sequential execution.

Parallel Execution:

Parallel execution aims to execute multiple tasks simultaneously. This can significantly improve performance when tasks are independent and do not need to wait for one another to complete.

Using Promise.all, multiple promises can be resolved in parallel. Here is how the previous example can be modified to run tasks in parallel:

```
async function executeInParallel(): Promise<void> {
  const taskPromises = [taskOne(), taskTwo(), taskThree()];
  await Promise.all(taskPromises);
}

executeInParallel();
```

The output of running this code is:

```
Task One starting
Task Two starting
Task Three starting
Task One completed
Task Two completed
Task Three completed
```

In this case, all tasks are initiated almost simultaneously, and they complete independently of each other. It's important to note that the tasks' completion order might vary depending on their individual execution time.

Handling Results of Parallel Execution:

Sometimes, the results of parallel tasks need to be aggregated or processed further. Promise.all returns an array of results, corresponding to the input promises:

```
async function fetchResource1(): Promise<string> {
  return new Promise((resolve) => setTimeout(() => resolve("Resource 1 data"),
        1000));
}

async function fetchResource2(): Promise<string> {
  return new Promise((resolve) => setTimeout(() => resolve("Resource 2 data"),
        2000));
}

async function fetchResource3(): Promise<string> {
  return new Promise((resolve) => setTimeout(() => resolve("Resource 3 data"),
        1500));
}

async function aggregateResults(): Promise<void> {
  const results = await Promise.all([fetchResource1(), fetchResource2(), fetchResource3
        ()]);
  console.log(results); // ["Resource 1 data", "Resource 2 data", "Resource 3 data"]
}

aggregateResults();
```

In this example, aggregateResults waits for all three resources to be fetched and then logs the results.

Error Handling in Parallel Executions:

When using Promise.all, if any of the promises reject, the entire Promise.all rejects. To handle errors gracefully:

```
async function fetchDataSafe(fetchFunction: () => Promise<string>): Promise<string
      > {
  try {
    return await fetchFunction();
  } catch (error) {
    console.error("Error fetching data:", error);
    return "default data";
  }
}
```

```
async function safeParallelExecution(): Promise<void> {
  const results = await Promise.all([
    fetchDataSafe(fetchResource1),
    fetchDataSafe(fetchResource2),
    fetchDataSafe(fetchResource3)
  ]);
  console.log(results);
}

safeParallelExecution();
```

Here, each fetch function is wrapped in fetchDataSafe, ensuring that an error in one does not disrupt the others.

Understanding and utilizing both parallel and sequential execution patterns in TypeScript leads to more efficient and maintainable asynchronous code.

9.8 Using Async Iterators

Async iterators offer a powerful tool in TypeScript to handle asynchronous data streams. Following the introduction of async and await, async iterators extend the capabilities of handling sequences of asynchronous operations. This section will delve into the specifics of async iterators in TypeScript, demonstrating their syntax, usage, and integration with existing asynchronous constructs such as Promise and async function.

AsyncIterator is an interface that represents the asynchronous iteration protocol, which allows consuming data sources asynchronously. Instead of blocking the execution while waiting for data, async iterators enable the implementation of a non-blocking code execution pattern. The primary operations of async iterators are encapsulated within for-await-of loops.

Firstly, let us define the basic syntax and demonstrate an example to solidify the concept:

```
async function* asyncGenerator() {
    yield 'First data chunk';
    yield new Promise(resolve => setTimeout(() => resolve('Second data chunk'),
          1000));
    yield 'Third data chunk';
}

async function processData() {
    for await (const chunk of asyncGenerator()) {
        console.log(chunk);
```

```
    }
}
processData();
```

The output of running the code above will be:

```
First data chunk
Second data chunk
Third data chunk
```

In the asyncGenerator function, each yield statement pauses the generator and returns a value. If the yielded value is a promise, the iteration waits for the promise to resolve before continuing. The loop in processData consumes these chunks as they become available, with for-await-of ensuring that each step completes before executing the next.

To elaborate further, consider the practical scenario where we might be fetching data from an API that pages the results. Here is an example integration:

```
async function* fetchPages(url: string) {
    let nextPageUrl: string | null = url;
    while (nextPageUrl) {
        const response = await fetch(nextPageUrl);
        if (!response.ok) break;
        const data = await response.json();
        yield data;
        nextPageUrl = data.nextPage; // Assuming the response has a 'nextPage' field
    }
}

async function processApiPages() {
    const apiUrl = 'https://api.example.com/data';
    for await (const page of fetchPages(apiUrl)) {
        console.log('Received page:', page);
    }
}

processApiPages();
```

The above code sequentially fetches and processes paginated API responses. fetchPages is an async generator function that continues to request additional pages as long as nextPageUrl is valid. Each page is yielded to the consumer of the iterator, processApiPages, which processes each page asynchronously.

Central to mastering async iterators is understanding the typical use cases and limitations. Async iterators excel in scenarios requiring handling of data streams where each chunk is processed one at a time. Examples include reading files, handling user input streams, or making successive API calls. However, if the use case involves simple promise chains or single asynchronous operations, async iterators may introduce unnecessary complexity.

Complex scenarios can further benefit from the integration with other asynchronous patterns. Consider using async iterators in combination with concurrency primitives or within complex workflows. For example, parallel processing chunks:

```
async function* parallelProcess(generator: AsyncGenerator<any>, concurrency:
    number) {
  const queue: Promise<void>[] = [];
  for await (const item of generator) {
    if (queue.length >= concurrency) {
      await Promise.race(queue);
    }
    const promise = processItem(item);
    queue.push(promise);
    promise.finally(() => {
      queue.splice(queue.indexOf(promise), 1);
    });
  }
  await Promise.all(queue);
}

async function processItem(item: any): Promise<void> {
  // Process item asynchronously
  console.log('Processing:', item);
}

// Usage
async function executeParallelProcessing() {
  const items = asyncGenerator();
  await parallelProcess(items, 3);
}

executeParallelProcessing();
```

In this code, parallelProcess allows parallel processing of items yielded by the asyncGenerator function, with a specified concurrency limit. By waiting for Promise.race(queue), the function maintains the desired level of concurrency, ensuring no more than the specified number of items are processed simultaneously.

Async iterators are thus integral to scalable and responsive TypeScript applications, enabling developers to write readable, efficient, and maintainable asynchronous code. By incorporating these constructs, asynchronous programming tasks become considerably more manageable, facilitating orderly and systematic data handling.

9.9 Working with Fetch API

The Fetch API is a modern interface that allows you to make HTTP requests to servers from web browsers. It provides a more powerful and flexible feature set than the traditional XMLHttpRequest API. In this section, we will explore how to integrate the Fetch API in TypeScript, focusing on making requests, handling responses, and managing errors effectively.

At its core, the Fetch API involves the fetch() function, which takes a URL as an argument and returns a promise that resolves to the response to that request.

```
fetch('https://api.example.com/data')
  .then(response => response.json())
  .then(data => {
    console.log(data);
  })
  .catch(error => {
    console.error('Error fetching data:', error);
  });
```

In the example above, the fetch() function makes a GET request to the specified URL. The response is then parsed into JSON format using the response.json() method. Finally, the parsed data is logged to the console. Any errors that occur during the request or parsing phases are caught and logged using the catch method.

Handling different types of responses is an essential aspect of working with the Fetch API. The response object provides various methods such as text(), json(), blob(), and formData(), corresponding to different content types.

```
fetch('https://api.example.com/image')
  .then(response => response.blob())
  .then(imageBlob => {
    const imageObjectURL = URL.createObjectURL(imageBlob);
    const imgElement = document.createElement('img');
    imgElement.src = imageObjectURL;
    document.body.appendChild(imgElement);
  })
  .catch(error => {
    console.error('Error fetching image:', error);
  });
```

The blob() method indicates that the response type is expected to be binary data (such as an image or PDF). After obtaining the binary data, we create an object URL using URL.createObjectURL() and set it as the source of an img element, which is then appended to the document.

When working with APIs that require authentication, headers must be included in the request options. The Fetch API supports adding headers via the Headers interface or directly in the fetch request options.

```
const headers = new Headers();
headers.append('Authorization', 'Bearer your-token-here');

fetch('https://api.example.com/secure-data', {
  method: 'GET',
  headers: headers
})
  .then(response => response.json())
  .then(data => {
    console.log('Secure data:', data);
  })
  .catch(error => {
    console.error('Error fetching secure data:', error);
  });
```

In this example, an Authorization header is added to the request to access secure data. The Headers interface provides a convenient way to manage multiple headers.

The Fetch API also supports other HTTP methods such as POST, PUT, PATCH, and DELETE. These methods can be specified in the request options by setting the method property.

```
const requestData = {
  name: 'John Doe',
  age: 30
};

fetch('https://api.example.com/users', {
  method: 'POST',
  headers: {
    'Content-Type': 'application/json'
  },
  body: JSON.stringify(requestData)
})
  .then(response => response.json())
  .then(data => {
    console.log('User created:', data);
  })
  .catch(error => {
    console.error('Error creating user:', error);
  });
```

Here, a POST request is made to create a new user. The request data is transformed into a JSON string using JSON.stringify() and included in the request body. The Content-Type header is set to application/json to indicate the request payload format.

Error handling is an integral part of working with the Fetch API. While the fetch() function's promise only rejects on network failure or if anything prevents the request from completing, it is important to check the response.ok property to handle HTTP response errors.

```
fetch('https://api.example.com/data')
  .then(response => {
    if (!response.ok) {
      throw new Error(`HTTP error! status: ${response.status}`);
    }
    return response.json();
  })
  .then(data => {
    console.log(data);
  })
  .catch(error => {
    console.error('Error fetching data:', error);
  });
```

In this example, an error is thrown if the response.ok property is false, which occurs for HTTP statuses outside the range 200–299. This approach ensures that only successful responses are processed further.

To improve the readability and maintainability of asynchronous code, the Fetch API can be combined with async and await. This allows asynchronous operations to be written in a synchronous style, making the code easier to follow.

```
async function fetchData(url: string): Promise<void> {
  try {
    const response = await fetch(url);
    if (!response.ok) {
      throw new Error(`HTTP error! status: ${response.status}`);
    }
    const data = await response.json();
    console.log(data);
  } catch (error) {
    console.error('Error fetching data:', error);
  }
}

fetchData('https://api.example.com/data');
```

In this example, the fetchData function is declared with the async keyword, allowing the use of await within its body. The await keyword pauses the execution of the fetchData function until the fetch promise and subsequent response.json() promise are resolved. Errors are handled using a normal try-catch block, which provides an intuitive way to catch and handle exceptions.

Combining the Fetch API with async and await not only enhances readability but also aligns with the modern ECMAScript features, making the code more maintainable and robust. Applying these patterns consistently results in cleaner and more efficient asynchronous operations.

9.10 Consuming Third-Party Asynchronous Libraries

When working on modern TypeScript projects, it is common to use third-party libraries to efficiently handle asynchronous operations. These libraries often provide pre-built functionalities that can simplify complex tasks, such as HTTP requests, database interactions, or file operations. This section delves into the practicalities of integrating and utilizing third-party asynchronous libraries in your TypeScript code, ensuring you take full advantage of their capabilities while maintaining code quality and readability.

One of the most widely used libraries for handling HTTP requests is Axios. Axios is a promise-based HTTP client for JavaScript and also supports TypeScript out of the box. We will start by exploring how to install, configure, and use Axios for making asynchronous HTTP requests.

To install Axios, you can use npm or yarn:

```
npm install axios
# or
yarn add axios
```

Once installed, you can import Axios into your TypeScript file and start making requests. Below is an example of how to perform a GET request to fetch data from an endpoint:

```
import axios from 'axios';

async function fetchData(url: string): Promise<void> {
    try {
        const response = await axios.get(url);
        console.log(response.data);
    } catch (error) {
        console.error('Error fetching data:', error);
    }
}

// Usage
fetchData('https://api.example.com/data');
```

In this example, the fetchData function is an asynchronous function that takes a URL string as an argument. It uses axios.get to make a GET request to the provided URL. The function logs the response data to the console if the request is successful; otherwise, it catches and logs any errors.

Axios also allows for configuration and customization, which can be beneficial when dealing with authentication, timeouts, or setting default headers. The following example demonstrates configuring Axios with a base URL and default headers:

```
const axiosInstance = axios.create({
    baseURL: 'https://api.example.com/',
    timeout: 1000,
    headers: { 'Authorization': 'Bearer YOUR_ACCESS_TOKEN' }
});

async function fetchUserData(userId: string): Promise<void> {
    try {
        const response = await axiosInstance.get(`users/${userId}`);
        console.log(response.data);
    } catch (error) {
        console.error('Error fetching user data:', error);
    }
}

// Usage
fetchUserData('12345');
```

In this instance, axios.create is used to create a new Axios instance with a base URL, a timeout of 1000 milliseconds, and a default Authorization header. The fetchUserData function leverages this instance to perform a GET request to fetch user data based on a user ID.

Another common third-party library used in asynchronous programming is node-fetch, which provides a fetch API for Node.js environments, similar to the browser's fetch. To install node-fetch, use the following command:

```
npm install node-fetch
# or
yarn add node-fetch
```

After installation, you can import and use node-fetch just like you would with the browser fetch API:

```
import fetch from 'node-fetch';

async function fetchData(url: string): Promise<void> {
    try {
        const response = await fetch(url);
        if (!response.ok) {
            throw new Error(`HTTP error! status: ${response.status}`);
        }
        const data = await response.json();
        console.log(data);
    } catch (error) {
        console.error('Error fetching data:', error);
    }
}

// Usage
fetchData('https://api.example.com/data');
```

In this example, the fetchData function performs a GET request to the provided URL using fetch. It checks if the response is ok and throws an error if not. It then parses the response as JSON and logs the data.

TypeScript provides excellent support for most popular JavaScript libraries, allowing you to utilize type definitions for better code completion, navigation, and error checking. For example, TypeScript automatically recognizes types from Axios, ensuring that you adhere to the library's API and catch type-related errors early during development.

When integrating third-party asynchronous libraries, it is essential to follow best practices to maintain code cleanliness and avoid common pitfalls like callback hell or unhandled promise rejections. Proper error handling using try...catch blocks and leveraging TypeScript's type checking can significantly improve the robustness and maintainability of your asynchronous code.

9.11 Concurrency Patterns

Concurrency in JavaScript and TypeScript involves managing multiple asynchronous operations efficiently to improve performance and resource utilization. TypeScript enhances this capability by adding type safety to asynchronous programming constructs. Various concurrency patterns exist to address different scenarios and requirements. This section delves into some of the widely-used patterns: async/await with error handling, the worker pattern, and task queues.

Async/Await with Error Handling:

The async/await syntax introduced in ES2017 simplifies writing and reading asynchronous code in TypeScript. By using async functions, the code resembles synchronous code, improving readability and maintainability. However, with the added benefit of type inference in TypeScript, error handling becomes more robust.

Consider the following example illustrating this pattern:

```
async function fetchData(url: string): Promise<any> {
    try {
        const response = await fetch(url);
        if (!response.ok) {
            throw new Error(`HTTP error! status: ${response.status}`);
        }
        const data = await response.json();
        return data;
    } catch (error) {
        console.error("Failed to fetch data:", error);
```

```
        throw error; // Propagate the error
    }
}
```

In this example, the fetchData function fetches data from a provided URL and handles potential errors using a try...catch block. The await expression pauses the function execution until the Promise is resolved or rejected, ensuring that any error thrown can be caught and properly managed.

The Worker Pattern:

The worker pattern is another essential concurrency pattern, leveraging web workers to offload heavy computational tasks away from the main thread. This pattern becomes increasingly relevant in the context of TypeScript, where strongly-typed interfaces improve the communication between the main script and the workers.

Here is an example demonstrating the worker pattern:

```
// worker.ts
addEventListener('message', (event) => {
    const { num1, num2 } = event.data;
    const result = num1 + num2; // Simulate a computation
    postMessage(result);
});
```

```
// main.ts
const worker = new Worker('worker.js');

worker.onmessage = (event) => {
    console.log('Result received from worker:', event.data);
};

worker.postMessage({ num1: 5, num2: 3 });
```

In the above code, the worker.ts file defines a worker that listens for messages, performs a computation, and posts the result back. The main thread, represented by main.ts, initiates the worker, sends data, and handles the result asynchronously. Utilizing TypeScript's type annotations can ensure the data communicated between the worker and the main thread adheres to the expected format, reducing runtime errors.

Task Queues:

Task queues facilitate the orderly execution of asynchronous tasks, often implementing priority and retry mechanisms. This pattern can be handy for managing network requests, background processing, and other delayed operations.

Here is an example of a simple task queue:

```
class TaskQueue {
    private queue: (() => Promise<void>)[] = [];

    constructor(private concurrency: number) {}

    async add(task: () => Promise<void>) {
        this.queue.push(task);
        if (this.queue.length <= this.concurrency) {
            this.run();
        }
    }

    private async run() {
        while (this.queue.length > 0) {
            const task = this.queue.shift();
            if (task) {
                try {
                    await task();
                } catch (error) {
                    console.error('Task failed:', error);
                    // Optionally, requeue the task or handle error
                }
            }
        }
    }
}

// Usage
const taskQueue = new TaskQueue(2);

taskQueue.add(async () => {
    await fetch('https://api.example.com/data1');
    // Process data
});

taskQueue.add(async () => {
    await fetch('https://api.example.com/data2');
    // Process data
});
```

In this illustration, the TaskQueue class maintains a queue of tasks and controls their execution according to a specified concurrency limit. The add method appends new tasks to the queue, while the run method ensures that tasks are executed up to the defined concurrency limit. Error handling within each task allows for fail-safe operations and optional retry mechanisms.

By integrating strong type checks and module interfaces, TypeScript enhances the robustness and maintainability of each concurrency pattern introduced here. Effective concurrency management not only boosts application performance but also leads to smoother and more responsive user experiences.

9.12 Asynchronous Programming Best Practices

Adhering to best practices in asynchronous programming is pivotal for creating robust, maintainable, and efficient applications. This section delineates these practices in the context of TypeScript, leveraging techniques discussed in previous sections to manipulate the asynchronous flow effectively.

1. *Use Promises Over Callbacks*

Using promises instead of callbacks is generally recommended. Promises provide a more straightforward and readable approach, avoiding callback hell, which often leads to convoluted and hard-to-maintain code. Promises also support chaining, making error handling more consistent and manageable.

```
function fetchData(url: string): Promise<Response> {
    return fetch(url);
}

fetchData('https://api.example.com/data')
    .then(response => response.json())
    .then(data => console.log(data))
    .catch(error => console.error('Error:', error));
```

2. *Embrace Async/Await*

Async/await syntax is more syntactically appealing and easier to interpret than the traditional promise syntax. It enables writing asynchronous code in a synchronous manner, enhancing readability and maintainability.

```
async function fetchData(url: string): Promise<void> {
    try {
        const response = await fetch(url);
        const data = await response.json();
        console.log(data);
    } catch (error) {
        console.error('Error:', error);
    }
}
```

3. *Error Handling Mechanisms*

Implement robust error handling in asynchronous code to prevent application crashes and ensure a better user experience. Use `try...catch` blocks for functions with async/await and `.catch()` for promises to handle errors gracefully.

```
async function fetchData(url: string): Promise<void> {
    try {
        const response = await fetch(url);
        if (!response.ok) {
            throw new Error(`HTTP error! status: ${response.status}`);
        }
        const data = await response.json();
        console.log(data);
    } catch (error) {
        console.error('Fetching error: ', error);
    }
}
```

4. *Avoiding Unnecessary Asynchrony*

Not every function needs to be asynchronous. If a function does not perform any asynchronous operations, avoid marking it with async. This will prevent unnecessary promise creation and improve execution efficiency.

```
function calculateSum(a: number, b: number): number {
    return a + b;
}

// This should not be marked async
const result = calculateSum(3, 5);
console.log(result);
```

5. *Rate Limiting and Throttling*

When making multiple asynchronous requests, particularly to external APIs, observe rate limits to avoid overwhelming the server or hitting request quotas. Implement throttling to space out requests.

```
function sleep(ms: number): Promise<void> {
    return new Promise(resolve => setTimeout(resolve, ms));
}

async function fetchWithRateLimit(urls: string[]): Promise<void> {
    for (const url of urls) {
        await fetchData(url);
        await sleep(500); // Waits for 500 milliseconds between requests
    }
}
```

6. *Leverage Concurrency Appropriately*

While writing asynchronous code, opt for concurrency when tasks are independent and can be executed simultaneously. Use Promise.all for executing multiple promises in parallel for improved efficiency.

```
async function fetchMultipleData(urls: string[]): Promise<void> {
    try {
        const promises = urls.map(url => fetch(url).then(response => response.json()))
            ;
```

```
        const results = await Promise.all(promises);
        console.log(results);
    } catch (error) {
        console.error('Error fetching multiple data:', error);
    }
}
```

7. *Use Asynchronous Iterators*

Asynchronous iterators (for await...of) are beneficial when working with streams or a series of asynchronous operations that produce results over time.

```
async function* asyncGenerator(urls: string[]) {
    for (const url of urls) {
        const response = await fetch(url);
        const data = await response.json();
        yield data;
    }
}

async function processData(urls: string[]): Promise<void> {
    for await (const data of asyncGenerator(urls)) {
        console.log(data);
    }
}
```

8. *Graceful Cancellation*

Introduce mechanisms to cancel long-running asynchronous operations when they are no longer needed. This can be achieved using AbortController or custom cancellation tokens.

```
const controller = new AbortController();
const signal = controller.signal;

async function fetchDataWithTimeout(url: string, timeout: number): Promise<void> {
    setTimeout(() => controller.abort(), timeout);

    try {
        const response = await fetch(url, { signal });
        const data = await response.json();
        console.log(data);
    } catch (error) {
        if (error.name === 'AbortError') {
            console.error('Fetch aborted due to timeout');
        } else {
            console.error('Fetch error:', error);
        }
    }
}
```

9. *Adopt Appropriate Concurrency Patterns*

Choose between parallelism and sequential execution based on the task requirements. Utilize Promise.all, Promise.race, Promise.allSettled, and Promise.any to tailor concurrency handling to specific needs.

```
// Example using Promise.race for the quickest response
async function fetchFirstData(urls: string[]): Promise<void> {
    try {
        const response = await Promise.race(urls.map(url => fetch(url)));
        const data = await response.json();
        console.log(data);
    } catch (error) {
        console.error('Error:', error);
    }
}
```

10. *Documentation and Code Comments*

Comprehensively document asynchronous functions and their behaviors. Include descriptions of input parameters, expectations, and error handling mechanisms. Code comments aid future maintenance and onboarding of new developers.

Prudently applying these best practices significantly enhances the performance, readability, and reliability of asynchronous code in TypeScript applications, fostering a more maintainable and scalable codebase.

Chapter 10

Testing and Debugging TypeScript

This chapter focuses on testing and debugging TypeScript applications, covering the setup of a testing environment, unit testing with Jest, and techniques for mocking and spying. It explores integration and end-to-end testing with tools like Cypress, and emphasizes writing testable code. For debugging, the chapter details using Visual Studio Code, leveraging source maps, and configuring TypeScript compiler options. Additionally, it addresses logging, error monitoring, and adopting best practices and strategies to ensure robust and reliable TypeScript code.

10.1 Introduction to Testing TypeScript

Testing is a fundamental aspect of software development that ensures code reliability, maintainability, and functionality. As TypeScript grows in popularity due to its robust type system and ability to enhance JavaScript development, understanding how to effectively test TypeScript code becomes increasingly important. This section delves into foundational concepts, providing a baseline for understanding the various testing paradigms applicable to TypeScript applications.

Importance of Testing in TypeScript

The primary objective of software testing is to identify and fix bugs before the application reaches end users. For TypeScript, testing is particularly crucial because it combines static type checking with dynamic behavior. TypeScript's type annotations help catch a variety of issues at compile time, but runtime errors, edge cases, and integration mishaps still need to be detected through rigorous testing.

Three main types of tests exist within the context of software development:

- **Unit Tests**: Focus on individual components or functions, verifying that each unit of the codebase works as intended.
- **Integration Tests**: Ensure that different modules or components work together correctly.
- **End-to-End (E2E) Tests**: Validate the complete functionality of the application by simulating real user interactions.

Effective TypeScript testing strategies incorporate all three test types to ensure comprehensive coverage.

Tooling for Testing TypeScript

Several tools are available for testing TypeScript applications, each catering to different aspects of the testing pyramid. Some widely used tools include:

- Jest: A testing framework maintained by Facebook, offering extensive features for unit and integration testing. Known for its simplicity, performance, and out-of-the-box TypeScript support.
- Mocha and Chai: Mocha is a feature-rich JavaScript test framework running on Node.js, while Chai is an assertion library that pairs complementarily with Mocha.
- Cypress: An E2E testing framework that provides a fast, reliable, and easy-to-setup environment to test web applications comprehensively.
- Sinon: A library to create spies, mocks, and stubs in JavaScript, frequently used within unit tests to emulate the behavior of complex components and provide control over their interactions.

Testing Setup

Setting up a testing environment in TypeScript typically involves configuring the appropriate tools and integrating them into the development workflow. For example, setting up Jest with TypeScript requires installing relevant packages and configuring the jest.config.js file.

A simple setup of Jest in a TypeScript environment involves the following steps:

```
npm install --save-dev jest @types/jest ts-jest
```

Next, create a jest.config.js file to define Jest configurations:

```
module.exports = {
    preset: 'ts-jest',
    testEnvironment: 'node',
    verbose: true,
};
```

Here, ts-jest serves as a preprocessor to compile TypeScript files during testing.

Basic Testing Syntax

A basic understanding of test syntax is crucial. Let's consider a test for a simple TypeScript function that adds two numbers:

```
function add(a: number, b: number): number {
    return a + b;
}
export { add };
```

And a corresponding test file might look like this:

```
import { add } from './path/to/module';

test('adds 1 + 2 to equal 3', () => {
    expect(add(1, 2)).toBe(3);
});
```

To execute these tests, run:

```
npx jest
```

Writing Effective Tests

Writing effective tests in TypeScript involves adhering to certain principles:

- **Clarity**: Tests should be easy to read and understand. Each test should focus on a single functionality or behavior.
- **Independence**: Tests should not depend on each other. The result of one test should not affect the execution of another.
- **Execution Time**: Tests should execute quickly to facilitate rapid feedback during the development process.
- **Coverage**: Aim to cover various paths and edge cases within the code. This ensures that a broad range of scenarios are tested.

Incorporating these principles ensures that the tests are instrumental in maintaining a healthy codebase. Subsequent sections will delve deeper into specific tools and techniques, enhancing the understanding established here.

10.2 Setting Up a Testing Environment

Setting up a testing environment for TypeScript involves installing and configuring various tools to ensure that your test suites run smoothly and efficiently. The primary tools you'll need are Node.js, npm (Node Package Manager), a test framework (such as Jest), and any necessary TypeScript configuration. This section provides a detailed guide on setting up these components.

First, ensure that you have Node.js and npm installed. You can download the latest versions from the [official Node.js website](https://nodejs.org/). Verify the installation by running the following commands in your terminal:

```
node -v
npm -v
```

The output should display the installed versions of Node.js and npm, for example:

```
v14.17.3
6.14.13
```

Next, initialize your project with npm. This will create a package.json file in your project directory, which is essential for managing project dependencies. Run the following command:

```
npm init -y
```

The -y flag automatically confirms the default configuration options. The generated package.json should look like this:

```
{
  "name": "project-name",
  "version": "1.0.0",
  "main": "index.js",
  "license": "MIT"
}
```

Now, install TypeScript and Jest as development dependencies:

```
npm install --save-dev typescript jest ts-jest @types/jest
```

Here, typescript is the core TypeScript compiler, jest is the testing framework, ts-jest provides a preprocessor to handle TypeScript files, and @types/jest includes TypeScript type definitions for Jest.

Next, create a TypeScript configuration file, tsconfig.json, in the root of your project. This file tells the TypeScript compiler how to compile your code. A typical tsconfig.json might look like this:

```
{
  "compilerOptions": {
    "target": "ES6",
    "module": "commonjs",
    "outDir": "./dist",
    "strict": true,
    "esModuleInterop": true,
    "skipLibCheck": true,
    "forceConsistentCasingInFileNames": true
  },
  "include": [
    "src/**/*"
  ],
  "exclude": [
    "node_modules",
    "**/*.spec.ts"
  ]
}
```

The compilerOptions object includes settings such as the target ECMAScript version (ES6), module system (commonjs), and the output directory for compiled files (./dist). The include and exclude arrays specify which files to compile.

Next, create a Jest configuration file, jest.config.js, in your project root. This file configures Jest for running tests with TypeScript:

```
module.exports = {
  preset: 'ts-jest',
  testEnvironment: 'node',
  testPathIgnorePatterns: [
    '/node_modules/',
    '/dist/'
  ],
  globals: {
    'ts-jest': {
      tsconfig: 'tsconfig.json'
    }
  }
};
```

The preset field specifies the use of ts-jest for transforming TypeScript files. The testEnvironment is set to node, which is suitable for most server-side tests. The testPathIgnorePatterns array ensures that Jest ignores unnecessary directories like node_modules and the TypeScript output directory (dist) when searching for tests.

Finally, let's create a couple of directories to organize our code and tests. Create src and tests directories in your project root:

```
mkdir src tests
```

Inside the tests directory, add a simple test file, example.spec.ts:

```
import { sum } from '../src/example';

test('adds 1 + 2 to equal 3', () => {
  expect(sum(1, 2)).toBe(3);
});
```

In this example, there's a sample test that checks if the sum function correctly adds two numbers. Now, create the corresponding example.ts file in the src directory:

```
export function sum(a: number, b: number): number {
  return a + b;
}
```

This simple sum function demonstrates how to write and test TypeScript code.

With everything set up, you can now run your tests using Jest. Add a test script to your package.json:

```
"scripts": {
  "test": "jest"
}
```

Then, run the tests with the following command:

```
npm test
```

The output should indicate that the tests have passed:

```
PASS tests/example.spec.ts
  adds 1 + 2 to equal 3 (3 ms)
```

This setup ensures that you have a robust testing environment for your TypeScript applications using Jest.

10.3 Unit Testing with Jest

Unit testing involves isolating and testing individual components or functions of an application to ensure they behave as expected. Jest is a widely adopted testing framework for JavaScript applications, and it integrates seamlessly with TypeScript. This section delves into setting up Jest for TypeScript, writing test cases, executing them, and interpreting the results.

Jest is chosen for its simplicity, ease of use, and extensive feature set, including snapshots, mocking, and a powerful assertion library. Additionally, Jest's zero-configuration approach makes it a favored tool for TypeScript developers.

To begin using Jest with TypeScript, you need to install the necessary dependencies:

```
npm install --save-dev jest @types/jest ts-jest
```

The jest package provides the testing framework, @types/jest offers TypeScript type definitions, and ts-jest serves as a preprocessor that compiles TypeScript code to JavaScript suitable for Jest.

Next, configure Jest by creating a jest.config.js file in your project's root directory:

```
module.exports = {
  preset: 'ts-jest',
  testEnvironment: 'node',
  verbose: true,
  globals: {
    'ts-jest': {
      tsconfig: 'tsconfig.json'
    }
  }
};
```

The configuration file specifies the use of ts-jest as the preset, which allows Jest to handle TypeScript files. The testEnvironment is set to node, making it suitable for testing backend applications. The verbose flag, when set to true, provides detailed test results.

Consider a simple function defined in a math.ts file:

```
export function add(a: number, b: number): number {
  return a + b;
}
```

To write a unit test for this function, create a corresponding test file math.test.ts:

```
import { add } from './math';

test('adds 1 + 2 to equal 3', () => {
  expect(add(1, 2)).toBe(3);
});

test('adds -1 + 1 to equal 0', () => {
  expect(add(-1, 1)).toBe(0);
});
```

In this test file, the test function defines individual test cases. Each test contains a descriptive string and a callback function with assertions. The expect function and matcher toBe verify the correctness of the add function's output.

To run the tests, execute the following command:

```
npm test
```

Upon execution, Jest outputs the test results in the console:

```
PASS ./math.test.ts
  adds 1 + 2 to equal 3 (3 ms)
  adds -1 + 1 to equal 0 (1 ms)

Test Suites: 1 passed, 1 total
Tests:       2 passed, 2 total
Snapshots:   0 total
Time:        1.21 s
```

Jest's default behavior is to discover and run tests in files with extensions such as .test.ts or .spec.ts. The output confirms that all tests have passed successfully.

Jest's assertion library provides various matchers enhancing the expressiveness of test cases. Simple equality checks use toBe, while object value comparisons use toEqual:

```
test('object assignment', () => {
  const data = {one: 1};
  data['two'] = 2;
  expect(data).toEqual({one: 1, two: 2});
```

```
});
```

There are additional matchers for more specific assertions, for example:

```
test('null', () => {
  const n = null;
  expect(n).toBeNull();
  expect(n).toBeDefined();
  expect(n).not.toBeUndefined();
  expect(n).not.toBeTruthy();
  expect(n).toBeFalsy();
});
```

For numbers, Jest includes matchers like toBeGreaterThan:

```
test('two plus two', () => {
  const value = 2 + 2;
  expect(value).toBeGreaterThan(3);
  expect(value).toBeGreaterThanOrEqual(3.5);
  expect(value).toBeLessThan(5);
  expect(value).toBeLessThanOrEqual(4.5);

  // toBe and toEqual are equivalent for numbers
  expect(value).toBe(4);
  expect(value).toEqual(4);
});
```

String matchers like toMatch handle regular expressions:

```
test('there is no I in team', () => {
  expect('team').not.toMatch(/I/);
});

test('but there is a "stop" in Christoph', () => {
  expect('Christoph').toMatch(/stop/);
});
```

Array and iterable matchers include toContain:

```
const shoppingList = [
  'diapers',
  'kleenex',
  'trash bags',
  'paper towels',
  'milk',
];

test('the shopping list has milk on it', () => {
  expect(shoppingList).toContain('milk');
  expect(new Set(shoppingList)).toContain('milk');
});
```

Testing exceptions can be managed with toThrow:

```
function compileAndroidCode() {
  throw new Error('you are using the wrong JDK');
```

```
}

test('compiling android goes as expected', () => {
  expect(compileAndroidCode).toThrow();
  expect(compileAndroidCode).toThrow(Error);

  // check the exact error message or a regexp
  expect(compileAndroidCode).toThrow('you are using the wrong JDK');
  expect(compileAndroidCode).toThrow(/JDK/);
});
```

Jest also supports running tests in parallel, reducing the overall test runtime. Additionally, it provides rich features for mocking functions and modules, which will be explored in later sections. Configuring Jest appropriately and leveraging its extensive matchers ensure comprehensive and maintainable unit tests for TypeScript applications.

10.4 Mocking and Spying

Mocking and spying are essential techniques in unit testing that enable developers to isolate components, monitor function calls, and simulate various behaviors and states. These techniques are particularly advantageous when testing TypeScript applications, as they assist in creating predictable and controlled test environments. This section elucidates the concepts and applications of mocking and spying using the Jest testing framework, widely adopted in the TypeScript ecosystem.

Mocking refers to the process of simulating the behavior of complex, real objects or components with simpler, controlled substitutes. This facilitates testing code functionality independently of external or potentially unreliable dependencies such as network requests, databases, or third-party services. Jest supports various forms of mocking including manual mocks, automocking, and jest.fn().

Consider a TypeScript module api.ts which contains a function fetchData that makes an HTTP GET request using Axios:

```
import axios from 'axios';

export const fetchData = async (url: string): Promise<any> => {
    const response = await axios.get(url);
    return response.data;
};
```

When unit testing a function that relies on fetchData, it is prudent to mock Axios' GET request to ensure the test is not dependent on an actual HTTP request. Jest provides jest.mock to automatically mock

Axios:

```
import axios from 'axios';
import { fetchData } from './api';

jest.mock('axios');
const mockedAxios = axios as jest.Mocked<typeof axios>;

test('fetchData makes a GET request and returns data', async () => {
  const fakeData = { data: 'test data' };
  mockedAxios.get.mockResolvedValue(fakeData);

  const data = await fetchData('https://example.com');
  expect(data).toEqual('test data');
  expect(mockedAxios.get).toHaveBeenCalledWith('https://example.com');
});
```

In the test above, jest.mock('axios') replaces all of Axios' methods with Jest mock functions. mockResolvedValue sets up a predefined response for axios.get, ensuring our test remains deterministic and fast. We assert that fetchData indeed returned the correct data and verify that Axios' GET request was called with the expected URL.

Spying is another valuable technique that involves observing and/or modifying the behavior of functions while retaining their original implementation. Jest provides jest.spyOn to create spies:

Consider a TypeScript module math.ts with a function multiply:

```
export const multiply = (a: number, b: number): number => {
    return a * b;
};
```

To verify that function multiply is invoked with the correct arguments within another function, a spy can be utilized:

```
import * as math from './math';
import { calculate } from './calculate';

jest.spyOn(math, 'multiply');

test('calculate calls multiply with correct arguments', () => {
  calculate(2, 3);
  expect(math.multiply).toHaveBeenCalledWith(2, 3);
});
```

In this example, jest.spyOn creates a spy on math.multiply. The test then checks whether math.multiply was called with the correct arguments, ensuring that calculate functions correctly.

Mocking and spying can also be combined to enhance test robustness. Consider a scenario where we need to mock some methods of a class while capturing other method calls. Here, Class Mocking will be instrumental:

First, let's define a simple TypeScript class UserService:

```
export class UserService {
    async fetchUser(id: string): Promise<any> {
        // simulate an api call
        return { id, name: 'John Doe' };
    }

    async deleteUser(id: string): Promise<boolean> {
        // simulate another api call
        return true;
    }
};
```

Now consider a module that uses UserService:

```
import { UserService } from './userService';

export const UserManager = {
    async deleteUserIfInactive(userId: string): Promise<boolean> {
        const userService = new UserService();
        const user = await userService.fetchUser(userId);
        if (user.isActive === false) {
            return userService.deleteUser(userId);
        }
        return false;
    }
};
```

To test deleteUserIfInactive without making actual API calls:

```
import { UserService } from './userService';
import { UserManager } from './userManager';

jest.mock('./userService');
const MockedUserService = UserService as jest.MockedClass<typeof UserService>;

test('deleteUserIfInactive deletes user if inactive', async () => {
  const mockFetchUser = jest.fn().mockResolvedValue({ id: '123', isActive: false });
  const mockDeleteUser = jest.fn().mockResolvedValue(true);

  MockedUserService.prototype.fetchUser = mockFetchUser;
  MockedUserService.prototype.deleteUser = mockDeleteUser;

  const result = await UserManager.deleteUserIfInactive('123');
  expect(mockFetchUser).toHaveBeenCalledWith('123');
  expect(mockDeleteUser).toHaveBeenCalledWith('123');
  expect(result).toBe(true);
});
```

In this scenario, we use Jest to mock the UserService class. We replace specific methods with jest mock functions that return controlled values. This approach allows us to validate the interactions between our methods and ensures the right ones are invoked based on the application's logic.

10.5 Integration Testing

In an application, individual units often interact with each other, forming a cohesive system. Integration testing aims to verify that different modules or services in the application work together as expected. This type of testing is crucial because an application's functionality often depends not just on individual units but also on their interplay and integration points. This section explores the methodologies, tools, and best practices for conducting integration tests in a TypeScript environment.

To perform integration testing, we typically use frameworks and libraries that facilitate interaction between multiple units of implementation. One popular framework is Jest with its extended functionality, along with tools like SuperTest for HTTP assertions in Node.js applications. Below, we illustrate setting up Jest and SuperTest for integration testing.

```
npm install --save-dev jest supertest ts-jest
```

Setting Up Integration Tests with Jest and SuperTest

Consider an example where a RESTful API service needs to be tested. We assume a Node.js application using Express with endpoints that interact with a database. Below, we set up the initial testing environment and write basic integration tests.

1. **Configure Jest for TypeScript**: Update the package.json to include Jest settings for TypeScript.

```
{
  "scripts": {
    "test": "jest"
  },
  "jest": {
    "preset": "ts-jest",
    "testEnvironment": "node"
  }
}
```

2. **Create a Test File**: Create a file named example.spec.ts in the __tests__ directory.

```
import request from 'supertest';
import app from '../src/app'; // Assume this is your Express app

describe('GET /users', () => {
  it('should return an array of users', async () => {
    const response = await request(app).get('/users');
    expect(response.status).toBe(200);
    expect(Array.isArray(response.body)).toBe(true);
  });
});
```

In this example, SuperTest sends an HTTP request to the /users endpoint, and Jest assertions validate the response status and data structure.

Mocking in Integration Testing

Although integration tests are about interactions between real modules, sometimes it is necessary to replace certain components (e.g., database connections) with mocks to isolate the test environment. jest.mock() is useful for this purpose.

```
import request from 'supertest';
import app from '../src/app';
import * as db from '../src/db';

jest.mock('../src/db');

describe('GET /users', () => {
  beforeAll(() => {
    (db.getUsers as jest.Mock).mockResolvedValue([
      { id: 1, name: 'John Doe' },
      { id: 2, name: 'Jane Doe' }
    ]);
  });

  it('should return an array of users', async () => {
    const response = await request(app).get('/users');
    expect(response.status).toBe(200);
    expect(response.body).toEqual([
      { id: 1, name: 'John Doe' },
      { id: 2, name: 'Jane Doe' }
    ]);
  });
});
```

In this scenario, the getUsers method in the database module is mocked to return a predefined array of user objects, ensuring the data source is controlled during the test execution.

Running the Integration Tests

To execute the integration tests, use the predefined npm script:

```
npm test
```

The console output should verify that the tests pass and provide feedback on any failures.

```
PASS __tests__/example.spec.ts
 GET /users
    should return an array of users (20 ms)
```

Best Practices for Integration Testing

- **Isolate Tests**: Ensure tests are isolated from each other, especially when dealing with external systems like databases. Use mock data or in-memory databases to achieve this. - **Automate Setup and Teardown**: Automate the setup and teardown processes of your test environment to maintain consistency and reliability. - **Granular Test Cases**: Create granular test cases that cover various integration points but avoid excessive overlap with unit tests. Focus on the interaction between modules rather than individual functionalities. - **Monitor Performance**: Keep an eye on the performance of integration tests, as they often run slower due to the involvement of multiple components and possible I/O operations.

This section has highlighted the methodologies and practices for conducting effective integration tests in a TypeScript environment, reinforcing their importance in delivering a robust software application.

10.6 End-to-End Testing with Cypress

End-to-end (E2E) testing is a critical phase in the testing lifecycle of TypeScript applications, ensuring that the entire application flow is functional and stable. Cypress is a robust end-to-end testing framework that enables developers to write, execute, and manage tests with ease. This section delves into the details of using Cypress for E2E testing, covering the installation, setup, and execution of tests, as well as best practices to follow.

Installation and Setup

To start using Cypress, install it via npm. It is recommended to install Cypress as a dev dependency to keep the project's production dependencies clean. Use the following command in your terminal:

```
npm install cypress --save-dev
```

After installation, the next step is to initialize Cypress in your project. Run the following command to open the Cypress Test Runner, and Cypress will automatically create the necessary files and folders:

```
npx cypress open
```

This command creates a directory named cypress in your project's root folder, containing default folders like fixtures, integration, plugins, and support. These folders are structured to organize your tests, test utilities, and support files. Additionally, a cypress.json configuration file is created, which is used to define your project's specific configurations.

Writing End-to-End Tests

Create a new test file within the cypress/integration directory. For example, name it login.spec.ts to write a test for the login feature of your application. Include the following content to test a basic login functionality:

```
describe('Login Functionality', () => {
  it('should be able to login with valid credentials', () => {
    cy.visit('http://localhost:3000/login');

    cy.get('input[name=username]').type('testuser');
    cy.get('input[name=password]').type('Password123');
    cy.get('button[type=submit]').click();

    cy.url().should('include', '/dashboard');
    cy.contains('Welcome, testuser');
  });
});
```

In this example, the test:

- cy.visit('http://localhost:3000/login'); navigates to the login page.
- cy.get('input[name=username]').type('testuser'); selects the username input field and types "testuser".
- cy.get('input[name=password]').type('Password123'); selects the password input field and types "Password123".
- cy.get('button[type=submit]').click(); clicks on the submit button.
- cy.url().should('include', '/dashboard'); asserts that the URL includes "/dashboard" after logging in.
- cy.contains('Welcome, testuser'); verifies that the welcome message containing "testuser" is displayed.

Running Cypress Tests

You can run Cypress tests in two modes: headed mode and headless mode. The headed mode opens the Cypress Test Runner, allowing you to see the tests execution in real-time. Use the following command to start Cypress in headed mode:

```
npx cypress open
```

To run the tests in headless mode, which is ideal for continuous integration environments, use:

```
npx cypress run
```

Headless mode executes the tests in the background without opening the browser GUI, providing a faster feedback loop during automated pipelines.

Best Practices for End-to-End Testing

Adhering to certain best practices ensures the efficiency and maintainability of your E2E tests:

- **Isolate Tests:** Ensure tests are isolated and independent by resetting the application state before each test. Use the beforeEach hook to perform actions such as database seeding and clearing cookies.
- **Use Selectors Wisely:** Prefer using data attributes for selectors (e.g., data-cy), which are less likely to change and break tests compared to class or ID selectors.
- **Avoid Testing Implementation Details:** Focus on testing the user interactions and application behavior instead of implementation details. This ensures tests remain stable even when internal changes occur.
- **Leverage Custom Commands:** Create custom Cypress commands for reusable actions (e.g., login) to keep tests DRY (Don't Repeat Yourself) and enhance readability. Custom commands can be defined in the cypress/support/commands.ts file.
- **Parallelism and Sharding:** For large test suites, leverage Cypress's parallelization and sharding features to distribute tests across multiple machines, reducing the overall execution time.

Here's an example of a custom command for logging in a user, defined in cypress/support/commands.ts:

```
Cypress.Commands.add('login', (username: string, password: string) => {
  cy.visit('http://localhost:3000/login');
  cy.get('input[name=username]').type(username);
  cy.get('input[name=password]').type(password);
  cy.get('button[type=submit]').click();
  cy.url().should('include', '/dashboard');
});
```

The custom command login can then be used in your tests:

```
describe('Dashboard Access', () => {
  it('should allow access to authenticated users', () => {
    cy.login('testuser', 'Password123');
    cy.contains('Dashboard');
  });
});
```

Using Cypress for E2E testing enhances the quality of TypeScript applications by verifying that all components interact seamlessly in real-world scenarios. Proper setup, judicious use of selectors, and adherence to best practices are fundamental to creating stable and reliable tests.

10.7 Writing Testable Code

Writing testable code ensures that applications are resilient, maintainable, and can be confidently modified or extended. Testability in TypeScript is achieved through careful design, following principles such as separation of concerns, dependency injection, and the use of interfaces. This section will delve into these principles and demonstrate practical techniques to make your TypeScript code more testable.

Separation of Concerns: Separation of concerns is a software design principle that promotes dividing a software system into distinct sections, where each section addresses a specific concern. This makes the system easier to understand, maintain, and test. In TypeScript, this can be achieved by breaking down functions and classes into smaller, more focused units.

For instance, consider a service that handles user authentication:

```
class AuthService {
  private apiUrl: string = 'https://api.example.com/auth';

  async login(username: string, password: string): Promise<boolean> {
    const response = await fetch(this.apiUrl, {
      method: 'POST',
      body: JSON.stringify({ username, password }),
      headers: { 'Content-Type': 'application/json' },
    });

    if (!response.ok) {
      throw new Error('Login failed');
    }

    const data = await response.json();
    return data.success;
  }
}
```

To improve testability, we should separate the concerns of making an HTTP request and handling authentication logic. This can be achieved by extracting the HTTP request into its own module:

```
class HttpClient {
  async post(url: string, body: any): Promise<any> {
    const response = await fetch(url, {
      method: 'POST',
      body: JSON.stringify(body),
      headers: { 'Content-Type': 'application/json' },
    });

    if (!response.ok) {
      throw new Error('HTTP request failed');
    }

    return response.json();
  }
}
```

The AuthService can now use HttpClient to perform its operations:

```
class AuthService {
  private apiUrl: string = 'https://api.example.com/auth';
  private httpClient: HttpClient;

  constructor(httpClient: HttpClient) {
    this.httpClient = httpClient;
  }

  async login(username: string, password: string): Promise<boolean> {
    const data = await this.httpClient.post(this.apiUrl, { username, password });
    return data.success;
  }
}
```

Dependency Injection: Dependency Injection (DI) is a design pattern used to implement Inversion of Control (IoC) between classes and their dependencies. DI facilitates the injection of dependencies, rather than having classes instantiate their dependencies. This practice enhances testability and flexibility.

Refactoring the AuthService to use DI improves testability, as dependencies can be mocked in tests. Consider the AuthService example:

```
class MockHttpClient {
  async post(url: string, body: any): Promise<any> {
    return { success: true }; // Mocked response
  }
}

const mockHttpClient = new MockHttpClient();
const authService = new AuthService(mockHttpClient);

(async () => {
  const result = await authService.login('user', 'password');
  console.log(result); // Should print: true
```

```
})();
```

```
true
```

By injecting MockHttpClient into AuthService, we can unit test the service without making actual HTTP requests, isolating the authentication logic.

Using Interfaces: Implementing interfaces in TypeScript is another strategy to enhance testability. Interfaces define contracts for classes, ensuring that they adhere to specific behaviors. This allows for easily swapping implementations in tests.

```
interface IHttpClient {
  post(url: string, body: any): Promise<any>;
}

class HttpClient implements IHttpClient {
  async post(url: string, body: any): Promise<any> {
    const response = await fetch(url, {
      method: 'POST',
      body: JSON.stringify(body),
      headers: { 'Content-Type': 'application/json' },
    });

    if (!response.ok) {
      throw new Error('HTTP request failed');
    }

    return response.json();
  }
}

class AuthService {
  private apiUrl: string = 'https://api.example.com/auth';
  private httpClient: IHttpClient;

  constructor(httpClient: IHttpClient) {
    this.httpClient = httpClient;
  }

  async login(username: string, password: string): Promise<boolean> {
    const data = await this.httpClient.post(this.apiUrl, { username, password });
    return data.success;
  }
}
```

In tests, you can now create a mock implementation of IHttpClient:

```
class MockHttpClient implements IHttpClient {
  async post(url: string, body: any): Promise<any> {
    return { success: true }; // Mocked response
  }
}

const mockHttpClient = new MockHttpClient();
const authService = new AuthService(mockHttpClient);
```

```
(async () => {
  const result = await authService.login('user', 'password');
  console.log(result); // Should print: true
})();
```

```
true
```

Avoiding Side Effects: Side effects occur when a function modifies some state outside its scope or relies on external states. Avoiding side effects makes code predictable and easier to test. Pure functions, which have no side effects, are the ideal for testing.

Consider a function that updates user data and saves it to local storage:

```
function updateUser(user: { name: string, age: number }) {
  // Update user data
  user.age += 1;

  // Save to local storage (side effect)
  localStorage.setItem('user', JSON.stringify(user));
}
```

To make this function more testable, split the logic to separate the side-effect operation:

```
function updateUser(user: { name: string, age: number }): { name: string, age: number
    } {
  return { ...user, age: user.age + 1 };
}

function saveUserToLocalStorage(user: { name: string, age: number }) {
  localStorage.setItem('user', JSON.stringify(user));
}
```

Testing the updateUser function now becomes straightforward, as it no longer has side effects:

```
const user = { name: 'Alice', age: 30 };
const updatedUser = updateUser(user);
console.log(updatedUser); // Should print: { name: 'Alice', age: 31 }
```

```
{ name: 'Alice', age: 31 }
```

Concentrating the side effects into isolated modules or functions makes it easier to stub or mock them during testing.

Modular Design: Breaking down the application into smaller modules enhances testability. Each module should encapsulate a single responsibility or functionality, which can be independently tested.

Consider a module responsible for user authentication:

```
// auth.ts
export class AuthService {
```

```
  private apiUrl: string = 'https://api.example.com/auth';
  private httpClient: IHttpClient;

  constructor(httpClient: IHttpClient) {
    this.httpClient = httpClient;
  }

  async login(username: string, password: string): Promise<boolean> {
    const data = await this.httpClient.post(this.apiUrl, { username, password });
    return data.success;
  }
}
```

Unit testing each module separately ensures that each part of the code is reliable before integrating them into a larger system.

By adhering to these principles and techniques, you will enhance the testability of your TypeScript applications, ensuring they are robust, maintainable, and reliable.

10.8 Debugging TypeScript with Visual Studio Code

Visual Studio Code (VS Code) provides a robust set of tools for debugging TypeScript applications. The integration of the VS Code debugger with TypeScript enhances the development experience by allowing inspection of variable states, stepping through code, and setting breakpoints, among other features.

Configuring the Debugger

To begin debugging TypeScript in VS Code, a configuration file launch.json must be created. This file specifies how the debugger should run the application. It resides in the .vscode directory within your project. Below is an example setup for a Node.js application:

```
{
    "version": "0.2.0",
    "configurations": [
        {
            "type": "node",
            "request": "launch",
            "name": "Launch Program",
            "skipFiles": ["<node_internals>/**"],
            "program": "${workspaceFolder}/src/index.ts",
            "preLaunchTask": "tsc: build - tsconfig.json",
            "outFiles": ["${workspaceFolder}/dist/**/*.js"],
            "sourceMaps": true
        }
    ]
}
```

- type: Defines the type of debugger; in this case, node for Node.js applications.
- request: Indicates whether to launch the program or attach the debugger to an existing process (e.g., "launch").
- name: A friendly name for the configuration.
- skipFiles: An optional array to specify files or folders that should be skipped in the debugging process.
- program: The entry point file of the TypeScript project.
- preLaunchTask: Specifies a task to run before starting the debugger, typically the TypeScript compiler.
- outFiles: An array indicating where to find the compiled JavaScript files.
- sourceMaps: A boolean flag to enable source map support.

Setting Breakpoints

Breakpoints can be set by clicking on the gutter next to the line numbers in the editor. They can also be modified to conditional breakpoints, which only trigger when a specific condition is met. Here is how to set a conditional breakpoint:

- Right-click on the existing breakpoint.
- Select "Edit Breakpoint".
- Enter the condition in the text field, such as $counter > 10$.

Variable Inspection and Watch Expressions

During a debugging session, variables within the current scope can be inspected by hovering over them with the mouse. Additionally, adding watch expressions provides the ability to monitor specific variables or expressions continuously.

- Open the Debug view by selecting the Debug icon in the Activity Bar.

- In the VARIABLES section, local variables and their values appear automatically.
- To add a watch expression, click on the + icon in the WATCH section and enter the variable or expression to track.

Debugging Commands

The Debug Toolbar in VS Code offers several commands to control the execution flow:

- Continue (F5): Resumes execution until the next breakpoint or the end of the program.
- Step Over (F10): Executes the current line of code and moves to the next line in the same function.
- Step Into (F11): Steps into the function call at the current line.
- Step Out (Shift+F11): Steps out of the current function and pauses at the first line after the function call.
- Restart (Ctrl+Shift+F5): Restarts the debugging session.
- Stop (Shift+F5): Stops the debugging session.

Exception Breakpoints

Exception breakpoints will halt execution whenever an exception occurs, allowing analysis of the context in which the error was thrown.

- Open the Debug view.
- Click on the icon at the top of the Breakpoints section to add an exception breakpoint.
- You can specify whether to break on all exceptions or only uncaught exceptions.

Console Logging

Console logging remains a useful tool for debugging. By inserting console.log() statements in code, developers can output variable values or program states to the integrated terminal.

```
console.log("The value of x is:", x);
```

```
The value of x is: 42
```

Integrated Terminal

The integrated terminal supports running tasks and scripts directly. It can be opened via View > Terminal or using the keyboard shortcut Ctrl+`. The terminal's output is helpful for monitoring build processes and scripts that are part of the development workflow.

This section provided a thorough guide on configuring and utilizing the debugging features within Visual Studio Code for TypeScript applications. By mastering these tools, developers can enhance their efficiency in pinpointing and resolving issues in their code, ensuring a more robust and reliable development process.

10.9 Using Source Maps in Debugging

When working with TypeScript in large projects, debugging can often become complex due to the transpilation process, where TypeScript code is compiled into JavaScript. The compiled JavaScript can sometimes be quite different from the original TypeScript code, making it challenging to pinpoint the exact source of errors or issues. Source maps provide a significant mitigation to this problem by maintaining a mapping between the TypeScript source and the resulting JavaScript code, allowing developers to debug TypeScript code directly.

A source map is a JSON file that creates a correspondence between a particular position in a minified file back to the position in the original source file. Let's explore how source maps can be used effectively in debugging TypeScript applications.

To enable source maps in a TypeScript project, modify the tsconfig.json file to include the sourceMap option set to true:

```
{
    "compilerOptions": {
        "sourceMap": true,
        ...
    },
    ...
}
```

When the sourceMap option is set to true, the TypeScript compiler generates `.map` files alongside the corresponding JavaScript files. These `.map` files contain the necessary information to construct a mapping between the TypeScript and JavaScript files.

Consider the following TypeScript function:

```
function greet(name: string): string {
    console.log("Hello, " + name);
    return "Hello, " + name;
}
```

When compiled with the sourceMap option enabled, the TypeScript compiler generates the following JavaScript and source map files:

```
"use strict";
function greet(name) {
    console.log("Hello, " + name);
    return "Hello, " + name;
}
//# sourceMappingURL=greet.js.map
```

The corresponding source map file may look like this:

```
{
    "version": 3,
    "file": "greet.js",
    "sources": ["greet.ts"],
    "names": [],
    "mappings": ";;;AAAA,IAAI,CAAC,GAAG,MAAM,CAAC,GAAG,CAAC,CAAC,
        ICAC,CAAC,GAAG,CAAC,CAAC,CAAC,CAAC,GAAC,CAAC,IAAC"
}
```

When debugging in a browser such as Chrome, Edge, or Firefox, the developer tools will utilize these source maps to allow inspection and stepping through the TypeScript code directly, rather than the down-leveled JavaScript. This ability to debug TypeScript code significantly simplifies the development and maintenance process.

To illustrate the practical application of source maps, let's consider a scenario where an error occurs in the greet function. Without source maps, the debugger would point to the transpiled JavaScript console statement, making it tedious to trace back to the TypeScript source. With source maps enabled, however, the developer can see the exact TypeScript line causing the issue, making the debugging process more intuitive and efficient.

For Node.js environments, source maps can also be used to enhance the debugging experience. Install the source-map-support package to enable source map support:

```
npm install source-map-support --save
```

Then, include the following line at the start of your application entry file to enable source map support:

```
import 'source-map-support/register';
```

By integrating source map support, any stack traces generated during runtime will accurately reflect the TypeScript source, thus aiding in quicker and more accurate identification of issues.

It is important to note that while source maps are invaluable during development and debugging, they should typically be excluded from production deployments to avoid revealing source code structure and to reduce the payload size. Configure build tools to exclude source maps from the production build artifacts. For instance, with Webpack, you can distinguish between development and production configurations:

```
module.exports = (env) => {
    return {
        devtool: env.production ? false : 'source-map',
        ...
    };
};
```

Being proficient with source maps and understanding their configuration and use are critical for debugging TypeScript applications efficiently. Proper usage of source maps allows developers to maintain high productivity and robust code integrity even as projects scale in size and complexity.

10.10 TypeScript Compiler Options for Debugging

When working with TypeScript, leveraging the compiler options effectively can significantly enhance the debugging process. The tsconfig.json file allows developers to specify the compiler configuration, which can be used to control various aspects of code compilation. For debugging purposes, several specific compiler options should be configured to ensure that developers have the necessary tools to identify and resolve issues efficiently. The primary compiler options of interest include sourceMap, outDir, strict, target, and module.

- sourceMap: This option makes it possible to generate source maps, which are essential for debugging TypeScript code. Source maps create a mapping between the compiled JavaScript code and the TypeScript source, allowing developers to set breakpoints, inspect variables, and step through code in a more intuitive manner.

- outDir: This option specifies the directory where the compiled JavaScript files will be output. By organizing the compiled files into a distinct directory, developers can easily locate and reference them during the debugging process.
- strict: Enabling strict type-checking options can help catch potential errors early in the development process. Although not a direct debugging tool, it enforces better coding practices and reduces the number of runtime errors.
- target: This option specifies the ECMAScript target version for the compiled JavaScript code. By setting the appropriate target, developers can ensure compatibility with the execution environment, which can aid in debugging.
- module: This option determines the module system for the generated JavaScript. Proper configuration ensures that module imports and exports function correctly, preventing issues related to module resolution.

Below is an example of a well-configured tsconfig.json file tailored for debugging purposes:

```
{
  "compilerOptions": {
    "sourceMap": true,
    "outDir": "./dist",
    "strict": true,
    "target": "es6",
    "module": "commonjs"
  },
  "include": ["src/**/*"],
  "exclude": ["node_modules", "dist"]
}
```

sourceMap: true generates source maps, creating an association between the TypeScript and JavaScript code. During debugging, this configuration enables developers to set breakpoints and step through TypeScript code directly within the browser or an integrated development environment (IDE) such as Visual Studio Code.

outDir: "./dist" directs the compiler to output the transpiled JavaScript files to the dist directory. This keeps the project's structure organized and assists in locating the output files generated during compilation.

strict: true activates all strict type-checking options in TypeScript, including noImplicitAny, strictNullChecks, strictFunctionTypes, and others. Although it may initially increase the effort required to handle type definitions, adhering to strict type-checking fosters more robust and error-free code.

target: "es6" specifies that the output JavaScript should be in ECMAScript 6 (ES6) syntax. Selecting the correct target version ensures that the compiled JavaScript code remains compatible with the intended runtime environment. This compatibility is crucial when debugging issues related to language features or interoperability.

module: "commonjs" sets the module system to CommonJS, which is widely used in Node.js environments. Proper module configuration helps avoid runtime errors related to incorrect module resolution, import, and export behaviors.

For more complex projects, additional options can be incorporated into the tsconfig.json file to further streamline the debugging process. For instance:

```
{
  "compilerOptions": {
    "sourceMap": true,
    "outDir": "./dist",
    "strict": true,
    "target": "es6",
    "module": "commonjs",
    "baseUrl": "./src",
    "paths": {
      "@models/*": ["models/*"],
      "@controllers/*": ["controllers/*"]
    },
    "removeComments": false
  },
  "include": ["src/**/*"],
  "exclude": ["node_modules", "dist"]
}
```

baseUrl: "./src" and paths allow for alias configuration, enabling shortened import paths. This setup not only improves code readability but also aids in debugging by making it clearer where specific modules are being sourced from.

removeComments: false ensures that comments are retained in the compiled JavaScript files. Retaining comments can be useful during debugging to reference notes and explanations added by the code author without needing to switch back to the TypeScript source files.

Understanding and configuring the TypeScript compiler options appropriately is a pivotal step in smoothing the debugging process. Proper setup optimizes the development workflow, mitigates potential errors, and provides a robust environment for addressing issues when they arise.

10.11 Logging and Error Monitoring

Logging and error monitoring are critical components for maintaining robust and reliable TypeScript applications. Effective logging provides insights into application behavior, making it easier to diagnose issues and understand user interactions. Error monitoring captures and reports runtime errors, enabling quick responses to potential problems. This section will delve into the strategies and tools available for logging and error monitoring in TypeScript applications.

To integrate logging into your TypeScript applications, consider using a logging library such as Winston or Bunyan. These libraries offer powerful features like multiple log levels, formatting options, and transport mechanisms to various outputs (e.g., console, files, remote servers). Below is an example of how to set up Winston for logging in a TypeScript application:

```
import * as winston from 'winston';

const logger = winston.createLogger({
  level: 'info',
  format: winston.format.combine(
    winston.format.timestamp(),
    winston.format.printf(({ timestamp, level, message }) => {
      return `${timestamp} [${level}]: ${message}`;
    })
  ),
  transports: [
    new winston.transports.Console(),
    new winston.transports.File({ filename: 'application.log' })
  ]
});

logger.info('Logging setup complete.');
```

This script initializes a Winston logger that outputs logs to the console and a file named application.log. The log format includes a timestamp, log level, and message, which is useful for debugging and monitoring purposes.

When dealing with asynchronous operations, ensuring that logs are flushed properly when an application exits or crashes is essential. The following code demonstrates how to gracefully handle log flushing:

```
process.on('uncaughtException', (err) => {
  logger.error(`Uncaught Exception: ${err.message}`);
  winston.end(() => {
```

```
    process.exit(1);
  });
});

process.on('unhandledRejection', (reason, promise) => {
  logger.error(`Unhandled Rejection at: ${promise}, reason: ${reason}`);
  winston.end(() => {
    process.exit(1);
  });
});
```

Monitoring unexpected errors ensures that they are logged and that the application can terminate safely after flushing the logs.

Error monitoring, on the other hand, involves capturing exceptions and reporting them to a centralized system. Services like Sentry and Rollbar integrate well with TypeScript applications and offer comprehensive dashboards for tracking and managing errors. Below is an example of integrating Sentry into a TypeScript project:

```
import * as Sentry from '@sentry/node';
import { RewriteFrames } from '@sentry/integrations';

Sentry.init({
  dsn: 'YOUR_SENTRY_DSN',
  integrations: [
    new RewriteFrames({
      root: global.__dirname,
    }),
  ],
});

function captureError(error: Error) {
  Sentry.captureException(error);
}

process.on('uncaughtException', (err) => {
  captureError(err);
  process.exit(1);
});

process.on('unhandledRejection', (reason, promise) => {
  captureError(reason as Error);
  process.exit(1);
});
```

This setup initializes Sentry with the provided Data Source Name (DSN) and configures it to capture both uncaught exceptions and unhandled promise rejections. The captured errors are sent to Sentry's dashboard for analysis.

When using TypeScript, enabling source maps is vital for effective debugging and monitoring. Source maps map the transpiled JavaScript code back to the original TypeScript source, making stack traces more readable. To enable source maps, add the following configuration to your tsconfig.json:

```
{
  "compilerOptions": {
    "sourceMap": true,
    ...
  }
}
```

Once source maps are enabled, ensure that your logging and monitoring libraries are correctly configured to use them. For instance, in our Sentry integration, we included the RewriteFrames integration to align the frames in the error stack trace with the source maps.

Furthermore, it's essential to adhere to best practices when implementing logging and monitoring. Here are some recommendations:

- Use appropriate log levels (debug, info, warn, error) to differentiate the importance and verbosity of log entries.
- Structure log messages uniformly to ease parsing and analysis (e.g., include timestamps, log levels, and contextual information).
- Avoid logging sensitive information (e.g., passwords, personal data) to comply with privacy regulations.
- Regularly review logs and monitor dashboards to proactively identify and address potential issues.
- Incorporate automated alerts to notify your team of critical errors promptly.

These practices ensure that logging and error monitoring are effective and help maintain high application reliability by providing insights and early warning signals for potential issues.

10.12 Testing Best Practices and Strategies

Effective testing practices and strategies are instrumental in ensuring the reliability, maintainability, and robustness of TypeScript applications. This section delves into key best practices and strategies that developers should adopt when testing their TypeScript code.

Test Naming Conventions

Adopting a clear and consistent naming convention for tests aids in understanding what a particular test is doing and why it is necessary. It is recommended to name test files to reflect the module or functionality they are testing. For example, if testing a UserService module, the test file could be named user.service.spec.ts.

Within each test file, function names should be descriptive. A common practice is to use the *describe-it* pattern as shown:

```
describe('UserService', () => {
  it('should return user data when getUser is called', () => {
    // Test implementation
  });

  it('should throw an error when user is not found', () => {
    // Test implementation
  });
});
```

Testing Coverage

Maximizing test coverage is essential but should not be the sole focus. Ensuring critical paths and edge cases are adequately tested is more practical. TypeScript projects should aim for comprehensive unit tests and functional tests to cover:

- All branches in conditional statements
- Critical business logic
- Edge cases and potential error conditions
- Integration points with external modules or services

Tools like jest can provide coverage reports. For example, to generate a code coverage report with jest, you can add the following script in package.json:

```
"scripts": {
  "test:coverage": "jest --coverage"
}
```

Running npm run test:coverage will then generate detailed coverage reports, helping identify untested parts of the codebase.

Isolation in Unit Tests

Unit tests should be isolated and independent. This means avoiding dependencies on the actual implementations of other modules, which is where mocking and spying come in handy. Using libraries such as jest.mock helps in creating mock modules that emulate the behavior of real modules:

```
jest.mock('../userRepository');
import { getUser } from '../userService';
import { userRepository } from '../userRepository';

describe('getUser', () => {
  it('returns user data when ID is valid', () => {
    userRepository.findById.mockResolvedValue({ id: 1, name: 'John Doe' });
    const result = getUser(1);
    expect(result).toEqual({ id: 1, name: 'John Doe' });
  });
});
```

Avoiding Shared States

Tests should avoid shared states due to the risk of side effects. Utilizing setup and teardown methods, such as beforeEach and afterEach, ensures each test starts with a clean slate:

```
describe('User Management', () => {
  let userService;

  beforeEach(() => {
    userService = new UserService();
  });

  // Test cases
});
```

Integration and End-to-End Testing

While unit tests are critical, integration tests and end-to-end tests offer a broader validation of the system's behavior. Cypress is a popular tool for such testing. Integration tests should focus on larger interaction between modules, while end-to-end tests validate user journeys through the application.

For example, a simple Cypress test that verifies the login flow might look like:

```
describe('Login Flow', () => {
  it('should login with valid credentials', () => {
    cy.visit('/login');
    cy.get('input[name="username"]').type('validUser');
    cy.get('input[name="password"]').type('validPassword');
    cy.get('button[type="submit"]').click();
    cy.url().should('include', '/dashboard');
  });
});
```

Continuous Integration (CI)

Incorporating tests into a Continuous Integration pipeline ensures that code changes are continuously validated. Popular CI tools like GitHub Actions, Travis CI, or CircleCI can run tests on each push or pull request. An example GitHub Actions workflow for running tests could be:

```
name: Node.js CI

on:
  push:
    branches: [ main ]
  pull_request:
    branches: [ main ]

jobs:
  build:
    runs-on: ubuntu-latest
    strategy:
      matrix:
        node-version: [14.x]

    steps:
    - uses: actions/checkout@v2
    - name: Use Node.js
      uses: actions/setup-node@v2
      with:
        node-version: \${{ matrix.node-version }}
    - run: npm install
    - run: npm test
```

All these best practices synergize to create a robust and maintainable testing strategy, ensuring the TypeScript codebase remains reliable and resilient to changes.

Made in the USA
Monee, IL
05 November 2026

67911514R00184